# Playing Around

## Women and
## Extramarital Sex

# Playing Around

## Women and Extramarital Sex

## BY LINDA WOLFE

WILLIAM MORROW AND COMPANY, INC.
NEW YORK    1975

Printed in the United States of America.

1 2 3 4 5   79 78 77 76 75

**Library of Congress Cataloging in Publication Data**

Wolfe, Linda.
    Playing around.

    Bibliography: p.
    1. Women—Sexual behavior. 2. Adultery—United States.
3. Women—Psychology. I. Title. [DNLM: 1. Marriage. 2. Sex
behavior. HQ806 W855p]
HQ29.W65        301.41'76'453        74-34056
ISBN 0-688-00290-0

*Book design by Helen Roberts*

*To Max*

# Acknowledgments

Many people helped me with this book. Those whom I want to thank the most were the women I interviewed. They were unstinting with their time, their confidences, their insights, but above all with their trust in me. I hope I have warranted their generous participation in this project.

I am very grateful to the late Professor Oscar Cargill of New York University, who first prompted my attention to the treatment of extramarital sex in the fiction of women writers by suggesting I do my thesis on Kate Chopin; to the New York Public Library for permission to investigate the literature of adultery in the Frederick Lewis Allen Room; and to Joan Goulianos, who helped me to focus some of my research.

Three young women helped me extraordinarily. One was my daughter Jessica, whose high spirits always revived me when writer's cramp or despair set in; another was my stepdaughter Debbie, who read and discerningly finecombed the manuscript; and the third was my stepdaughter Judith, who offered both encouragement and critiques characteristically profound beyond her years.

But there would have been no book without the constant enthusiasm and tough-minded perceptions of my husband, Max Pollack, who, above all others, has always helped me the most in whatever.

# Contents

Men are like the earth and we are the moon; we turn always one side to them, and they think there is no other, because they don't see it—but there is.

—OLIVE SCHREINER, *The Story of an African Farm*

# Part I

*From Adultery to Extramarital Sex*

# (1)
# *The Spirit of the Times*

I knew only the fiction and very few of the realities about women who were having extramarital sexual affairs until the mid-1960s. In those days, married to my first husband, I was working part-time as a researcher and journalist, raising my baby daughter, and living in a populous section of Manhattan's West Side. The neighborhood, filled with parks and expansive river views, seemed to me a conventional, orderly place, dominated by the playground on the corner. It was the year-round headquarters—a steaming desert in summer where we mothers sat in milk-dripped slacks, eating popsicle leftovers and trying to keep from melting away ourselves, the Siberian steppes in winter, when we braved the ten-degree cold and howling river winds to give colicky babies their fill of air.

The street itself seemed just a corridor to the real stage of our lives, the public school down the corner. On it, before nine and after three, balletic mothers hurried to and from the school, swooping the ground after a trailing shoelace, stooping one-legged to retrieve a fallen lunchbox, waving on tiptoe to a friend down the block, moving, moving fast.

It was only after I had lived there a while that I came to see my surroundings differently, and to discover that what had seemed a world exclusively of mothers and children was actually an environment shared extensively by male lovers, some of them fantasied, others quite real. In the small apartment building in which I lived, there were eight married mothers with small children. In a few months' time, four of them confided to me that they had been involved in extramarital sexual relationships. A neighbor further down the street was picked up by Cadillac by her lover every morning about half a block from her house right after she had walked her three children to school. Another met hers for breakfast at the local luncheonette three times a week, then escorted him past her doorman, each carrying a briefcase underarm, as if they were colleagues on a lengthy research project.

For those who did not have lovers, the subject of extramarital sex was nevertheless conversationally prominent. It is true it was discussed with lower voices than those used on feedings, the air, the permissiveness or lack of it at private schools, or the drunken superintendent who stole the TV in the co-op. But who was or wasn't having extramarital sex, how to, whether, and why filled up hours of park bench time.

The phrase that was most often used by my neighbors to describe sexual experience outside marriage was "playing around." They used it in preference to the others in the roster of imprecise and harsh expressions available in the English language, a roster that went from the obscene, like screwing or fucking around, to the degrading, like two-timing or cheating. A few women called extramarital sexual experience "having affairs," but they were sometimes challenged as to whether the expression was precise for some of the short-term sexual activity they were describing; one woman said she thought that in German there was a useful word that translated as sidestepping; another liked the connotation of dalliance. But playing around was the most frequent expression, even though when a woman used it, it was always with a touch of irony; playing around might have gains and losses, but there were no rules or umpires or clearcut goals, and those who participated were rarely playful or lighthearted.

Despite my attempts at sophistication, I found I was uneasy. I had been raised, like so many of us, on Anna Karenina face up beneath a railroad carriage, on Emma Bovary pale and vomiting arsenic, on Hester Prynne shamed in the marketplace. But these were women of fiction. I had grown up with the knowledge of the affairs of Madame de Staël and George Sand and of the trial of Queen Caroline of England for adultery. But these were rich women, women of another class. Middle-class women didn't have affairs once they married. I think I learned this at my mother's knee. So my reactions to my neighbors who were having extramarital sex were complicated, contradictory. On the one hand, I condemned them, considered them cruel; they were betraying their husbands, their children, even their sex, which from time past had been assigned the victim role when it came to adultery; husbands wandered from wives, not the other way around; and there was comfort in that role. But on the other hand, something in me admired them, admired their ability to find lovers, their know-how at secrecy and their determination not to be victims, not to let life plough them underground in Riverside Park.

I found myself wondering about their lives, listening avidly to their stories, and experiencing vicarious enjoyment as well as anxiety at each new saga they reported. I think it was then that the idea for this book first occurred to me. My own confusion of feelings was part of what interested me about the subject. I was also interested in it because, while I knew that extramarital sex had not been reported as having increased since Kinsey's time (he had stated in 1953 that about one-fourth of the married women and one-half of the married men he had surveyed had had at least one extramarital affair), it did seem to me that among tne women in my milieu, the rate was inordinately high. That milieu consisted of non-religious, economically secure, highly educated women; they were spirited and a little rebellious, but not particularly radical.

But I didn't turn to writing about the subject back then.

My own life was undergoing considerable upheaval. My first marriage broke up. My work as a journalist became full time and more demanding. I began to concentrate on articles about marriage, divorce, and sexual behavior and therapy for various national and East Coast magazines, traveling the country to research some of them, examining my immediate environment for others. The women's movement had emerged and for a while, my consciousness raised, I lost interest in the whys and wherefores of female extramarital sex. I suppose the topic seemed retrogressive. Once I discussed it with a friend, a divorced woman and an activist in the movement, who said to me, "Affairs are married women's opiate. If women are unhappy in marriage and seek their pleasure outside it, it is because marriage itself is an untenable institution. Ending it, not keeping it going with panaceas, is the only sensible solution and those who have extramarital affairs are simply slowing down the revolution."

Nevertheless in 1971, the year I remarried, I decided that I wanted to write a book about women and extramarital sex. Two exchanges took place shortly after my wedding that strengthened my determination. The first occurred the day one of my favorite long-married friends came over to the apartment to wish me congratulations. Rachel was pleased that I had remarried and wanted to tell me so. I was delighted to see her. Of all the brilliant and beautiful women I know, she is the most brilliant and beautiful. But her view of herself is dim. There is a well of depression at her center. She used to tell me there were days she woke, sent the children off to school, and simply, merely stared at her four walls.

"I would have told you sooner," she said quite exuberantly the day she came over, "but you've seemed so busy with your remarriage. I've got a lover. What do you think of that?"

"I think, *you too*. So what else is new?"

"You don't mean that," Rachel said.

"No," I said. "But I'm not as surprised as I would have been a while back. Does Bob know?"

"Are you kidding?"

"How come you have?" I asked.

She said, "The *Zeitgeist.*"

Now it was my turn. "The spirit of the times? You can't mean that," I said.

"No," she said. "Not altogether." Then, "Look, I don't like the idea of myself as an adulterous wife. But there comes a time in every woman's marriage when she just doesn't feel the bedsheets under her, the quilt over her. Forget about bodies. She doesn't know what's under her or on top of her or if the pillow is soft. And playing around, adultery, makes her know that the pillow is down, the sheet is woven of rough cotton, the blanket's wool."

It wasn't exactly the wedding present I had wanted from Rachel. Actually, I didn't even want to discuss Rachel's situation. Remarrying had made me complacent and sentimental and I didn't want to think about marital difficulties. I told Rachel this. I told her that the old-fashioned provisos still dominated my thinking and that I expected that my husband and I would be faithful to each other, emotionally and sexually. Exclusivity, I told Rachel, that's what the sociologists say is the basis for marriage, or, for that matter, any sexual liaisons that are meant to last.

Rachel merely wished me good luck. I remember her looking at me disdainfully as if I had insisted on some intellectually inferior notion, as if I had said the world was flat.

The other exchange arose during a conversation several months after our wedding when my husband said to me, over lunch, "What I want from a relationship is the sense that I will never want to wander. You give me that. I want you always to give me that."

At first I felt touched. I thought, how flattering. Later, on reflection, it seemed extraordinary. What a thing to say. It wasn't that I was surprised at the thought, but at the expression. I'm sure many people want from a love relationship the feeling of never again having to wander. Choosing anew is time-consuming; distracting; full of anguish. But still, how extraordinary. I would never have expressed what I wanted in such a fashion. It seemed to me peculiarly and exclusively male.

It reminded me of something I had read years before in the words of a fourteenth-century bourgeois called the Menagier de Paris who, upon marrying, had tried to instruct his fifteen-year-old bride in morality and domestic care. The menagier had also wanted never again to wander. "In God's name, I believe that when two good and honorable people are wed, all other loves are put far off, destroyed and forgotten, save only the love of each for the other. And meseems that when they are in each other's presence, they look upon each other more than upon the others, they clasp and hold each other and they do not willingly speak or make sign save to each other." But it was part of his upbringing, part of his male expertise, to know that men *did* explore beyond their wives. How to prevent it?

He first warned his young wife that should he ever do so, it needn't be the end of her pretty world. Men had wandered and, when their wives were patient enough or wily enough, returned. But the menagier realized that more useful than knowing how to outwait or win back a husband would be to know how to keep a spouse's love at such a peak that he would never flee. After thinking how his wife might best accomplish this, he came up with this prescription: "I pray you to bewitch and bewitch again your husband, and beware of dripping roof and smoking fire, and scold him not, and be unto him gentle and amiable and peaceable. Be careful that in winter he has good fire without smoke, and let him rest well and be well-covered between your breasts and thus bewitch him . . ."

I did not find the menagier's equation of fidelity with material comforts strange. For all I know, such comforts are the very things that do keep people sexually loyal to each other. But what I found strange was how unlikely it would be for a woman, five hundred years ago or today, to say to her husband, "If you do such and so for me, you will keep me from adultery." Many women today have an intellectual awareness of the prevalence of female extramarital sex; they know that according to statistics one out of four of them is likely to have at least one extramarital affair. But despite this, they rarely prepare for the possibility that they may one day be tempted to have such relations, even to the extent of discussing with their husbands how to ward them off. Extramarital sexual encounters seem always to take a woman unawares and she invariably feels like the first woman in the world to have had the experience. I remember thinking that there might be value in loosening the covers that still shroud women's extramarital experiences just so that the woman who finds herself in an adulterous situation would know that others had been there before her and survived.

Whatever the motivating event, it had by then occurred to me that the openness concerning extramarital sex that I had experienced among my neighbors was not just a phenomenon unique to a few perhaps neurotic lives but rather, a reflection of a change in the mores, a *Zeitgeist,* as Rachel had said. By then I was reading in a variety of sources that just as we had moved through a period which had caused our society at large to relinquish taboos on premarital sex, so we were now traversing one which would end by abandoning strictures on extramarital sex. A number of factors seemed to support this assumption.

There were public revelations which only ten years ago would have been kept secret: Mrs. Lyndon B. Johnson intimating the adulteries of her husband, our president; Buzz Aldrin, our great astro-hero detailing his in the pages of *McCall's*; Viet Nam prisoners of war returning home and announcing that one of their frequent emotional chores had been to deal with their wives' extramarital liaisons; Nigel Nicholson lauding the homosexual adulteries of his parents; Barbara Howar handling the trauma of turning thirty by buying a diamond necklace and having an affair.

Beyond revelations, there were semantics. More revealing

to me than the outspoken confessions of individuals was a more subtle change that I observed in the field of marriage counseling. Many psychologists, psychiatrists, and marriage counselors had taken to using the term "extramarital sex" as if it were a euphemism to replace the old familiar word "adultery." *Why,* I would ask some two dozen of them. The two terms have precisely the same meanings. Adultery means sexual intercourse between a married man and someone other than his wife, or between a married woman and someone other than her husband; extramarital sex means sex outside, beyond, besides marriage. But invariably when I asked mental health workers why they preferred "extramarital sex," they would reply, "Because 'adultery' has negative connotations," and they would say, somewhat ostrich-like I thought, that perhaps by changing the word, the connotation of the act would alter.

And beyond semantics, there were pronouncements: Dr. Lonny Myers, Director of Medical Education for Chicago's Midwest Population Center, declaring that extramarital sex is not the messy disturbed experience we view it but that "it can be related to maturity, personal growth, better marriages and joy"; Corliss Lamont writing in *The New York Times* that one way to forestall the ever-blossoming divorce rate is to make extramarital sexual relations the privilege of every married person, male or female; Dr. Alex Comfort writing at The Center for the Study of Democratic Institutions that sexual jealousy in marriage is disappearing so rapidly that he is convinced our children, and certainly our grandchildren will be unable to comprehend the themes of nineteenth-century opera.

It sounds apocalyptic, if you believe it; I don't, quite. Nevertheless, there has been a significant change in the occurance of extramarital sexual experience among American women: they have sexual relationships outside their marriages by an earlier age than woman did in Kinsey's time. This change has been reported in two recent reliable and large-scale studies of American sexual behavior. One study of 2,372 married women was conducted by Robert R. Bell and Dorthyann Peltz; the results were published in March, 1974, in *Medical Aspects of Human Sexuality*. The other, a study of some 1,500 married men and women, was conducted in 1972 by the Playboy Foundation and published as a book in 1974 with a text by Morton Hunt.

In Kinsey's day, it was only by the age of forty that a little over a quarter of the women he surveyed had had extramarital experience. Bell and Peltz found that such experience had been had by the same percentage of women they surveyed by the time their women were thirty-five; they predicted that when all members of the group they had chosen to investigate reached the age of forty, 40 percent of them would have had extramarital experience. The Playboy Foundation's statistics were even more startling. Their figures showed that while in Kinsey's time only 8 percent of young wives—those under age twenty-four—had reported extramarital sexual experience, by 1972, 24 percent did.

There had been no comparable or even considerable change in extramarital activity among men in any age group since Kinsey's time. Therefore, Morton Hunt interpreted the change of "historic dimensions" among women as indicating not that the nation as a whole was becoming less monogamous but that women were becoming less so; there had been, he said, not a "radical break with the ideal of sexual fidelity, but a radical break with the double standard." Although Hunt found it in very young wives, I believe that this radical break with the double standard was already underway among the slightly older women who were my neighbors back in the mid-sixties.

But we are all inhabited by history, and it is not a simple matter for women to break with this particular aspect of the double standard. In Stith Thompson's definitive *Motif-Index of Folk Literature*, the punishments meted out in folk stories for adultery merit examination. There was one listing for an adulterer; he was punished by madness. But the adulteress was another matter. She was:

> blackmailed by lover
> drowned in leaky vessel with paramour
> caused unwittingly to eat her lover's heart
> fettered with paramour
> hurled from a high rock (admittedly she escaped injury and there was a legal decision handed down that she might not be punished for the same crime again)
> kicked to death by a mule as punishment
> killed by her husband when she returned
> ridden through the street on a bull
> roughly treated by her lover
> caused to fall down a flight of stairs from which the steps had been removed
> transformed into a mare and stirruped

And so on.

Certainly I have known men for whom sexual wandering was deeply guilt-provoking; who felt as troubled by deceiving their spouses as ever any woman did. I don't believe we all act and respond according to inflexible sex-determined patterns but that there are widespread individual differences among us, within both sexes. Still, to the extent that we are formed not only by our own personal pasts but by our historical pasts—our culture—adultery for a woman is more complicated and potentially guilt-producing than it is for a man.

So if women were defying the age-old precepts, what I wanted to know was who were they? Why were they? How could they? What had happened among individual consciences to make it possible for centuries of proscription to be overridden? What could women themselves tell me about how their adulteries affected their marriages? Their main motivations in seeking extramarital sex? Their attitudes toward the double standard in this realm? And whether they believed affairs preserved or destroyed marriage?

There were innumerable ways to pursue these questions, but I decided I wanted to write a book that would be a voyage, not a survey, so that I myself could travel with the social adventurers. I would go back into the past—where most of the documentation about women and extramarital sex is fictional—but then I would accompany living women, allowing their voices and steps to guide me. I decided to survey the fictional and historical accounts of adultery with particular attention to what women writers of the past had expressed about the subject. I also decided to interview some contemporary women novelists because it seemed to me that female adultery had increasingly come under their scrutiny. But above all, I would interview those who had been adulterous, the old as well as the young. I would interview as widely but as intimately as I could, and include women who were pursuing traditional secret adultery as well as those who had chosen experimental open adultery, known to and agreed upon with their spouses. I wanted to record the thoughts and experiences of women who had broken the code concerning extramarital sex because, if we were really at or even just approaching a moment in history when one of the oldest strictures of society was altering, a report on those who had traversed this path of social change seemed to me to be of significant documentary importance. It would be a story of a major flight of our century as surely as were reports of trips to the moon or political revolution.

# (2)
# Clues to the Adulterous Woman from Literature and History

Most reports about female extramarital sex have been filed by male novelists and story writers. But in the last few years the subject has come increasingly under the scrutiny of female novelists. Indeed, it has provided them with so many portraits and so many plots that it seems not just a preoccupation of women writers, but their metaphor for life lived on the keen edge of experience.

In the early 1970s alone, female adultery was explored in Doris Lessing's *Summer Before the Dark*, Erica Jong's *Fear of Flying*, Judith Rossner's *Any Minute I Can Split*, Ann Birstein's *Dickie's List*, Barbara Raskin's *Loose Ends*, and Joyce Carol Oates' short story collection *Marriages and Infidelities*—to mention but a few of the more well-received titles. Most of these writers had previously tackled the subject, as had Mary McCarthy, Anaïs Nin, Lois Gould, Joan Didion, Sandra Hochman, Margaret Drabble, Alix Kates Shulman, Penelope Mortimer, and many other contemporary female novelists. It is as if women writers were all of them and all at once reflecting the sentiment expressed in the poet Erica Jong's "Going to School in Bed":

> If it is impossible to promise
> absolute fidelity,
> this is because
> we learn so much geography

from the shifting of one body
on another.

If it is impossible to promise
absolute fidelity,
this is because
we learn so much history
from the lying of one body
on another.

If it is impossible to promise
absolute fidelity,
this is because
we learn so much psychology
from the dreaming of one body
of another.

Life writes so many letters
on the naked bodies of lovers.
What a tattoo artist!
What an ingenious teacher!

Is it any wonder we appear
like schoolchildren dreaming:
naked
& anxious to learn?

Perhaps the burst of books on female extramarital sex can
be traced to the fact that freedom to explore the subject is
new among women writers. Until our own era, it was an
impolitic subject for women, even given the safe harbor provided by fiction. Thus the majority of the great investigations
of the matter had been done by men. Admittedly they were
written by men who became, at least for the duration of their
novelistic exploration, intensely sensitive to their adulterous
heroines, men who were able, like Tolstoy, to draw a dreamy

Anna Karenina who feels "as though everything were beginning to be double in her soul, just as objects sometimes appear double to over-tired eyes. She hardly knew at times what it was she feared, and what she hoped for. Whether she feared or desired what had happened, or what was going to happen, and exactly what she longed for, she could not have said." Or they were men like Joyce, able to create a defiant Molly Bloom who says of her adultery, "O much about it if thats all the harm ever we did in this vale of tears God knows its not much doesn't everybody only they hide it I suppose thats what a women is supposed to be there for or He wouldnt have made us the way He did."

But until our own era, the subject of women's extramarital sex was primarily a male writer's province. And even today, some women writers report being uneasy about exploring it. When I interviewed a number of women novelists whose works had dealt with female extramarital sex, several spoke to me of experiencing or fearing negative reactions to their work because of the subject matter. Erica Jong explained, "After I finished *Fear of Flying* I went through the heebie-jeebies. I had a terrible struggle with myself. Something inside me was still saying that I shouldn't end the book the way I had, with the adulterous heroine returning unscathed to her husband. I felt that perhaps it was still necessary for the plot to punish her, for her to get knocked-up or killed. And then, when the manuscript was sent off to be printed, the first printer it went to wouldn't set the type. In 1973, post-Portnoy, post-*Ulysses*, there was nevertheless a printer refusing to set type! They had to find another compositor. Why? Because it was written by a woman, I guess. It may have been because he opened the manuscript to chapter one and it said 'Fuck' or it may have been because of the attitude toward monogamy. All that summer I was depressed. My family will hate me. My husband will leave me. It sounds funny now, since none of that happened, but it's what I expected. I kept wishing I could take it all back, that I had never written it, that I could just give back the money."

The novelist Ann Birstein reported that for many years her novella *Love in the Dunes,* a politely worded story of female adultery, "went begging for a publisher. Nobody would buy it. Women who read the story always liked it, but the men in publishing wouldn't buy it." Alix Kates Shulman suggested to me that she had escaped a ticklish problem by using scenes of fantasied rather than real adultery in *Memoirs of an Ex-Prom Queen.*

Nevertheless, these authors, and many others, have begun writing about women's extramarital sex, often focusing on heroines whose adultery does not involve great love but passion alone. One of the first women writers to explore adultery in this way was the remarkable turn-of-the-century novelist, Kate Chopin. In her 1899 novel, *The Awakening,* buried and unread for many years, but currently experiencing a revival as Chopin's pertinence to today's women has been discovered, a dissatisfied wife leaves her husband and children to embark on a voyage of self-discovery. It starts with the wife's romantic dalliance with a young intellectual who reads de Goncourt to her, pauses at her sexual liaison with a flighty roué who, unlike her husband, makes her feel joyous about her body, and ends, in the expected nineteenth-century fashion, with the suicide of the heroine. While the book bears some resemblance to Madame Bovary, Chopin's heroine Edna, unlike Flaubert's Emma, is seen sympathetically throughout the novel and even her suicide is not presented as retribution for a life of hysteria and self-delusion but rather as a triumphant act of the will. As Emma dies, she curses her poison; her tongue hangs out of her mouth; her eyes roll and her ribs shake. Her death is "horrible, frantic, desperate." Edna moves slowly, with composure, to her death. She prefers to die rather than live as wife to any man she knows, and as she drowns she peacefully recalls the sounds and smells of childhood.

*The Awakening* was shocking for its day and its country. The very fact that a woman had written it added to the antagonism it aroused. The book was "sensual and devilish" said one critic; it should be "marked poison" said another; and a third, ostrich-minded, found Kate Chopin's truths about women's yearnings "unseemly," and therefore not really true at all. "A fact . . . which we have all agreed shall not be acknowledged is as good as no fact at all." The book was banned from libraries, most painfully from the author's hometown St. Louis library, and Kate Chopin never again wrote for publication, despite the fact that she had been well known and well respected previously as a local colorist. But she continued to write, and one of the works that she turned to after *The Awakening* might be considered radical and startling even in our own era. It is the 1904 short story "The Storm," a light-hearted, amusing story that nevertheless seriously insists that a woman's grasping of her right to sexual pleasure outside marriage need not upset the marital applecart.

In "The Storm," a young wife has an unplanned sexual encounter with an old boyfriend which not only proves sexually satisfying but which has no repercussions of retribution or even guilt for the lovers, and which seems to bring nothing but pleasure all around. Calixta, the heroine, has stayed at home while her husband and little son have gone off to do some marketing. While they are away a storm blows up. Calixta goes out on the front porch to gather in her child's laundry before the rain descends and just at this moment, her old beau Alcée Laballière rides by. He asks whether he may take shelter on her porch until the rain stops, and then helps her to pull in the clothes.

The storm itself—reminiscent to the modern reader of D. H. Lawrence's use of nature's elements for sexual imagery— evokes the sexual tension between the two. Calixta is frightened of the rain, calls it a cyclone, cannot compose herself.

Alcée tries to comfort her but when he clasps her shoulders to do so, "The contact of her warm palpitating body when he had unthinkingly drawn her into his arms, had aroused all the old-time infatuation and desire for her flesh."

Each of the pair recalls, separately, their passionate impulses when they were young and single. As the storm continues to rage around them, they draw closer and embrace. When Alcée touches Calixta's breasts "they gave themselves up in quivering ecstasy, inviting his lips." And when he has intercourse with her, Calixta experiences her first orgasm, an inner storm that shakes "her firm elastic flesh that was knowing for the first time its birthright . . ." Yet, when the rain is over and the sun "was turning the glistening green world into a palace of gems," the two part happily; Calixta smiles, lifts her chin in the air, and laughs aloud.

She busies herself preparing supper and when her husband and son come home is gay and effusive. They have brought her a special present, some shrimps she adores, and the three sit down to supper laughing "much and so loud that anyone might have heard then as far away as Laballière's." And Laballière? He too is happy that night as he sends a tender loving letter to his wife. And his wife is happy when she receives it. "So the storm passed and everyone was happy."

It was 1960 when I first read Kate Chopin, yet I felt an immediate across-the-century intimacy with her. She had read de Maupassant and Zola and perhaps Flaubert in a provincial era when few American writers, male or female, knew what was being written or thought about in Europe. She didn't start to write until she was thirty-four when, suddenly widowed, she found herself in charge of supporting her six young children. But then, child-interrupted and chorebound, she plugged away at her material, exploring the mainstreams that were to feed the fictional treatment of the adulterous woman in the twentieth century—the matter-of-fact earthiness of Molly Bloom, the orgasmic discoveries of

Lady Chatterley, and the conviction of so many women writers who followed Chopin that perhaps adultery did not involve great love but merely a storm of passion.

Even prior to modern times, the adulterous woman exerted a unique pull on the imagination and provided for authors and readers alike a preoccupying figure. She made her first appearance, as far as I can tell, in an ancient Egyptian legend written down in the XVIIIth Dynasty, but describing events that took place long before in the IIIrd Dynasty reign of the Pharaoh Nabka. We don't know the woman's name; she is referred to throughout as "Ubaû-anir's wife," but what happens to her has the rattle of familiarity.

When the Pharaoh and his entourage paid a call on her husband, who was high up in court circles, she happened to be introduced to a royal vassal, a man of more humble station than herself but apparently the possessor of great bodily charm. Ubaû-anir's wife felt physical attraction at first start. "From the hour that she beheld him she no longer knew in what part of the world she was." So she asked her maid to approach him and set up a rendezvous. "Come, that we may lie together for the space of an hour; put on thy festival garments."

The stranger and Ubaû-anir's wife did lie together. It was presumably a pleasurable encounter, since they then determined to explore their relationship further by sneaking a few days together at her husband's vacation retreat on the shores of an ancient lake.

Ubaû-anir's wife directed the overseer of the vacation property to get everything ready for her arrival, and "it was done as she had said, and she stayed there, drinking with the vassal until the sun set." But the overseer was not to be trusted; he had informed Ubaû-anir of his wife's goings-on. When the lover decided to take a swim at twilight he disappeared into the dark waters of the lake; Ubaû-anir, using sorcery, had created a magic wax crocodile which turned real and carried off the vassal. Once the lover was taken care of, it was time to attend to the wife. She was brought back to the palace by her husband, under the Pharaoh's express command, and there she was promptly burned to death.

The severity of the punishment meted out to Ubaû-anir's wife has been taken as evidence of how rigorously the Egyptians condemned women's adultery. Not only was she killed, but her body was destroyed. Since the ancient Egyptians favored entering death with intact mummified bodies, burning a body not only destroyed life but made even afterlife uncertain. Still, despite the cruelty displayed in this story, there must have been some recognition on men's parts that they themselves, not women alone, coveted female extramarital adventuring. Another Egyptian Pharaoh was buried with a pornographic papyrus that assured him that the afterworld to which he was going was not so altogether dreadful a place since in it he could "at his pleasure take the wives away from the husbands."

Certainly there were real-life rewards as well as punishments for women who engaged in extramarital sex, even in the ancient world, and even in places where the laws were harshest concerning female adultery. In ancient Assyria the legal code provided that a woman who had intercourse with a man not her husband could be mutilated by having her nose cut off or could be put to death. The choice was her husband's. And yet the only female name which has come down to us from that bleak civilization is that of Semiramis, a semilegendary figure who, according to the Greek historian Diodorus, was an adulteress before she became a queen. In Semiramis' case, her adultery was rewarded rather than punished because she abandoned a husband who was a mere officer in King Ninus' army to have an affair with the king himself. Ninus later married her, died, and thus paved the way for Semiramis herself to rule through her young son.

There is a similar happy rise in station for the Biblical Bathsheba. King David had seen her washing herself as he

walked upon his rooftop, and although he knew she was
another man's wife, "took her; and she came in unto him;
and he lay with her." Later, he arranged to get her husband
out of the way by sending him unaided into the front lines
of the hottest battle. There is punishment inflicted on David
and Bathsheba; the child conceived during their first adulterous union dies. But Bathsheba goes on to become David's
wife and the mother of Solomon, again a dynastic adulteress.
Of course, Bathsheba's fate was in direct contradiction to
ancient Hebrew law as stated in Leviticus: "And the man
that commiteth adultery with another man's wife, even he
that commiteth adultery with his neighbour's wife, the adulterer and the adulteress shall surely be put to death."

Still most of the time, the adulteress came to a bad end,
or brought misery to others. She is Helen, whose affair with
Paris starts the Trojan war. She is Phaedra, whose sexual lust,
albeit administered by a god, causes the death of Hippolytus.
In Euripides' version of the story, Hippolytus voices the pre-
vailing Greek contempt for female sexuality: "Animals! Let
someone teach them to smother their hot wishes. Or don't
ask me not to despise the lot of them." Euripides was present-
ing in drama what numerous Greek philosophers were to
complain of in treatises: women were almost by nature adulterous. Much later, St. Jerome, basing his words on a lost tract
on marriage written by Aristotle's protégé Theophrastus, implied that there was no end to women's interest in extramarital seduction. The beautiful ones couldn't help but at-
tract lovers; the ugly ones were easily seduced because they
wanted to gain reassurance about their appearance. *Anything*
could start a woman on an adulterous course. "If you introduce old women, and soothsayers, and prophets, and vendors
of jewels and silken clothing, you imperil her chastity."

The Hebraic and Greek view of women as unpleasantly,
dangerously sexual had entered the thinking of the first Chris-
tians and was to linger through much of Christianity, even
in periods when women were upgraded and idolized. Early

Christianity set great store by celibacy, and women were seen as the stumbling block that prevented right-minded men from avoiding sex. Women were a veritable pollutant. Thus the second-century theologian Tertullian longed to have every woman veiled or else all men would be put in peril, and the fourth-century theologian St. John Chrysostom warned men that behind the superficial appeal of women's pretty faces and bodies there lay nothing but death and disaster. If men were to "consider what is stored up inside those beautiful eyes and that straight nose, and the mouth and cheeks, you will affirm the well-shaped body to be nothing else than a white sepulchre; the parts within are full of so much uncleanness." Down into the Middle Ages, such warnings continued, often with implications of woman's adulterous nature. The thirteenth-century Franciscan Friar Salimbene offered, "Wouldst thou define or know what woman is? She is glittering mud, a stinking rose, sweet poison, ever leaning toward that which is forbidden her."

And yet gradually a new prestige adhered to women. They became the objects of courtly or romantic love, a love that stressed adoration of women. Men were to accomplish great deeds of heroism for women, and to worship them with despairing even tragic sentiments. But debate still flourishes as to the essential nature of courtly love. It was certainly adulterous, in that the object of a man's dedication was often a married woman, wife of a lord to whom the lover owed fealty. But was this adulterous love sexual or not? Some explicators of medieval poetry stress that courtly love was nonsexual and that the married woman was a perfect object of admiration precisely because she was unattainable, thus adding to the intensity and spirituality of a passion.

But there is no doubt that some such loves were not only consummated but even ended in cheerful domesticity. The twelfth-century poet Marie de France, for example, disarmingly tells the story of Gugemar, a virile knight who fell in love with a married exotic queen. The queen, a woman "of tender age," was the wife of a king much older than she. When Gugemar happened along, the queen and the knight fell intensely in love. They met secretly and joyously in her bedchamber before they were discovered and parted by the queen's husband who wounded Gugemar and left him to die in an unmanned ship on the sea. The queen was locked in a prison. Miraculously Gugemar made it to Brittany and one day the queen too escaped and she also sailed to France. There, she was again imprisoned, but this time she was rescued by Gugemar, with whom she ended up living happily ever after "in peace in his own land."

But most of the time when medievalists wrote of adulterous love that was consummated, their stories ended tragically. A favorite and often-told legend was that of Tristan and Isolde. Their adulterous love ended in death for both even though they had never meant to become sexual with one another and had only done so because of a magic potion.

Dante popularized the story of Francesca da Rimini, another adulteress whose physical passion for a man not her husband brought death to both herself and her lover. When her lengthy passionate attachment to her husband's brother was finally discovered, she and her lover were murdered by her husband and ended up in the Inferno. There Dante, perhaps the first person ever to interview an adulteress, questioned Francesca about just what exactly made her turn to adultery. She offered an explanation that was to linger throughout history and figure in the speculations of Flaubert, Tolstoy, and even modern writers. It was that books—romantic stories of other impassioned lovers—had brought her low. Had she and her brother-in-law not read the story of Lancelot together, they might never have thought of exchanging their first kiss.

How did an adulterous woman feel in those long-ago years? We have little to go on in the way of personal accounts except for one written early in the fifteenth century by the mystic

Margery Kempe, author of the first extant autobiography in English.

When Margery Kempe had been married several years, "it so fell that a man she loved well, said unto her on Saint Margaret's Eve before evensong that, for anything, he would lie by her and have his lust of his body." Kempe was immensely troubled by the man's words, so disturbed "that she could not hear her evensong, nor say her Paternoster." But what was troubling her was not, as one might expect, fear of the man's threat or even anger at his boldness. She was distressed because she recognized in herself an enormous temptation to agree to the sexual encounter. All that night she thought about it. "She lay by her husband, and to commune with him was so abominable to her that she could not endure it." Finally, "through the importunity of temptation and lack of discretion she was overcome and consented in her mind" to adultery.

Shortly afterwards she went to her admired friend to arrange their assignation. Suddenly, completely to her surprise, he turned on her, rejected her, and, adding insult to injury, made her feel the whole thing had been *her* idea. He told her he would "rather be hewn as small as flesh for the pot" than have intercourse with her.

Margery Kempe went home and did extreme penance. Yet all year she was tempted to "lechery and despair," until finally she felt God's forgiveness. She seems to have believed she actually spoke with God about her lustfulness and that He helped her overcome it by suggesting that she turn her thoughts to religious, but nevertheless still sexualized fantasies about Himself. God said,

> When thou art in thy bed, take Me to thee as thy wedded husband, as thy dearworthy darling, and as thy sweet son, for I will be loved as a son should be loved by the mother, and I will that thou lovest Me, daughter, as a good wife ought to love her husband. Therefore

thou mayest boldly take Me in the arms of thy soul and kiss My mouth, My head, and My feet, as sweetly as thou wilt.

Loving God, Kempe eschewed further efforts at adultery.

Women's confessional accounts of adulterous feelings are rare almost until our own day, but gradually their fictional and reportorial accounts began to accumulate. One of the most charming was Madame de Lafayette's 1678 psychological novel about a woman tempted to adultery, *The Princess of Cleves.*

In a pattern that is already familiar in the literature of the adulterous woman, the underage princess admires but cannot love her older husband. Therefore, surrounded by a frivolous court in which adultery is the norm, she inevitably falls in love with someone else—the handsome and accomplished Duke of Nemours. But although the duke ardently returns the princess' love, he is never able to convince her to sexualize their love, even when at last her husband's death leaves her free and available for marriage. She has "an austere virtue which is almost without a precedent." She parts from the court, spends much of her time in a convent, and dies.

But despite the princess' sturdy religiosity, there is no doubt that something besides religion holds her back from adultery. Madame de Lafayette supported her heroine's religious argument against adultery with another, psychological deterrent. One cannot fall in love and live by its consequences, for who knows whether love has any stability? When M. de Cleves is dead and by all moral rules the princess is at liberty to marry the duke, she still refuses, saying to her lover,

> I cannot confess to you without deep shame that the certainty of not being loved by you as I am, seems to me a horrible misfortune. . . . I know that you are free, as I am, and that we are so situated that the world would

probably blame neither of us if we should marry; but do
men keep their love in these permanent unions? Ought
I to expect a miracle in my case, and can I run the risk
of seeing this passion, which would be my only happiness, fade away?

Madame de Lafayette had added a new insight to the literature of adultery. She recognized that a married woman might
cherish adulterous fantasies but fear translating romantic into
mundane love. Today psychologists often list as a major cause
of adultery people's inability to commit themselves to their
spouses. It is amusing to note that in *The Princess of
Cleves* the fear of commitment works in two directions; it
isolates the princess from her husband but also from her lover.

In England, a little later than the period in which Madame
de Lafayette wrote, the adventurous Lady Mary Wortley
Montagu was to question the wisdom of the Christian world's
insistence on sweeping under the rug all traces of women's
adultery. She had observed while visiting Constantinople in
1716 that many Turkish women had lovers and that they
even appeared publicly with both husbands and lovers. She
wrote that among these women "getting a lover is so far from
losing, that 'tis properly getting reputation; ladies being
much more respected in regard to the rank of their lovers
than that of their husbands." Corresponding with an English
friend about the liaisons of Turkish women, she ended her
letter with a plea for relativism. "Thus you see, my dear,
gallantry and good-breeding are as different, in different cli-
mates, as morality and religion. Who have the rightest no-
tions of both, we shall never know till the day of judg-
ment . . ."

As Lady Montagu implied, the major difference between
the English women she knew and the Turkish women she was
observing was not that the former group did not take lovers,
but that they hid their extramarital activities out of concern

for their reputations. At no period in Western history does it appear that female adultery was unknown. This was true even when dire governmental laws attempted to restrict its occurrence. The English Puritans had tried. In 1650 they had passed an act requiring the death penalty for adultery and in 1653, they had actually executed an adulterer, an eighty-nine-year-old man. But even under Puritan rule, juries were loath to hand down convictions, and most of the time, in Western countries, moral responsibility rather than law was urged as the means to prevent adultery. Preachers and priests were the guardians of morality, and in their sermons and writings they propagandized the dangers of adultery.

In *The Natural, Civil and Religious Mischiefs Arising From Conjugal Infidelity,* a text published in 1700, the author presented a myriad of reasons, beyond respect of God's law, for eschewing adultery. Male adultery, he warned, would "consume the Strength, and melt down the Courage of the Nation." Women's adultery was even worse. It produced either crippled or temperamentally deformed offspring, or it could render a wife sterile, incapable of producing any heir at all, since "the beaten Paths are always barren, and never productive of Fruit."

One of my favorite explicators of the dangers of female adultery was Mason Locke Weems, an eighteenth-century American Episcopalian clergyman, a purveyor of legends—notably the one about George Washington and the cherry tree—and a vibrant proselytizer who, while determined to make sin nasty, often merely succeeded in making it read well.

In *God's Revenge Against Adultery,* Weems told the hair-raising story of Nancy Wiley, wife of a Pennsylvania tavern keeper, and her affair with the local physician, Doctor Wilson, "an Apollo in his form and a Chesterfield in his manners." The upshot of the affair was particularly tragic. When Mr. Wiley discovered it, he shot Dr. Wilson, thereby widowing the doctor's wife and orphaning his young children; later, consumed with depression, he caused even his own seemingly natural death.

In trying to analyze Nancy Wiley's fall into adultery, Weems fastened the blame on the poor education given to girls. Digging back into her past, he unearthed a friend of her parents who reported telling the girl's mother years before that Nancy would be an angel "if she could but receive the polish of a good education," only to be rebuffed by the mother's retort, "Never mind! Let Nancy alone. She will be angel enough, I'll be bound for her, without education."

Weems felt that

> such cruel neglect of parents to direct their daughters to the pleasures of the mind has been the ruin of many a fine girl. It proved, in the sequel, the ruin of beautiful Mrs. Wiley. Having never been taught to polish that immortal jewel, her soul, she had nothing left but to polish the poor casket, her body—to trick it up in gaudy attire—to perfume it with sweet odours—to blanch its skin—to whiten its teeth—to curl its tresses, making it in this way, the goddess of her devotions. Thus idolized by herself, she expected, of course, that her dear person should be idolized by all others. And those were most sure of her favour who most flattered her vanity.

But despite the efforts of even the most dynamic moralists, female adultery persisted. By the mid-eighteenth century there was evidence of its frequency in the records of trials for adultery which were published in both the American colonies and England.

There are many such documents. They seem to have been popular almost as a kind of pornography. A publisher would send a clerk to court and the clerk would write out whatever testimony he could copy down, and the result would be published for the amusement of the general public. At least this is the impression the title pages of these trials convey. Like book advertisements of today, they were filled with seductive promises. One announces itself as "Being the particulars of an adulterous intercourse for the space of several years in which the partners showed as little attention to decency as to fidelity"; another features "the amorous love letters" exchanged by the two people on trial; a third is advertised as "The whole trial of Mrs. Harriet Errington, with nine amorous scenes elegantly engraved," including, "The Breeches scene . . . the Hiding scene . . . the Bed scene." This particular trial report promised that "the Essence and Quintessence of all the trials for Adultery that ever appeared in the Rambler's magazine or any other publication is Chastity to this."

A typical case is that of Mrs. Ann Wood, tried for adultery in 1785. Her husband, stationed in the colonies as a paymaster of artillery for his Majesty during the period of the American Revolution, sent her home to England so that she could be safe from the ravages of war. The Woods had been married fifteen years at the time they experienced this first separation. Poor Mrs. Wood must have felt sexually deprived. After doing without a man for three years, she began to entertain frequent visits in her Mayfair home from Mr. Quintin Dick, a merchant of King Street. Although she went to great lengths not to let her neighbors know, the servants began to spy on her. They took to examining her sofa and bed each morning, "plainly distinguishing the marks of two persons having lain therein, and also such marks and stains on the sheets, as convinced them that a man and a woman had been in the act of carnal copulation therein." No matter that Mr. Wood had stayed away for six years, returning home only in 1784. He was enraged at his wife and demanded, and obtained, a divorce.

Not every husband whose wife had had an affair wanted or could obtain a divorce. With a few exceptions, divorce was granted not by the courts but only through an act of Parliament. This was a costly and scandalous procedure and sometimes husbands preferred merely to separate from their adulterous wives. But whether they divorced or not, it was customary for them to go to court to try to obtain financial rewards from their wives' paramours to pay for "the outrage on their feelings and happiness" or for the loss of "the Aid and Comfort" of a wife's society. Most eighteenth- and early nineteenth-century trials for adultery were held for damages, not divorce. Financial awards were granted more often than not although usually the husband had to prove that he and his wife had lived amicably until a seducer appeared on the scene. This was what had happened in 1815 to the charming and loving Trelawneys.

They were in their early twenties, a delightful couple fond of living in retirement and filling up their leisure hours with reading. Trelawney, a lieutenant, had served in India until he had been wounded in a naval engagement; Caroline, his wife, was "extremely beautiful" and of a cultured, sensitive frame of mind. The pair had one child and were living in perfect harmony in a Bristol lodging house when a man almost twice Caroline's age, a Captain Coleman, "a military man, aged forty, a man of the world, of great experience" set his sights on her. He had moved into the same lodging house and was quickly attracted by her good looks and elegant manners. He was accused of having carefully planned his seduction by figuring out Caroline's weak points. He discovered that she was fond of reading. Although Caroline had a very moral, upright nature, by lending her books and holding literary discussions, Coleman soon "obtained the enjoyment of her person."

The two began seeing each other whenever Lieutenant Trelawney was away. The trusting husband was unaware of any difficulty. It was true that Caroline now requested that they sleep in separate beds, but she was pregnant again and he figured she was uncomfortable and restless at night. But one day he picked up a note which dropped out of a book that was lying about and which was filled with the most passionate expressions of tenderness. It was addressed to "Dearest Anne" not "Dearest Caroline," but somehow it aroused his suspicions.

Trelawney thereupon asked the landlady whether she had noticed anything odd in Caroline's habits when he was out of the house. She hadn't, but after he mentioned his distrust, the landlady took to spying. One day she climbed on top of an outhouse which adjoined Captain Coleman's bedroom, and, casting her eyes toward the room, saw there Mrs. Trelawney's shoes. She took a "more enlarged view of the room, and she saw the Defendant and Mrs. Trelawney in bed together; and she had no doubt, from what she saw, that the adulterous intercourse had taken place." In the end, the jury decided that Trelawney had indeed been sorely damaged by the seducer Captain Coleman, and awarded him five hundred pounds in damages.

That was small pickings. Lord Elgin, who brought to England the Greek sculptures called the Elgin marbles, sued a man who had had an affair with Lady Elgin and obtained a monumental award. The lover, R. J. Fergusson, at one time Elgin's secretary, was accused of adopting a "deliberate system" to break down Lady Elgin's morality. That system was a series of impassioned love letters, filled with pronouncements like, "Till I breathe my last, Mary, I boast of loving you with a passion never known before; never was there such a perfect union."

Fergusson's lawyer argued that his client, a young man without a shilling, wasn't scheming but, rather, suffering from a form of temporary insanity. He said the letters "appear to be the effusions of a man in a frenzy, persuading himself that he and this lady were born for one another, and to live in a state of bliss more than was possible to be enjoyed by mortals upon this earth . . . [it is] impossible that any man could read them without being convinced that such romantic ideas of happiness could not exist in a sane mind." Nevertheless, Lord Elgin was granted an award of ten thousand pounds.

Of course, husbands didn't always get the rewards they asked for. One rather famous case was brought by the actor Theophilus Cibber, son of England's highly-respected dramatist and poet laureate, Colley Cibber. It ended in Cibber's being denied his requested award of five thousand pounds for a Mr. Sloper's adultery with Cibber's wife Susannah Maria because the jury felt that not only Cibber but even Susannah Maria had arranged the adultery as a get-rich-quick scheme.

What was motivating these eighteenth- and early nineteenth-century women to be adulterous, to push so brazenly against the morality of their day? One reason may have been that adultery was the only grounds for divorce. At least, this was the opinion expressed in many English documents of the period, although two entirely different cures for the situation were recommended. One group of social critics argued that adultery would decrease only if additional grounds for divorce were permitted. Their position was that unhappy marriages were breeding grounds for adultery. Pointing to the fact that repeatedly people who had been abandoned by their spouses and people whose marriages had never been consummated failed in their legal efforts to divorce, they insisted that in a peculiar albeit unintentional way the law rewarded the adulterous.

One particularly touching case that was brought to trial involved Mary Forester and George Downing, who had been married in 1701 when she was thirteen years old and he a mere two years her elder. They had been "put to Bed, in the Day Time, according to Custom, and continued there a little while, but . . . they touch'd not One the Other." Immediately afterwards, perhaps ashamed of his inadequate performance, George left his bride and went abroad, disappearing from her life, avoiding all contact and communication. He traveled for three or four years and, when he eventually returned to England, wanted nothing to do with the young woman with whom he had been so unaroused. Fourteen years later both the young people's families attempted to have the marriage dissolved.

The House of Peers debated the situation for a strenuous three hours, but in the end voted against the dissolution, citing the "solemn words used by Our Saviour, that those whom God hath joined, let no man put asunder."

Eloquently, the counsel for the young couple argued that it was appalling that a pair so young should be forced to waste their entire lives because of their early disastrous marriage. And he made the radical assertion that it was incredibly unfair that in a case like this where "the parties are each of them untouched, pure and unsullyed, even in thought" no divorce should be possible, whereas in cases of adultery, where one or both partners had done "such things as I have neither will nor leave to mention," divorce "follows of course." But the House of Peers remained adamant. "Nothing but adultery can dissolve a marriage."

While one group of social critics was arguing that divorce should be made more accessible, so as not to reward the adulterous, another maintained the reverse. They held that adultery could only be eliminated if the adulterous could be prohibited from divorcing or at least from marrying again and especially from marrying their adulterous paramours. On occasion they proposed laws to ensure this.

In one curious document, women were portrayed as the greatest obstacle to the passage of such laws. It is *The House of Peeresses or Female Oratory,* published in 1779, in which a group of unnamed but identifiable English peeresses strenuously oppose the passage of a law proposed by the Bishop of Landaff to prohibit the adulterous from remarrying for twelve months after divorce. In the debate, the peeresses express their fear that such a restriction might indeed hinder them and they assert that adultery has been for them a treasure "surpassing the descriptive fire of eloquence, a treasure your mothers and grandmothers have maintained with

united and irresistible torrents of threats, prayers, ill language, and omnipotent invective." One dynamic orator sums
up the case: adultery is woman's "last expedient," her only
outlet from "her Lord's imperious government." Rather
than give up the privilege, the women should riot as the
American Colonists have done.

It is, of course, a satire, but it reflects the very serious concern of the period over the uses of adultery.

In France, even adultery did not lead to the dissolution of
marriage. Divorce was unknown until 1792, although a husband (but not a wife) could obtain a separation from an unfaithful spouse. During the Revolution the law was changed
to permit divorce on the grounds of incompatibility, but it
was quickly revoked, then reinstituted by Napoleon with
some restrictions, and at last suppressed again under the
Bourbons. It remained impossible to divorce in France until
1884.

Adultery nevertheless appears to have been common in
France as well as in England, at least among rich and powerful women. It was not the carrot of divorce that dangled at the
end of the stick of extramarital liaisons. Other enticements
were suspended there. Women found themselves in pursuit
not of remarriage but of love. "Love is above the laws, above
the opinion of men; it is the truth, the flame, the pure ele-
ment, the primary idea of the moral world," wrote Madame
de Staël in a novel, while living her life in demonstration.
It was the dawn of a period in which declarations of independence flourished. De Staël had married her husband in
1786; by 1789 she had already taken at least two lovers, and
was smartly outwitting her husband. Did he say she had spent
twelve hours with a lover? Madame de Staël acted outraged,
insulted. It had only been six.

Like many other women of her day, de Staël was an
admirer of Rousseau, a believer in tempestuous passion and
the stormy majesty of the emotions. Her husband had disap-

pointed her. He may have been a homosexual. But whether
he was or wasn't, he was certainly never able to produce in
her the torrents of passion she had envisioned. She grew depressed and for the rest of her life used affairs as a form
of therapy—they countered her depression and maintained
her ego. She may have been one of the first women writers
to recognize how this worked—there have been many since.
Writing to one lover who had angered her, she provocatively
explained why she had let another man "love me madly";
she had done so in order to pick up "a sort of excitement that
would relieve for a moment the terrible weight that was
pressing on my heart."

George Sand, who also had her first affair within a few
short years of marriage, was to attempt later in life to describe
to her husband the lack of uxorious appreciation which provoked her adultery.

> At nineteen, freed from all real anxieties and troubles,
> married to a man of excellent qualities and mother of a
> fine child, surrounded by everything calculated to flatter
> my tastes, I yet lived a life of utter boredom. This mood
> of mine can be easily explained. There is a period in the
> life of every woman when she needs to love, and to love
> exclusively. When she is in that state of mind, it needs
> must be that her every action is concentrated upon the
> beloved object. She values her charms and her talents
> only insofar as they give delight to him. You never no-
> ticed mine. Such knowledge as I had was wasted, since
> you did not share it. I did not put all this into words,
> even to myself, but I felt it. I pressed you in my arms,
> I was loved by you, and yet, something, I knew not what,
> was lacking to my happiness . . .

Sand, Madame de Staël, most other heiresses in the eighteenth and nineteenth centuries, and indeed most middle-
class women, were married when very young. Marriages were
arranged for economic convenience by parental command.

Sand had actually tried to resist early marriage. But when she was eighteen, her mother threatened that unless she married she would be locked up until she reached twenty-one in a particularly punitive convent where "no one will listen to your complaints, and neither you nor your friends will know the name and whereabouts of your retreat." Her mother actually went so far as to take Sand to the door of the proposed convent-jail, and Sand married the next man who asked.

Many advanced nineteenth-century social thinkers concluded from examples like this that the marriage of parental command or economic convenience was itself what was provoking female adultery. Harriet Martineau, the mid-nineteenth-century sociologist, argued that if love marriages could replace "mercenary marriages," extramarital sex would diminish. She felt that when people married for economic reasons "the sanctity of marriage is impaired, and vice succeeds. Anyone must see at a glance that if men and women marry those whom they do not love, they must love those whom they do not marry."

The love that nineteenth-century women sought was not usually envisioned as a carnal pursuit. In fact, often it was the opposite. Women craved sentimental and spiritual attachment to men who, unlike their husbands, did not demand sex of them. Sand found her husband's sexuality brutal, degrading. She was to write, "Men do not know that what is fun for them is hell for us." Her first love affair was with a young man with whom she exchanged merely kisses and passionate letters. Confessing her attachment in an eighteen-page letter to her husband, she swore the affair would never become physical, but begged her husband's permission to send her lover "one letter a month. . . . You shall read all his letters to me, and all my answers."

When Leo Tolstoy's wife at age fifty-three developed an attachment to a musician who was a frequent visitor to the Tolstoy home, she wrote in her diary how much more enticing she found the thought of spiritual love than the sexual love in her marriage. "I yearn for a poetic, spiritual, even a sentimental relationship with someone—only to get away from this eternal sex."

In England, it was the period of Victorianism and the sexologist William Acton wrote, "I should say that the majority of women (happily for society) are not very much troubled with sexual feeling of any kind." In the United States, even leaders of the women's rights movement like Sarah Grimké did not put much stock in women's sexuality. Grimké, who believed that women were naturally superior to men, thought that the superiority had to do with the very fact that "the sexual passion in man is ten times stronger than in woman."

With the flowering of the psychological novel in the nineteenth century, the adulterous woman now emerged as heroine or central figure in many analytic novels, plays, and stories. Almost always her emotional rather than her physical yearnings were stressed. Who did not have a go at her? She was examined by Pushkin, Dostoyevsky, Tolstoy, Hawthorne, Balzac, Flaubert and many other writers. Many of the attitudes that still dominate our understanding of female adultery are drawn from the careful observations of nineteenth-century writers.

We see the adulteress as self-absorbed and narcissistic, the way Dostoyevsky saw her in *The Eternal Husband*. His Natalya Vassilyevna is

> resolute and domineering. . . . She never thought herself wrong or to blame in anything. Her continual unfaithfulness to her husband did not weigh on her conscience in the least. . . . She was faithful to her lover, but only as long as he did not bore her.

Simultaneously we see her as a kind of noble savage, as Pushkin saw her in his dramatic poem *The Gypsies*. His Zemfira has lived only a few years with the adoring Aleko, but she finds his love monotonous and so she almost frivolously takes a gypsy lover.

But most of all, we see her as she was presented in *The Scarlet Letter, Madame Bovary,* and *Anna Karenina.* All three novels, each so different and so wonderful, share one view in common: the adulteress is seeking emotional fulfillment, whether authentically, as are Anna and Hester Prynne, or shallowly, hysterically, as is Emma Bovary. These women may victimize their husbands, but they are themselves victims of their societies' emphasis upon finding love.

For one thing, each of the heroines shares a biographical fact that we have come to assume common to all nineteenth-century women. Each, like the real-life adulteresses who left journals and letters, had married husbands they did not love. Emma had married her husband to get away from her father's farm where she wore wooden shoes and roughened her hands. It took her little time to realize that although her husband brought her material comfort, he was no savior. "Charles' conversation was flat as a sidewalk, a place of passage for the ideas of everyman . . . *This* man could teach you nothing; he knew nothing; he wished for nothing." Hawthorne's Hester considers her "crime most to be repented of" not her adultery with Dimmesdale, but the fact that she "had ever endured, and reciprocated, the lukewarm grasp" of her elderly, scholarly husband's hands, "and had suffered the smile of her lips and eyes to mingle and melt into his own." And Anna's husband, although innately kind, is pompous and frigid, with "an habitual sarcastic smile" and "big tired eyes."

It is important to note that not one of the authors of these three most compelling novels of female adultery was, in his personal attitudes or literary intentions, sympathetic to women's sexual experimentation. Hawthorne had once refused to meet George Eliot because she was living with a man without marrying him; Tolstoy had in mind, when he started *Anna Karenina,* the story of a heartless, flirtatious and crude woman, "not guilty but merely pitiful"; and Flaubert wanted to expose the banality of adultery. When Baudelaire praised him for discussing this "tritest possible human situation" he thanked him, saying, "You have entered into the secret of my book as though my brain were yours." Yet Hawthorne's Hester emerges as an honorable figure, ennobled by her never-wavering love for the unworthy Dimmesdale. Anna grew sympathetic and complex, so overtaking Tolstoy's original conception of her character that he had to rewrite the novel several times. And even Emma so overcame Flaubert's distaste for her that at times he wept over her troubles and, almost despite himself, seems to have felt some tenderheartedness for her, however banal he painted her. There is certainly a tinge of tenderness toward Emma in his explanation of why she desires a male and not a female child:

> A man is free, at least—free to range the passions and the world, to surmount obstacles, to taste the rarest pleasures. Whereas a woman is continually thwarted. Inert, compliant, she has to struggle against her physical weakness and legal subjection. Her will, like the veil tied to her hat, quivers with every breeze; there is always a desire that entices, always a convention that restrains.

It is against this background of the great nineteenth-century novels that today's women novelists explore the adulteress. But along the way her passion has become sexualized.

Perhaps it was inevitable once sex no longer led inexorably to pregnancy, with its ever-present tragic risks. Male contraceptives—condoms—were in use in the eighteenth century but they were uncomfortable and inadequate. Madame de Staël had described them as "a breast plate against pleasure and a cobweb against danger." In the nineteenth century they were improved, and female contraceptives—cervical caps— were invented, but both types caught on very slowly. There were powerful religious proscriptions against their use even until our own day. Thus nineteenth-century opponents of adultery used to urge women to eschew it not just because of moral scruples but because their sexual wandering brought with it the danger of polluting family blood—the possibility of illegitimate children. As an American physician explained in 1866, an adulterous wife might easily become pregnant, thereby introducing into her family an illegitimate child "which must either be maintained by a man not its father, or cruelly driven from the household for a sin not its own." With contraception, illegitimacy became less fearsome, and so too did sex itself.

Just as powerful as contraception in lessening women's fear of sex, and consequent avoidance of it, were the medical advances that reduced the dangers of that so common killer of women, childbirth complications, and that so common killer of infants, early childhood diseases. In England, as late as the 1890s, the average wife had a life expectancy of only forty-six years. It was expected rather than astonishing that several of the children she gave birth to would die in infancy or that she herself might die in childbirth. No wonder then that women loved for emotional rather than sexual pleasure.

It was, I believe, the removal of these two awesome negative consequences of sex—continual pregnancy and the concomitant fear of death either for the self or young offspring—that turned women's thoughts about sex to joy rather than dread. I don't mean that it turned women's thoughts to extramarital relations, but rather that the adulterous began to add to their emotional pursuits the quest for sexual pleasure.

Thus, in the twentieth century and among women writers, the adulteress is usually portrayed as a woman seeking not only emotional but sexual gratification. On occasion it is even sexual gratification of the no-strings-attached variety that heroines pursue—what Kate Chopin presented as Calixta's "birthright" in 1904, and Erica Jong as Isadora Wing's "zipless fuck" in 1973.

Curiously, the contemporary adulterous heroine is still out of love with her husband, despite the fact that she has presumably married in the twentieth-century fashion, for love.

Here is something that has not changed. Adultery has not withered away along with the withering of the marriage of parental command. There are two different points of view among women novelists as to why their heroines do not love their husbands.

One view holds that even though parents and economic necessity no longer dominate the young woman's choice of a husband, there are nevertheless powerful social pressures that make her marry with as little thought to her future needs as did her nineteenth-century sister.

In Judith Rossner's *Any Minute I Can Split* the heroine seems to have been aware of potential disappointments in her husband-to-be before they married. "Even then he would pinch her hard or kick her in the shins under the table if they had an argument when her parents were around, coming attractions for his proclivity to hit below the belt." But yet, as the author points out, these prickings of anxiety do not constitute reasons not to marry. "Once you decided to get married there was a kind of impetus that carried you through without leaving room in your thoughts for questions of mistakes." In Barbara Raskin's *Loose Ends,* the author explains that her heroine "married Gavin for a variety of reasons among which was the fact that Gavin was the first man to propose."

Another, perhaps more pessimistic group of writers, attributes adultery to alienation: either a woman's alienation from the goals of her society or her personal alienation from her husband. One can feel as alienated from a loved spouse as from an unloved one. Alienation develops like a disease. Psychoanalyst Leon Salzman, author of numerous articles on the psychology of adultery, says that even in marriages that begin with devotion, loyalty, and mutual commitment, alienation may set in as a result of "disappointed, unreal expectations and other exaggerated demands that cannot be fulfilled." Adultery follows as inevitably as it does in loveless matches.

"Dear Dr. Reuben," asks the heroine of *Fear of Flying,*

"Why does the fucking always become like processed cheese?"
A marriage that has at least the grace note of good sex has
deteriorated. Isadora, the heroine, had once loved her husband—had even loved his tendency to be silent. Yet eventually
this very trait began to dismay her. Bennett Wing had

> appeared as in a dream. On the wing, you might
> say. Tall, good-looking, inscrutably Oriental. Long thin
> fingers, hairless balls, a lovely swivel to his hips when he
> screwed—at which he seemed to be absolutely indefat-
> igable. But he was also mute and at that point his silence
> was music to my ears. How did I know that a few years
> later, I'd feel like I was fucking Helen Keller?

In Sandra Hochman's *Walking Papers* a similar alienation
has overcome the heroine, destroying what once she assumed
was love. In the case of Hochman's heroine, not only communication but sex too has deteriorated.

> I ask myself, what went wrong with Jason?
> And me? It's hard to explain. Suddenly there was no
> more sweetness. No more kindness. The talking stopped.
> And the lovemaking. No talk. No touch. How else do
> people reach out? By eyes. By the eyes. But he never
> looked at my eyes. I kept searching his eyes for looks
> that would mean something to me. And nothing was
> there. . . . I was being wrapped in bandages. Nothing
> to look forward to but my mummification.

Sometimes the husband has lost his wife's respect. This is
the situation in Doris Lessing's *Summer Before the Dark*.
Kate, many years married, feels disappointed with her husband because he has begun having casual sexual affairs with
women who are emotionally unimportant to him. ". . . she
was feeling about him, had felt for some time, rather as if
he had a weakness for eating sweets and would not restrain it.
He was diminished; there was no doubt about that."
In Mary McCarthy's *A Charmed Life* there is a chilling

insistence on the fact that love itself breeds alienation. Martha and her husband actually still love each other, but this in itself makes them depressed. There is no longer anything to hope for.

> If they could have chosen over again, neither would have chosen differently. Neither of them knew anyone they would have preferred to the other. They could not even imagine an ideal companion they would put in the other's place. From their point of view, for their purposes, they had the best there was. There lay the bleakness; for them, as they were constituted, through all eternity, this had been the optimum—there was no beyond. There was nothing.

Yet when the wife in a contemporary novel of adultery falls into a love affair, she does not fall in love. Something is always wrong with the lovers. Jong's heroine, Lady Chatterley in reverse, chooses an impotent man. Hochman's chooses a man whom she despises for his emotional cruelty. McCarthy's heroine chooses her ex-husband, a man she has previously rejected and fled. The lover in the Rossner novel is a puerile youth who asks the heroine, "How do you get attached to people?" while she can only wonder, "How could you *not* get attached to people?" Lessing's heroine knew at the start of her affair that "Jeffrey Merton, in retrospect, when she looked back, would seem to her all dryness and repetition."

Sometimes the men selected must be seduced into love affairs. This is a great humiliation for heroines and a surefire deterrent to love. In Ann Birstein's novels and stories, lovers are incapable or unwilling to make arrangements for liaisons. In *Love in the Dunes* Mrs. Kane thinks:

> Charlie make arrangements? That was the best joke yet. Poor Charlie, what had he ever done, except be willing? It was she who had dreamed the whole thing up single-

handed, she who had planned and schemed and even—
she blushed to think of it now—dragged him off bodily
this morning.

In Birstein's *Dickie's List,* the heroine suggests any number of
romantic or at least comfortable lovemaking situations but
the lover rejects them all. There will be no idyllic overnight
trains to Chicago—"They've discontinued the run, love"—no
day at a country inn or even an afternoon at a Plaza suite.
The lover merely offers a hasty grab at the heroine while they
are both attending a party. Dismayed, she means to refuse
him, but ends by agreeing to the abrupt intercourse. She has
come to realize "This was how you bought an ounce of love."

Small portions—millimeters—are the only quantities of love
the contemporary heroine seeks or obtains. The big passions
are beyond her calculation.

When the affair is over, the contemporary heroine usually
returns home to husband and family. If she never physically
but merely psychologically and sexually wandered, she nevertheless has traversed a path, even though she has ended up,
to the outsider's eye, exactly where she started out. We have
lived through the era of suicide as fiction's conventional
retribution for women's adultery. Mary McCarthy in *A
Charmed Life* was the last modern female author to kill off
a funtioning adulteress at plot's end. (Joan Didion's Maria
does kill herself in *Play It As It Lays,* but she is already only
half-conscious at the start of this dirgeful novel.)

But retribution itself is not dead. The return to marriage
may be the new fictional convention of retribution, as suicide
was in nineteenth-century novels. When I interviewed Ann
Birstein, she stated that in her novels at least, "the heroines'
marriages *are* their retribution. Although they don't walk
into the sea, they're treading water while living. Although
they don't die, something in them is dead because of the
death of their aspirations."

If the contemporary adulterous heroine is not seeking or

finding great love, what is it she pursues? It is still emotional fulfillment, although this frequently comes garbed now in an almost mystical belief in the healing powers of explosive sexuality. Alfred Kazin found such insistence on the holiness of sex nostalgic—for men—when *Lady Chatterley's Lover* was at last issued in America in 1959. He wrote of that book that it brought back "memories of a time when men still believed in establishing freedom as their destiny on earth, when sex was the major symbol of the imprisoned energies of man, for when *that* castle was razed, life would break open and flow free." Kazin was suggesting that such a belief, fashionable in the twenties, was already outmoded in 1959 and that contemporary men no longer held illusions about the power of sex.

Perhaps so, but it was not so for women. Women were just then beginning to cotton to such beliefs. They came late to an absorption with sexuality. And it is not yet outmoded or illusory for them. They are still pondering what will make *their* imprisoned energies flow free, and sex—along with many other things—seems at times a likely key. Therefore, it is no surprise that the figure of the adulterous woman—the woman who gambles security for sex—is so preoccupying for today's women novelists. They do not necessarily find her admirable, nor do they represent her sexual encounters as particularly rewarding. Nevertheless, they focus on her, if only because she is so enigmatic a heroine, a self-determined but mysterious guerrilla fighting in the underbrush of social custom. She has figured in so many plots, yet neither her full story nor her ultimate aims has altogether unfolded.

# Part II

*Interviewing: Marriage*

## Who the Women Are

I began to gather the stories which unfold here by talking with a handful of friends and some of my former neighbors who had, in the past, described their extramarital sexual experiences to me. But I quickly abandoned doing interviews in this way. It seemed at once too close and too distancing; I felt I would be uncomfortable in my future relationships with friends and neighbors (and their husbands) if I knew too much personal history. For me, friendship equates with slow disclosure; I get to know friends gradually, at their pace and not at my insistence. So I determined to do my interviews primarily among women not known to me before the time I began formal work on this book.

But how to reach them? I did it by discussing the nature of my project in the wide circle of my friends, acquaintances, and professional associates. I had the theory that many women involved in extramarital affairs confided in someone; that without a friend who knew the ins and outs of her erotic life, an adulterous woman would feel divided, unreal, perhaps depersonalized. I suppose I had gotten the idea from Flaubert. Even Madame Bovary had a confidante, her maid Felicité, who ultimately knew all Emma's sexual arrangements, and shared with her certain feminine sorrows.

The theory proved valid. There were hosts of women whose paths crossed mine who had friends, neighbors, colleagues who had confided affairs, and who urged their peers to speak with me. Everyone knew someone. A friend in suburban Connecticut, herself a faithful wife for twenty-five years, had nevertheless been the confidante and emotional barometer for two neighbors whose lives were less fixed than her own. A woman in a Midwestern city who was the friend of a friend called and said she knew four women in her town whom I might interview; I flew out and spoke with them all. At a party a woman I merely chatted with about my work responded with interest to the project. "I've never played around," she said. "And wouldn't. But my sister has been doing it for two years now, and I think she'd be grateful for a chance to speak with you." My phone rang constantly. "I have a friend." "There's a woman I work with." "My neighbor has been having a turbulent affair." Following leads like these, I interviewed women in a miscellany of middle-class Manhattan neighborhoods and, ultimately, in unfamiliar, sometimes distant suburbs and cities.

I arbitrarily stopped collecting informants when I had conducted lengthy interviews with sixty-six women whom I had selected from a preliminary list of a hundred. The accounts I heard by then seemed to me sufficient for a presentation of the characteristic patterns of female extramarital sexual behavior—its causes, its outcomes, its pleasures, its pains.

I have not included every story I was told. Some were not related with enough detail for me to translate authentic character or the particularities of experience onto paper; some were too similar to accounts I was already determined to use and would, therefore, have made the book repetitious; some were not especially interesting or telling. But those stories I have used are the reports of individual women, not of composites or types.

The accounts are organized within under two major headings, "Marriage" and "Experimental Marriage." Traditionally, marriage is a relationship between a man and a woman that requires two significant promises. One is that the participants to marriage will love each other for their lifetimes—the vow of permanence; the other is that they will love only each other—the vow of exclusivity. Most of us who marry, today just as in the past, make either ceremonial public or intimate private vows on these matters. Both vows are, however, often breached. What has happened to permanence can be observed in the ever-mounting divorce rate. Exclusivity is breached by extramarital sex.

In "Marriage," I present accounts of women who, by virtue of traditional marriage vows, attempt to be secretive about extramarital sexual experiences. In "Experimental Marriage," I present accounts of women who are committed to acknowledging such experience to their husbands. Marriages with this commitment are sometimes called open marriages or new marital life-styles or alternatives. In them, the vow concerning exclusivity has been revised. It avoids infidelity—the breaking of a faith or trust—but permits and sometimes even encourages adultery—extramarital sex.

Within the sections devoted to "Marriage" and "Experimental Marriage," I have further subdivided the book into chapters that begin with the phrases "Staying Married" or "Breaking Up." Both traditional adulterous marriages and experimental adulterous marriages sometimes hold—that is, the partners stay married—and sometimes cease holding and come apart; this is of course true for monogamous marriages as well. I have not made these subdivisions because I have found the answer to the perennial question of whether extramarital sex bolsters marriage or weakens it. The division merely reflects my interviewees' marital status at the time of the interview.

Why were these women who spoke with me willing to discuss with a stranger so personal and usually secret a subject as extramarital sex? One friend said to me, "I should think the only women you'll get will be the braggers and the exhibitionists." But this wasn't so. There were some of those, but there were shy women and embarrassed women as well.

What I discovered was that there was so often pain and confusion associated with women's affairs that many women accepted, even welcomed, the invitation to discuss their feelings and experiences. I had promised to try to be as nonjudgmental as possible and I believe this helped. I had also promised that I would use fictitious names in recounting their experiences, and that I would alter identifying details by choosing appropriate substitutes for such matters as occupation or residence. I think it helped, too, that I was known to be serious. I always used to chide myself for a certain brow-furrowing sobriety, but now my very failing served me well. Women who confided in me knew I wouldn't mock.

Finally, the women who spoke with me came because they were interested in seeing a change in the pejorative atmosphere surrounding female extramarital sex. They felt their experiences, when known, were judged more harshly than were men's, that there was no justification for this double standard hangover, and that opening up the subject might begin to clear the air.

When I was interviewing, I tried to give as much of myself as I could. All interviewers do. Many of my meetings with women took place over lunches and dinners; often I was invited to their homes; I met children, husbands, lovers. It was necessary to have dialogues, to be more than a questioner, more than a collector of monologues. In writing the results of my research, I again have tried to give something of myself, to include, wherever craft permitted, my reactions and response. I wanted to let the women speak. I love the authenticity of tape, but I often find mere transcribed and edited tape recordings dull and lifeless. Just as it is the interviewer's reaction and response that determines whether an interview will come alive, so, it seems to me, does his or her reaction and response determine whether the final transcribed and edited version has life. The technique didn't always work— sometimes my responses lay buried or confused—but it always seemed worth the effort, largely because I eventually realized that there was more than style at stake. It had become clear to me that the most important aspect of women's stories of their extramarital adventuring lay not in the social explorers themselves but in how the rest of us observe, receive, and screen out their news.

# (1)
# Staying Married:
## *Long-term Affairs*

I was always most curious about women who had long-term affairs, women who maintained both husbands and lovers over a period of many years. How did they pilot their years of secrecy? Were the rewards worth the price they paid?

I had known such a woman once. Like a general, she had always seemed prepared for every contingency. She knew exactly which restaurants to avoid because they were too big, noisy, and popular, and which to avoid because they were too small, quiet, and compromising. She was an expert on where to get one's hair cut, washed, and set in record time and where to buy children's clothes without having to rummage through stacks of mis-sized items. She had friends who could cover for her on days the housekeeper was sick; friends to help account for the sudden presence in her closet of expensive gifts from her lover ("Let's say you gave me this alligator bag. No, not gave. Why would you have given it to me? It wasn't my birthday. Let's say your cousin is in the wholesale handbag business and you sold it to me at a third its real price."); friends who would go to movies *for* her, which meant tell her exactly what happened in a film, down to details no reviews had mentioned, so that her report on it to her husband could be eminently credible.

Everyone in her circle (except, of course, her husband) had known about her lover. No one had approved, but no one had ever said a word to her husband. We all knew him for a nice fellow, a generous man. None of us wanted to hurt him; to be the bearer of cruel tidings. But more than this, we figured if he'd wanted to know, he could have. Overused psychology provided a way out; obviously he didn't *want* to know, we'd say. Besides, we figured that one day they would work the whole thing out; the situation would be "resolved."

I looked up this woman when I was starting this project. I had lost touch with her a year before when she moved across town. Now I telephoned her and asked if she would be willing to be formally interviewed. She was agreeable, and I ended up by interviewing her twice, once at the start of my research, the second time a year and a half later.

## Sylvia Shusky / I Can't Bear Loneliness

That first time we sat around Sylvia's living room. Her daughter and a friend were eating peanut butter sandwiches in the kitchen, making a mess, giggling their heads off, joyous. Her son was in his bedroom, watching TV and drinking Hawaiian Punch. Sylvia got up from time to time and wiped up spills. A slim, attractive blonde of thirty-four, she seemed awkward and absent-minded in the kitchen. Once she used a potholder to mop up some punch. Once the girls asked for spreading knives and she gave them small, elegant bone-handled steak knives.

"My lover picks me up in the car," she told me. "We've been together five years now. I still walk the kids to school and then I wait on the corner at York Avenue. He comes down the East River Drive from Westchester, gets off the highway and picks me up. Then we spend the day in his office.

"It wasn't always like that. In the beginning it was the usual thing: lunch once a week, the rest of the afternoon in a hotel room. But it gave us a creepy feeling. We felt we were in love, but we couldn't tell because we never did anything but go to bed together. So one day he said, 'Come down to my office. No one will say anything. They don't know you and your family from Adam. And the people who work for me are all loyal; old friends and loyal; none of them would dream of saying anything to my wife. They like her and know it would break her heart.'

"So I started going down there once, twice a week. Later I hired a housekeeper because I wanted to be sure of getting out and if a kid got sick I couldn't be sure. But with the housekeeper I can. I meet Tom every day during the week except holidays. I sit around his office in the mornings while he works. I write letters to my friends. I keep cookbooks there and plan my night's menu. Then I call up for the groceries and have them delivered to the housekeeper. I do my hair there a lot. In the sink in the ladies' room. That way my husband thinks I've been to the hairdresser."

She also pays her bills from her lover's office, does her nails, and reads the magazines. It makes Tom, her lover, feel good to have her working beside him, she said, giving an air of domesticity to their lives. When she calls Gristede's and orders fruits, he smacks his lips at her choices and says, "Delicious," quite as if they were being ordered for his own snacking that night. He works more rapidly than he used to, finishes what once took a whole day in only half, and then he and Sylvia daily go off for lunch and for the remainder of the afternoon to a studio apartment he has rented under Sylvia's maiden name. She is always home by five; her husband gets in around six; and she regales him with stories of her day's adventures out shopping, lunching with friends, touring the galleries.

She and Tom actually do go shopping a couple of times a week. "We look around in Saks or Altman's. We never spend much time at it, but about twice a week I make a purchase—whether it's a dress or slacks for me, a toy or sweater for the kids, new towels or a kitchen gadget. On those nights I tell my husband, 'Look what I found today!' Whatever the thing costs I always quote a lower price. Then if he is in the mood to chide me, either for going shopping as frequently as I do or because by his reckoning I've spent the whole day at it and made just a single small purchase, he can't. He thinks of me as a crazy, meticulous shopper and is impressed each time at how little I have spent. And of course, since Tom pays for almost half of everything I buy, our house really is nicely furnished on very little, the kids have better toys than anyone else on the street, and I have a stunning wardrobe. And it doesn't cost Bill very much money."

I found Sylvia startling, even when I came to know many other women whose affairs were as elaborate or complex as hers. I think it was because she focused so squarely on the economic conveniences of her double life. But convenience had always been uppermost to her. It had made her quick to marry, she told me. She had come to New York from the suburbs right after college and worked for an insurance company briefly, sharing an East Side apartment with three other girls. "That was terrible," she said. "We had to sign up for the bedroom on weekends. And the food situation was worse. Each girl had a yogurt container with her own name written on it and at any one time there were four half-eaten grapefruits and four sticks of butter turning into cheese in each quadrant of the box."

Bill Shusky, who was to become her husband, was a friend of family friends. He looked her up and took her out. To East Side movies. To dinners. "Five-course French dinners," are still uppermost in her memories. He was a joke-cracker and fond of remarks like "Where there's a will, there's a way," and "Laugh and the world laughs with you; cry and you cry alone." Just finishing engineering school, he wanted a wife, a home, furniture, children, respectability. They were married four months after they met, basking in their families' approval.

They had been to bed together during the four months of courtship, and Sylvia remembers, "Bed was boring from the start. We used to get laid in the early evening so we could top the experience with a movie or dinner. But I didn't think it made too much difference. I didn't know what it was going to feel like five years later."

A year after they were married they had a child; three years later, another. Sylvia had not liked her time in the work force; there was nothing she wanted to study; so she furnished her home, learned to cook, took care of the babies, and then looked up one day and noticed that her husband seemed fonder of them than he was of her. Or they were fonder of him than she was.

"He used to work late and was always tired when he came home. Sometimes he'd have supper and just go right to bed. But if the children woke up he was always willing to feed them, diaper them, play with them. He used to hold them on his lap, brush their hair, and feed them endlessly with the baby spoon. Big mouths gaping, tidbits going down. Daddy. It made me sick.

"I hated going to parties with him," she said, "with his color photographs of the kids zipping out of his pocket the minute someone breathed, 'Do you have children?' I hated that I was stuck at home while he was forever complaining, 'Oh, if I only had more time to spend with my family.' "

The winter that the second baby was two years old, Sylvia became very depressed. She made no social engagements with any of their friends. She no longer went to school to meet the older child's teachers. She stopped buying clothing, slept ten or twelve hours a night, napped in the afternoon, and read nothing but *Vogue*.

On weekends her husband took the children sleighing or skating and she was angry with them when they came home, either cold and hungry or, when he had tried to keep them longer out of her hair, warmed and sedated on a snack at the Chinese restaurant. Those nights he brought her a Chinese supper home in containers since she insisted she hated the smoky place. But she rarely ate it. It was the wrong dish;

didn't he remember what she liked; she was angry, furious, fierce. The children were afraid of her.

Then, that spring, a friend introduced her to Tom. Sylvia described how it happened: "My best girlfriend from my single days called and said, 'Sylvia, there's this guy I ran into who we used to know. He makes toys. He remembered me from the days we were working at the insurance company. He remembers you too, but he says you'll never recognize him now. He used to be fat and now he's gone to Weight Watchers and he's positively skinny. What about a lunch for old times' sake? He says you and I were the most beautiful girls in New York in those days and that I'm still one and he wants to see about you.' "

It was enough to get Sylvia up and out of bed that day. She bought a hat and had her hair done. The three of them had lunch at The Sign of the Dove, a setting Sylvia found very romantic, and by the time they were into their third martinis, Tom Brower had confessed how badly life had treated him. His wife was an invalid.

The friend who had brought Sylvia and Tom together was herself having an affair, the details of which had been known to Sylvia for some time. During lunch Sylvia sensed why her friend had presented her with Tom. "It was the same as when you get married and you keep trying to get your single friends to do the same as you," Sylvia said.

Sylvia had two or three more lunches with Tom and then they went to bed together. From the beginning, she found him more sexually stimulating than her husband. "We made love that first time for what seemed like hours. It seemed as if he just couldn't get enough of me. He'd had another mistress before me but she'd left him some months before to get married, and he was really hard up. But the strange thing was that our sex life pretty much stayed this intense. Maybe it's because of the secrecy. I've read there are some people who can screw better just because they're a little scared. In any event, it's been three years now and I'm just as excited every time we make love as I was the first time."

I told Sylvia my notion that probably her husband knew about her affair but had decided for his own reasons to keep silent. Her reaction was odd. She seemed hurt by the suggestion, indignant. "He doesn't know," she said. "If he knew, he'd want to divorce me. What man could just stand by and let his wife have an affair with another man and not do anything about it?"

"Maybe he has a girlfriend and he likes things the way they are."

"Impossible. He's become absolutely asexual."

"Maybe with you."

"No. I'm sure of it. And I'm sure he loves me. It's got to be that he doesn't know."

The next time I spoke to Sylvia about her affair it was a year and a half later. This time she agreed to meet me for lunch. I remember being troubled when I arrived in the restaurant a few minutes late and noticed that Sylvia was already seated at the table and in the company of another woman. I was sure it meant that she had decided not to confide in me further, that she was angry at me for the questions I had already asked. She had brought a friend along as armor.

As I came up to them Sylvia introduced me. "This is my friend Roberta," she said, "you know, the one who introduced me to Tom. She called this morning and I said I was meeting you and that I didn't think you'd mind meeting another one of us." She smiled coyly. She was in a club with Roberta. They were campfire girls, scouts, companions in tying and untying sexual knots. I realized I would still get my interview and I relaxed, annoyed with myself for having assumed that Sylvia was angry when in actuality she was trying to help me.

Her friend Roberta was, it turned out, a theoretician of affairs. She could always tell when a woman needed an affair, she said, and when she had actually started one. The need took the form of what she had recognized in Sylvia: depression, withdrawal. Starting had coiffure clues. "Most women change their hair style," Roberta told me. "They go from long to short in a rush, or from straight to curly." She had just noticed such a hairdressing change in a neighbor and extricated a confession: the neighbor had begun an affair with a cabdriver. Roberta frowned. Her own affair, five years in duration, was with a wealthy businessman. "I like all the trimmings," she said. "The lunches; the gifts; the trips when we can manage them."

Sylvia, it developed, was still seeing Tom but she had been through a crisis. During the past year she had begun to pressure Tom to leave his wife. She had grown edgy about lying to her husband, anxious about her future. She and Tom had begun to squabble. He had pleaded the illness of his wife, saying, "If I left her, I could never forgive myself." Sylvia had said, "If you don't, I'll never be able to forgive *myself.*"

Through all the quarrels, Roberta had been Sylvia's confidante, helpmeet, therapist. "You were wacky!" Roberta said now, prodding Sylvia. And to me, she said, "She's telling you the facts but she's leaving out how wacky she was. The phone calls in the middle of the night! The vomiting!" Both women laughed now. It had been said. It was a while ago. Things were different now, settled once again.

Sylvia had made a decision. She no longer wanted to leave her husband. "I have the best of both worlds," she said, "a husband who asks no questions. A lover who cares about me. It's fun going places with Bill and the children on weekends. And it's good being able to get away from them during the week and see Tom. He wouldn't leave his wife, but I decided it was just as well. I'd be scared to marry Tom. The thing, the real thing, that worries me, is he's fifty and I'm thirty-five. Suppose I married him, and let's say we lived happily for the next fifteen years. Well, let's say he's sixty-five, and he dies. And me, I'm fifty, still young, a fairly young widow. I just don't know. I just don't see how I'd find another man easily at that age."

I felt Sylvia really meant this, felt that her acceptance of the *status quo* of her affair had not come about because of Tom's reluctance to leave his wife but because she had a mammoth fear of loneliness and, to relieve it, two men seemed to her geometrically more effective than one.

## Evelyn Clement /
## Just How Worthwhile Is That Self?

Sylvia was of course a very idle woman. Whenever I told her story to friends, they would say, "Well, certainly she could conduct an elaborate affair like that. It's because she's so underemployed." They read into her daily grooming and domestic habits with her lover an exquisite variation on the boring drudgery of housewifery. Several friends said, "She's a double sufferer," and they were sure that if Sylvia had had a career, she might have been faithful.

But I interviewed several working women whose affairs were just as extravagant. They seemed to exemplify the old notion that the busier one is, the more time one finds.

This was what had happened to Evelyn Clement, an accomplished forty-year-old lawyer. She was one of the most articulate women I met, and a very successful one. She objected to the proposed title of my book, *Playing Around*. Extramarital sex wasn't playing; it was really work, in her opinion.

She lived in Washington, where she had been having an affair with the same man, a colleague, for over ten years. It had been an exquisitely private affair. Both Evelyn and her lover were prominent, in the public eye, and only a few people knew their connection. One of them was the woman who put me in touch with Evelyn.

Evelyn said she was interested in my project but wasn't certain she cared to discuss it. She would buy the book. Yet several days later she telephoned me and said she had decided to speak with me. "Perhaps it will help me sort things out," she said. She would get in touch with me, she promised, when she came to New York in the summer. She and her husband had rented a house at Fire Island, "to get away from it all," she explained, and I *could* interview her there.

I went to see her on a hot August day. Her house was in a community composed almost solely of married people and small children. Life there seemed deliciously stable and extravagantly boring. Women, for the most part alone, were sprawled on the white sand beyond Evelyn's enormous sun deck, tanning themselves and gaily supervising blistering, sandy children. Evelyn confessed to being restless. Taking the house for a month had been her husband's idea, she explained. He liked sailing and was out on the bay now with friends. But besides, she had been working hard all winter and he had wanted her to unwind.

She looked quite relaxed to me. Wearing a bikini and deeply suntanned, she seemed almost too young to be the mother of the two pre-teen-aged girls she introduced as her daughters, although they resembled her: all three were blond and freckled and fishing rod-thin. The girls were barefoot and clamoring to go musseling and soon disappeared, reappearing much later in the afternoon with their catch, which they washed and set to steaming for dinner. Evelyn and I lay down in deck chairs on her porch. But yes, as she had said, she was restless. While I sprawled in the chair, she paced. When I commented on her energy she said it was at once her most valuable asset and her biggest human defect.

She had always had it, she said. She attributed the first affair she had had—some four or five years after her marriage—to her abundant energy. "I hadn't thought of law school at the time and was working as a secretary for a publishing company. It was a dead-end job and my mind was often on ways out of the tedium. So when a very attractive and rather well-known writer I met there began flirting with me, it wasn't long at all before I was available. It started with lunches, of course. I thought him the most exciting man in the world—much more exciting than my husband—and at that point in my life, had this man been deeply interested in me, I might have left my husband. But although I was very committed to him, he just considered our relationship a romp. He was used to adulation. I was just another autograph hound to him, a bedhound, trying to get his unique sexual signature. He had in mind one-night stands in hotels while I had in mind changing my life."

Evelyn went on to describe the defects in her marriage at that long-ago time. "I was very attached to my husband and thought him very good and decent. But I believed that somehow I was stronger, smarter. He didn't really meet all the things I needed in a man." She had felt this from the beginning of her marriage. "I remember crying when I was packing for my honeymoon trip. It was right after the wedding and my husband, Peter, was in the room with me and I knew my crying was making him feel bewildered and betrayed, but I couldn't stop. My mother came in then and tried to smooth things over. She said, 'All girls cry on their wedding day. It's from all the fuss; too much emotion.' Peter and I were both comforted, and I stopped crying.

"But I no longer believe what she said is true. I believe a lot of girls cry on their wedding day, but that when they do, it's not unimportant. It really is a sign of feeling bad, and the idea that it's *just* emotion is hogwash. The woman may not wander from the husband she cried about getting, but the longing is always going to be there in the back of her mind."

In recent years Evelyn had become active in the women's movement. She had made a name for herself as a legal defender of women's rights. She told me that her reputation, with which I was familiar, was making her self-conscious about telling her story. "I suppose the young women of today would condemn me. They'd say, 'If you felt that way about your husband, why didn't you just get out? But it was different twenty years ago. We were raised differently. Even today women my age don't think in terms of giving up a marriage just like that. We look undercover for a substitute husband and only when we have one do we let go."

She had looked for close to fifteen years. After the writer, there was a publicist. After him, there was a professor at the law school to which she had now determined to go, "a very tortured, bizarre person," she said. "I think I've always had a thing for troubled men. Perhaps I viewed myself as capable of saving them. But I wasn't just a missionary. I enjoyed being a little scared. With this man I was always scared. He was married and the whole notion of having an affair was, for him, a notion of perversity. It had to be everything his marriage was not. Had to be dirty, perverse. He didn't want to have intercourse with me, for example. He would keep me in his office late and tell me how much I turned him on, though we didn't call it that then. Probably he said something like how much I excited him. But he wouldn't, couldn't have intercourse with me. He said it would hurt his wife. Probably he was impotent, but I didn't understand it all at the time. In any event, he would insist, plead that I masturbate in front of him. He would raise my skirt and pull down my pants and make me stand, while he stared, handing me different objects from his desk. 'Do it with the pencil,' he would say. 'Just rub yourself with the pencil.' And then, 'Do it with the pen. Stick it in a little. I'll be able to smell you on it all day.' I found the whole thing very humiliating."

Engrossed in her memory, she was frowning, annoyed. I didn't need to ask her why, then, if it had been so humiliating, she had participated, since she offered, "I think the thing about me then, and maybe still today, was that if the man was important, I wanted to collect him. I was, in my job at the publishing company and later in law school, a celebrity-fucker. It's not an unusual madness among women. It's the madness that makes us willing to have relationships in which we're uncomfortable and even scared as long as the men are prominent. We're willing because we imagine that the power of prominent men will somehow rub off on us. It's a form of masochism that occurs when a woman can't invest herself or her husband with stature."

I asked her why she had not been able to invest Peter with stature. "Just because he and I were agemates," she said, pondering it. "Just because I knew him from Day One. A woman meeting Peter today would probably consider him important and a little scary; he's a top childrens' book illustrator, quite successful. But I knew him when we were both nobodies, and so I always felt he was inferior. And since I also felt inferior, I felt I needed someone who was in some way superior to myself to give me ideas or at least surround me with a climate that was intellectually stimulating; it was as if I couldn't get ideas on my own."

At this point we were interrupted by the girls returning with their catch. Evelyn was attentive but quick with them. She set them to washing the mussels. I remember that they used the washing machine, which I thought very innovative.

When she returned to the deck she continued: "But actually none of what I've been telling you is important. What is important is the relationship I've been having for the last ten years with Marcus Roth. I'm sure that's what you meant to ask me about."

I said it was all important, that I was trying to understand the origins of women's wishes for extramarital sex as well as the current events. Evelyn said, "Well, you've got a good subject in me. I'm an analyzer, I've lived with this thing fifteen years and I'm not one of these people who just lets things happen to her, who specializes in shifting responsibility. I know a woman like that. She says, 'I don't know how it happened. It just came over me. Nothing was planned.' To me, that's irresponsible, self-deluding."

Evelyn revealed now that she had carefully plotted her affair with Marcus, to whom she had been introduced at a dinner party. "I had heard him lecture once when I was in school. I was flattered by his attention to me at the dinner party. When, some days later, he called me up for a drink, I knew I was going to try to push us into getting to bed."

Still, the little-girl awkwardness was there. "I didn't know what to call him," she said ruefully. "I remember how excruciatingly awkward it was, that first time in bed. I didn't feel right using his first name. In fact, I don't think I called him by any name for maybe six months."

She must have gotten over her awkwardness, however, since soon she and Marcus were using his apartment regularly when his wife was away, and taking afternoon excursions to motels. But the first arrangement was too erratic and the second too time-consuming. Both Evelyn and her lover were bent on success at work. So after the first six months they rented an apartment together.

"We took it in his name. We usually met just about every afternoon or late afternoon, the first couple of years. As the years went on, we did other things there besides screw. We both loved cooking, and we'd make these opulent lunches for each other, with wine and good French cheese and elaborate sauces. We were trying to get some simulation of real life, because in the back of both our minds was the idea, 'This can't go on forever. Sooner or later we're going to have to give it up or give up our spouses and make a stab at living together.' But cooking lunches wasn't real life, and we never felt quite sure enough of whether we loved each other, I guess. So the sooner or later dragged on and on."

Curiously, Evelyn insisted that despite her sexual experimentations, sex with her husband was better than with her lovers. She said, "I had a better sex life with Peter than with any of them. Still have, for that matter. I think partly this is because it is the most honest. I can feel much freer with Peter to sift out what I like, and to tell him. And he is always very responsive to me. With Marcus I am often dishonest. I feel I always have to pretend to something, have to protect him. He has a lot of potency problems and he always has to prove to himself that he is best at whatever he does. Like if he goes skiing, he has to master it. He took up the piano at forty and after three years he was playing Beethoven's *Appassionata*. He's always testing himself, and he craves evaluation. But I have very few orgasms with him. If I tell him I haven't had one, he always feels upset and obsessed about it, so I have to pretend a lot of the time. Whereas with Peter I can be myself and be honest. But I don't want to deny that there's a strong turn-on for me about Marcus. I always find him stimulating. In some ways sex with him is more exciting because the tension between us mounts and mounts. Still I am freer with Peter."

She followed this with, "In fact, there are many things about this affair, and perhaps about all women's affairs, that are extremely peculiar. For example, I have built up a lot of resentment toward Marcus over the years. Conducting the affair has been much more taxing for me than for him. I have children, lots of home responsibilities. He is on a much looser schedule. He is filling up free time with me, whereas I am sandwiching him into a very crowded life. Every summer I am aware of my unhappiness. Mostly I never want to go away on vacations at all. I am afraid to be out of contact with Marcus. So I am always slipping away to make long distance phone calls. My life is filled with subterfuge and it isn't fun. As a result, even out here, I'm not relaxed. I've taken this month off because I need a rest, but I'm not really getting one.

"It's this masochism I hope you're going to be able to convey," she said. "The married woman who has an affair is really making her own life difficult. She may think it's delicious, but actually it's damn hard work."

I asked Evelyn whether there was any possibility that she and Marcus would end their respective marriages and stage a life together. I was surprised at how adamantly she said no. They had apparently tried it once, about three years ago. Each had separated, and they had attempted to consolidate their relationship. It had been a dismal failure. She had found that she was no longer turned on by him; that she did not enjoy his company over long periods of time; that to her astonishment, she missed her husband. She had gone back to Peter and Marcus had gone back to his wife. When they resumed their affair it was far less intense. "You must understand that all this time there were fights, screaming fights, between Marcus and me. And letters, dozens of letters going back over everything that had ever happened, finecombing every detail of how we'd met, how we'd ended up this way. And tears. Sometimes I'd be sitting at the wheel of my car and for no reason at all I would get so flooded-up with tears I couldn't see the lights change. Now it's different. It's become a matter of convenience. I can't quite bring myself to let go, but I have no high hopes for a life with Marcus."

She was convinced, instead, that fairly soon their affair was going to terminate. The way she saw it, she said, she had two choices. One was to find someone else with whom she could anticipate a new marriage, someone she resented less than she did Marcus. The other was to give up seeking a new man altogether and settle down emotionally with Peter. She was, she said, leaning toward this resolution. "Now that I've at last become *somebody* on my own, now that I have a reputation and external success, I find I've begun to believe in myself more. I've begun to believe in my own ability to give myself ideas. And along with this development, I have greater and greater respect for Peter, who must on some level have known about all this but who has put up with it, put up with me, waited me out. I know he loves me, and more and more, I'd like to be able to spend at least some years of our life in which I am all his.

"That's where I'm heading. But it would give a very false impression to say that I'm there. I'm not there yet. The truth of the matter is I feel very bereft these days just because the guts have gone out of my relationship with Marcus. It's almost worse to have no emotion than to have bad emotion.

My life in the past was so characterized by big emotion that
now I often feel empty. Still, sometimes I think that after all
I really could fill up the space with Peter."

Evelyn and I became friends. Once I went down to Washington and had lunch with her and Marcus, dinner the next
night with her and Peter. I understood more after those two
meals than I had before. With Marcus, this articulate woman
became kittenish and quiet, leaving him to direct the conversation. With Peter, it was Evelyn who was the star. Peter
was a frowning, slightly critical audience who nevertheless
would not walk out in the middle of the show; the tickets had
cost him too much and the play moved him almost despite
himself. There was no question but that Evelyn was more
comfortable with Peter, more herself. But when I said this as
I was leaving and she was handing me my coat, she whispered,
"Yes, but just how worthwhile is that self?"

I remember standing in the carpeted hallway outside
Evelyn's apartment and realizing that more than any other
characteristic, self-doubt and a striking fear of loneliness,
even future loneliness, seemed to characterize the women I
spoke with who were engaged in long-term affairs. Although
they went through turbulent periods in which they tried to
exchange lovers for husbands, they apparently felt less fearful
of solitude having two men rather than just one. It occurred
to me then that these women were curiously well mated. The
husbands they had chosen seemed not only to respect their
wives' apprehensiveness but to share it. They were men who
were willing to close their eyes to a certain amount of emotional deprivation rather than risk abandonment.

# (2)
# Staying Married:
## *Sporadic Affairs*

Very few women I spoke with had long-term affairs. It was much more usual for me to meet women who had short affairs with men they saw only occasionally or sporadically for a year or two. Often such affairs seemed to flourish when women entered their mid-thirties. Suddenly wives who had previously perceived their marriages as comfortable and even happy, would experience a blossoming of fantasies and then attachments to men. These women talked of physiological changes that had occurred in their bodies as they passed certain chronological milestones. Or they talked of psychological changes equally related to the putting on of years.

Those who stressed psychological change had experienced a lack of direction as they had grown older. Their children had ceased to preoccupy them; if they did not work, they longed to do so or to go back to school; but if they did work, they found their jobs had grown repetitive or isolating. Sometimes these women felt their bodies and their beauty declining, and they could almost hear death's klaxon at their backs. They knew there was nothing their husbands could do to stop life's degenerative process. But they seemed to hope that by turning to men they didn't yet know, they might discover in these men magical transformative powers. Sometimes they even did.

## Regina Beaudeker /
## Is It Just the Fact of a New Body?

Regina Beaudeker, a thirty-eight-year-old school teacher who was one of the first such women I interviewed, had found a lover revitalizing. She had been married seventeen years and had just had her first affair the previous summer. She was deep into the throes of it when I spoke with her and had awakened on the morning of our interview—and indeed on so many other mornings lately—with a glow, a sense of pride in her appearance, that she had not felt in years. "Whatever the bad results of all this—and I want you to know I feel very guilty because I'm certain my husband has wanted to play around but has never done so—whatever the bad results, I think I will always feel this experience was worthwhile, just because it's given me these days since summer of feeling young and beautiful again."

She had come to see me in the office I sometimes work in, a dusty borrowed studio. Another writer and I shared it, and whenever I arrived the ashtrays were little pyramids of ground-down paper and ash. My colleague's work must go badly, I often thought, and it seemed ominous to me the day Regina came. How would I talk to this stranger without making my own cigarette mounds? Regina herself was uneasy with me and smoking heavily already. Why was it that since the Government warnings against cigarette smoking ten years ago, more men than women have given up smoking? What self-destructiveness holds us in its grip?

Regina said, "When I was in college I was vibrant. A lot of why I felt good about myself in those days was having men seek me out. Even when I went steady with a guy there were always others waiting in the wings; other men to choose from. I was never pretty, but lots of people told me I was sexy."

I was able to see her sexiness. She was small, olive-skinned, taut. She had a mouth too wide for her face, what used to be called a generous mouth. When she was not smoking, her fingers were at play on her lower lip. She was never still.

Regina told me first that she had been quite sexually experienced before marrying her husband whom she met at college, so it was not, she insisted, a feeling of sexual curiosity that had motivated her affair. For seventeen years she had been faithful to her husband, but, she explained, throughout those years she had felt herself growing wasted and old and dull. "There was something missing. I felt dissatisfied. End of life. Even at work, with the children yelling in the corridors, I would suddenly feel an unbearable stillness within me."

Then this past summer at the beach she had found herself intensely attracted to a neighbor. He was also married but his wife, a narcissist, said Regina, used to spend hours and hours in the sun and he, fair and quick to burn, would wander away from her to visit friends. "My own husband was working during the week and just coming up weekends. This man, my neighbor, proposed we sleep together. The most important thing I have to tell you is how shocked I was when he said that. I literally had never given such matters a thought. Marriage was the closing of that door, the ringing down of that curtain. I knew that married men sometimes played around. But not married women. And I figured the men had their affairs with sex-starved office girls. So I was shocked. And even indignant. Who did this guy think I was? My opinion of him went *down,* not up. I rejected him."

But after that, the idea was never far from her mind. She said, "I began asking myself 'Why not? Who would know? Why not once?' It wasn't as if I cared for my neighbor. I didn't then and I don't now. No, what happened was that just through thinking about it, something began to change. I began looking at myself in mirrors. Began asking myself, 'Does he really find me attractive?' Began fantasizing. Began, in short, feeling better about myself."

Regina moved constantly during our conversation. To the windows. To the couch. She wanted to be interviewed standing up. Whatever was going on with her, it was clear to me she was not really at peace with herself. She had come to see me at the prompting of a friend, and she told me she felt that investigating the subject of women and extramarital sex was, in her view, extremely important; yet, I felt throughout the conversation that she was ready to flee.

"I suppose," she said in explanation, "that my ego had gotten flattened out during all those years of marriage. It swelled back up to normal after my neighbor's proposition, I came out of a slump I had been in for years. It was classic. Of course, as I began to come out of the slump, I had the illusion that I was the only married woman in the world who had ever faced this conflict between duty and liberty. I had the insane illusion that nobody else had ever been in the same boat as me. Certainly nobody I knew admitted to adultery. So there was no one to talk to. I felt guilty, sick, angry at myself. But in September I called this guy and we met in a hotel after school. The Hilton, no less. And made love. It was really a joke. That first time, he came almost the minute he entered me. My husband was a much better lover. We always spent a lot of time in foreplay; intercourse was always long and slow; he knew what I liked and I knew what he liked. My lover was in an awful rush. Of course, he told me it would get better the next time.

"And to some extent it did get better. But he never took the time over me that my husband did. Never licked me, which is a thing I like very much. Didn't even especially want me to go down on him though there was one time I insisted; he squirmed a lot."

I found myself surprised at this description and told Regina so. Yet she continued to maintain that sex with her husband was better than with her lover. I concluded that extramarital sex had more significance to Regina as a balm for some emotional ache than for a strictly physical one.

"I had the feeling I was imposing on him," Regina went on. "So it was never what you could really call good sex. And yet I felt I had to continue because a very strange thing happened to me, a sexual thing. I started to feel damp between my legs whenever I thought of him. Sometimes just when I'd be out buying clothes. Or just watching TV. Or standing at the blackboard at school.

"It seemed to have nothing to do with what was happening. And then I remembered that I was that way too, when I was young and in the early days of my marriage. So what I'm wondering is, is it just the fact of a new body? Is it something hormonal that happens when you're with somebody new that just disappears within a long sexual relationship? And if that's the case, what am I to do? Because if I haven't made all this clear, my husband is the kind of man I can share everything with. All my thoughts and feelings, except of course about this. He's my intellectual equal and a delicious man. My lover isn't. And yet, for reasons I can't explain, whenever I start feeling my familiar depression, the sense that life is pale, or even sometimes when I'm not thinking, I get this surge of sexual excitement and although it makes me feel guilty, it also makes me feel so pleased with myself."

I didn't know what to tell Regina and for a long time after our interview I felt confused by what she had said. She had been asking me for answers, but how could I give answers to questions that have but barely begun to be raised. I had read animal research that showed that male rats became more stimulated when a new female was introduced into their cage. But I knew of no comparable findings concerning female animal sexuality. Female animals, even those closer in the evolutionary scale to ourselves, are locked into their estrogen cycles in ways that human females are not. Students of human behavior, on the other hand, have suggested that women, like men, may experience greater arousal toward new sexual partners, or at least a deadening of sexual response toward the long-familiar. I had read Simone de Beauvoir's devastating view of sexual relations in marriage in *The Second Sex:*

> "Eroticism is a movement toward the *Other,* this is its essential character; but in the deep intimacy of the couple, husband and wife become for one another the *Same;* no exchange is any longer possible between them, no giving and no conquering. Thus if they do continue to make love, it is often with a sense of shame: they feel that the sexual act is no longer an intersubjective experience in which each goes beyond self, but rather a kind of joint masturbation. That they each regard the other as a utensil necessary for the satisfaction of their needs is a fact that conjugal politeness ignores . . ."

De Beauvoir is of course a pessimist, but even Masters and Johnson, marital optimists, had stated at a meeting in 1972 held by the Sex Information and Education Council of the United States that "Sex in a warm, committed relationship does tend to become diffused after a time and may not always reach the peaks of excitement that are sometimes experienced in early, experimental encounters between a man and a woman." They had predicted that this diffusion was less likely to occur to couples who were not "goal-oriented" when it came to sex, couples who focused not just on orgasm but on the emotional value of their marital partner. Yet Regina did seem to be focusing on her marital partner and I felt perplexed by her.

## Catherine Lewyt /
## Maybe I'll Be President of the P.T.A.

Catherine Lewyt, a housewife from suburban New Jersey, had also turned to extramarital sex in her thirties—not because she found such activity more physically satisfying than the sex in her marriage, but because she found it emotionally satisfying. I had been given Catherine's name by a mutual friend who knew several women who were conducting extramarital sexual affairs. Of all of them, Catherine interested her the most. When I had asked why, the friend had said, "Because she's really not interested in sex at all."

We met at Catherine's house, a low-slung ranch set down in a maze of similar homes, all with picture windows looking out on a flattened landscape where only occasionally a tree was still standing on a lawn beside swings and ping-pong tables, barbecue pits, and croquet sets, and then only because its roots were too tenacious to be driven completely from the environment.

Catherine appeared to be in her early forties, a heavy woman, a blonde who was visibly graying. She must once have been voluptuous but now she had the massive sexuality of a Lachaise sculpture. I felt slight and childish beside Catherine. She enveloped me. She was not only big but garrulous.

She took me at once into her living room and began showing off to me the elements in the room that were the products of her husband's skillful hands. There were intricate built-in cupboards, a custom-made hi-fi system, drapes that were electrically controlled. She seemed extraordinarily proud of her husband's achievements, but at the same time she clearly resented his preoccupation with hobbies and objects. "He goes into his shop in the basement right after dinner and he's there until bedtime," she said, pouring coffee and shifting piles of comic books and records, the artifacts of her three children.

It was, she said, Henry's reclusiveness that had led her to her first extramarital experience seven years ago. At that time her children, female twins and an older boy, had already entered school and her major occupation, besides the children, had been charitable work with the local Episcopalian Church, a church she had converted to after her early years as a Catholic. It was the church of her husband and of her very beloved mother-in-law. But her major conflict in the early years of marriage had been Henry's unwillingness to participate in her various church-related activities. "He's the kind of man who's absent even when he's present," she complained, "and he'd much rather just be absent."

Still, he was kind, and recognized her needs for activity. So at his urging, she had gone on a church-sponsored trip to Florida one spring. There were mostly couples on the chartered flight, and a few unattached wives and husbands. The first night away from home, relaxed by her sudden freedom from the children and by the spirit and friendliness of the group, she had gone to bed with one of the men who had been on the flight. It had happened suddenly and hastily after partying.

A neighbor and a friend, he had talked about it afterwards and told her to consider it a meaningless, isolated event. They knew each other's spouses. They must not let the relationship continue. They agreed to consider it trivial.

But for Catherine, nothing was the same afterwards. For the first time since she had married Henry ten years before, a man had danced with her, been attentive, talked to her after lovemaking. She found that she had responded vigorously to the attention if not the lovemaking.

"When I came home the next day I felt like a different woman. I knew what I had done was wrong. But I couldn't believe it was entirely wrong if it made me feel this good. I couldn't hide from Henry how much more cheerful I was when I came home than when I went away. So I explained to him it had something to do with my having been able to get out. He, to my surprise, agreed. He urged me to get out more often, either with the church group or in some other fashion. 'Why don't you take a night off each week?' he said. 'I know I'm dull at night; I just like to get home and putter; and it's boring for you.' "

"Didn't that make you angry in a way?" I asked. I was searching her face for clues. Surely there had been anger toward Henry when she slept with the neighbor and felt herself reawakened.

But Catherine said, "No. I never felt angry. I started doing just that. Taking a night off. I like dancing, so I started going with girlfriends, later by myself, to a discotheque bar in the next town. And for a long while it was really true that just this business of getting out alone once a week kept me cheerful. Then one night some guy asked me to have a drink with him afterwards; which I did. One thing led to another and I slept with him. It was in his car. I felt terribly guilty afterwards. And yet, you know, there were some good feelings. I mean that when I looked in the mirror I didn't see thirty-seven-year-old Catherine Lewyt, but a woman somehow much younger, much more appealing.

"It wasn't just a sex thing. I'm not terribly keen on sex. I've only had two orgasms in my life and they were both with my husband, some years ago. But being with other men makes me feel better about myself.

"Henry is the kind of man whose idea of fun on weekends is mowing the lawn. And his idea of making love is you just do it, no preliminaries, no conversation. I've been turned off about sex for years. But I like so much to be where there's music and action and lots of people."

For Catherine, staying married was all-important. Her affairs were for her a way of smoothing out difficulties in her marriage, and she offered me an example of how her new freedom worked to accomplish this goal. "I think Henry is actually grateful to me that I'm willing to go out by myself to places where he would be miserable," she said. "Before, if he wouldn't go, I'd stay home and grump at him. Now I just go. We go to parties in our two cars so that he can leave when it grows boring for him.

"I've been going on this way for seven years," she explained. "I go out a couple of times a month. I meet guys at the bowling alley, at bars near here, sometimes at parties.

If I go to bed with them they always say, 'When can I see you again? Can I call you?' and I say yes a few times. But if they start showing possessiveness, I say, 'No. No more.'

"I've come to realize that this is the best thing for me to do. Actually, I've had some guidance in this. About four years ago, you see, I had an affair with a guy who became very attached to me. And I let it happen. It was immensely flattering; he was younger than me, unattached, and very intense. I saw him a lot, and he even visited me at home when my husband was away. But then he got it into his head that if I was sleeping with him so regularly I ought to leave my husband and marry him. He kept bothering me about this, and I kept saying no.

"I felt I loved my husband. I had been a real nobody when Henry married me, a file clerk, a fifty-dollar-a-week clerk with an unpronounceable last name. And Henry, and Henry's family, especially his mother, took me in and changed all that. My mother-in-law, when he called her to say he was marrying me and gave my name, which is Polish, didn't say as I'd dreamed she would, '*Who?* How do you spell it?' She just said, 'That's nice.' And that was all there was to it. I couldn't let her down by divorcing Henry. She's been a second mother to me. Is it her fault, or my fault or his that Henry is uncommunicative and I like gaiety?

"So I told my boyfriend I didn't want to marry him. Next thing I know, he goes around to the priest at my church and tells him the whole story. Only the way he told it was he said to the priest that we were going to run off together to make this thing all right with God.

"Next thing I know I get a phone call from the priest, I should come down and talk. Since he already knew so much, I told him my side of the story. I said I wasn't in love with this fellow and didn't want to run off with him but that I seemed to need men other than Henry, and I didn't know what to do.

"I was very nervous at the time, very troubled and depressed. The priest made me promise to stop the relationship and not run off from my husband and children, or even take the children away from Henry. 'You're a family,' he said. 'Everyone here knows you, respects you. You'd be wrecking your life, causing yourself and the children misery.' He said he could understand my wanting to sleep with men occasionally, and that I should go for marriage counseling with the church's pastoral counselor.

"I did all that. I'm still getting counseling. When I told my boyfriend I wouldn't leave my home for him, he left me. And from then on, I began looking for men I wouldn't risk much with. I mean men who wouldn't risk much of themselves for me. Wouldn't fall in love with me.

"I've gotten so I'm good at this. I can tell the kind of guy who's looking for an occasional fling from the kind of guy who wants a relationship, who maybe is in a bad marriage himself and thinks if he had a girlfriend he could work his way out. I avoid those like the plague. I feel now that as long as I don't break up my family, don't get divorced, don't hurt anyone, what I'm doing can't be too bad. I love Henry, but I can't help myself because every once in a while I need to be sure I'm still attractive."

She was settled. She was sure. The only time she showed any doubt as we talked, the only time her face clouded over, was when we discussed her children. It turned out she worried a lot about the possibility that as they grew older they would become suspicious of her behavior. She would feel ashamed if they found out.

She said, "I wouldn't ever want my children to know about any of this. Part of what is so remarkable about Henry is that he silences my teen-aged son's suspicions. The boy will say, 'Are you going out this week too, Ma?' and Henry will say, 'Mind your own business. Your mother is as entitled to fun as anyone is.'

"But if it gets to the point where I feel my son is really suspicious—or if it gets to the point where I'm too old or unattractive to find men—well, I guess I'll just take up hooking rugs or needlepoint. I'll be the president of the P.T.A. or chairman of the church social committee and do all the things other people do to keep themselves from thinking about where they are. But I won't ever let anything disturb my marriage. If we were bickering it would be a different story. But we almost never fight, and the children, no matter how old they get, will always need the both of us, their family. It would upset us all terribly if we were to divorce."

Because of these initial interviews with women who stressed that the sex they experienced in their affairs was inferior to or no better than the sex in their marriages, I had at first assumed that women turned toward extramarital sex in their thirties because of boredom, of lack of direction, of a reduction in childcare duties or a despair over aging. But as I continued interviewing I met just as many women who presented a reverse experience: they enjoyed the sex in their affairs more than that in their marriages. Indeed, a number of women felt quite strongly that they had taken lovers because at some point in their thirties they had undergone a physiological change that altered their sexual needs. One cluster of these women felt that the sex they had in their early years of marriage, while good, was no longer adequate to their present needs; another felt that the sex in their marriages had never been good, but that prior to their thirties this had not presented a problem.

## Sara Nichols / Am I Imitating the Behavior of Our Oppressors?

Sara Nichols, a prominent theorist of the women's movement, a psychotherapist with two children and a husband with whom she has lived for sixteen years, belonged to the first camp. Sex with her husband had been fine and perfectly suited to her needs until a few years ago. Now, as a result of a sexual upsurge in herself, simultaneous with a lessening sex drive in her husband, she had taken as a lover a man considerably younger than herself, and had been seeing him for the past year.

I was introduced to Sara by a colleague who had warned me that while she thought Sara might be very interested in my project, she would probably be too busy to speak with me. But I remember how generously Sara said she would make time because the subject was so important.

She was always making time for people. Periodically during our interview in her office, the telephone rang and Sara Nichols was consoling patients, making speaking commitments, spreading herself enthusiastically across a thousand requests and interruptions.

We began by discussing the feminist position on extramarital sex. Sara said, "If there were such a thing as a feminist position it would probably be that if I take a lover, I am imitating the worst behavior of our oppressors."

"Is that the way you feel about yourself?" I asked.

"No, of course not," she said. "I feel I am looking for myself, for what will make me happiest, and that this is not only my necessity but my obligation. For one thing, women my age face real sexual difficulties. They are still at their sexual peak, while their husbands—assuming they married men around their own age—are on a decline."

Sara's husband, it developed, had not for years made love to her more than four or five times a week and, on those nights he did, it was only once per night, whereas in their past they had always had repeated sexual episodes. Sara had come to experience the change as a physical deprivation. "You see, these days if I have one good orgasm, then that's the time when I want to go on and have three or four more episodes. The better the orgasm, the more I want to go on. And while my husband is potent, there's no question but that my sexual capacity now is greater than his."

Sara appreciated the fact that her husband wasn't bored

with her, either sexually or emotionally. "In fact," she conceded, "he is even fun to sleep with. I mean *sleep,* and that's terribly important. He's affectionate in his sleep. He makes me feel that he really knows I'm there and that he appreciates my presence. He doesn't turn off after sex the way some men do. But, as I said, he's not really likely to perform again, the way young men can, or even the way older men can when they're in new relationships."

The sexual disparity between Sara and her husband had apparently started troubling her about five or six years ago. "The more I would feel sexy, the more I would go around feeling frustrated all the time. And then there was an additional problem. I meet a lot of men through my work. There were always other men approaching me. But I didn't want an affair, so I turned my sexuality off altogether for a while, or so it seemed. It was a terrible dilemma. Some of my friends are very into masturbation and they think that's the answer. They look terrific. They seem happy and healthy. But it's just not for me. It's a relief, but it doesn't do for me what intercourse does. There's something about a nice warm body next to you. Then of course, I've got friends who have recommended I try women. But I think I'm afraid to start a relationship with another woman. I've read and thought and talked about this a lot. I'm not sure I quite understand my hesitation. I think I'm phallus-fixated."

Sara was very pleased with the man she had chosen as lover. "He's beautiful," she said, "with a face like the young Shelley. And for the first time in my life I can understand what men mean when they talk about young bodies—young, firm bodies. I used to get angry with men when they followed a bouncing young *tuccus* with their eyes and let whatever you were saying to them disappear into thin air. But I have empathy now."

Still, there were problems. Sara's husband was a firm believer in monogamy and Sara didn't want to rock the stately ship of her marriage. She said with a subdued voice, toward the end of our interview, "I'm afraid I'm stuck right now, stuck just where I don't want to be. I have to keep quiet about my affair, have to cool it down, even have to take the risk that because I can't see my lover as often as he'd like, he'll fall in love with someone else. I expect it every time I see him. Why should he hang on to me, a woman who's so rarely available to him? I don't look forward to this happening. I'll be devastated. But at least at this point in time I don't see I have any choice. The trouble is, I like being married."

## Prudence Phillips / My Body Changed after I Turned Thirty

Prudence Phillips, a thirty-five-year-old magazine researcher, felt that the sex in her marriage had never been adequate, but that this had not distressed her until, at about the time she turned thirty, she began to experience increased and specific sexual longings. When this happened she felt as if a pall had been cast over her life, and she became lethargic and subdued. But about a year and a half before I interviewed her, she had started an affair which was still going on with a lover who had, she said, resuscitated her. "It's been like a youth treatment," she told me. "Like a trip to one of those health farms."

We met at Prudence's house, about forty-five minutes out of New York City. She worked in the city, part-time, three days a week, and it was on those days, on her lunch hour, that she met her lover regularly. She couldn't see me in the city, she explained; every minute of her time there was overloaded. But if I wanted to ride up to her house on one of her nonworking days, she'd have plenty of leisure. Her son, five years old, was in school in the mornings and that would be a good time to come.

The house was big and sprawling, a Victorian house, intricate with bay windows and fireplaces and strips of carved wood molding. Prudence was fair-skinned, sunburned, and wearing blond braids, a pretty woman on whom well-worn dungarees looked like a second skin. She had been working in her garden before I arrived, getting ready for a summer crop of beans and zucchini which she and her husband would clean, cook, and freeze for the winter.

I turned on my tape recorder and Prudence just sat and talked into it, quite unself-consciously. She said, "My husband loves me and I guess I love him. But *making* love was never our forte. In fact, when I was twenty-eight and we were married only four years, he used to talk about my growing old gracefully and not being as sexually demanding as I was when we first met; he wanted it that way. I really hated going to bed with him after a while and only did it because I felt ashamed to just masturbate, but actually being sexually dependent on him was humiliating. He'd touch me and feel me all over, get me all aroused, then enter and come one second later. Then he'd masturbate me. I never felt anything inside me, never felt myself caring while coming.

"Of course, I had nothing to compare it to. I had been experienced before we met, but I was so young then that intercourse meant nothing to me. I cared only about being masturbated and caressed. I came that way. Only when I got older did I have the feeling of something being missing. But of course it wasn't until I actually started an affair that I knew what it was.

"It's hard to explain it exactly, but I guess what happened was that after about eight years of marriage I started to feel frustrated. I started looking over every guy I met—at work, at parties, even in the street—wondering how a married woman like myself could ever get into an affair with one of them. I felt horny. Just a touch on the arm from a guy at work would arouse me. My mouth would go dry.

"I should point out that my son was born a year before those feelings started. It was four years ago; I had been married seven years and I was thirty-one. One didn't see as much material then as one does now about women's sexuality. It's really astonishing and wonderful how this subject is finally being aired. But four years ago, when I began to feel so turned on all over my body, I had no way of knowing whether what was happening to me was something physical or something psychological."

I asked Prudence, "Do you know that now?" and she said, "Yes, I do. My body changed around the time I turned thirty. It needn't have been age. It could have just been that now I'd given birth. Let's say it was both, or one or the other. These were physiological things and they did something to my body. Suddenly I had nothing on my mind but sex. I really understand now the way teen-age boys must feel, the way they're led around by their cocks at seventeen. I could never again be angry at recollecting adolescent scenes of fighting off boys, never again agree with the complaints of some of my friends about how they were victimized by male sex drive. Once I turned thirty and once I had my baby, I was as led around by my genitals as ever any boy was, and if I could have had the opportunity to screw 'em and leave 'em, which is to some extent culturally permitted to boys, I assure you I would have.

"But no, it doesn't work that way for a woman. For one thing, before you can screw 'em and leave 'em, you have to find them. And that was the hardest part for me."

Prudence had, surprisingly, experienced a number of rejections once she began to look for a sexual partner. The men she met, now that she was in her thirties, men her own age or a little older, did not seem quite as enthusiastic about sex as the men she had known when she was single and in her early twenties. An old boyfriend, who had kissed her once after an intimate confiding lunch, had wanted just that, a kiss. A friend at work, with whom she rode to the railroad station one night after an office Christmas party, "got drunk, and he was caressing me in the cab. I was drunk too, because I found myself sucking his thumb in the cab and not wanting to stop for dear life. He said how sexy I was, and how he hadn't been near a woman who turned him on the way I did for years, and that passion had been dead between his wife and him for years. But that was all he said. He didn't seem to want to work anything out with me, to see me again. In fact, the next day I was at work, he apologized for having flirted with me in the cab. I said, 'That's okay. It was as much me as you,' and he looked at me unbelievingly and said, 'Oh, no; it was all my fault.'

"Things like this kept happening and happening. I was trying to transfer some of this sexy feeling I had to my husband, but he just wasn't very interested either. Once a week has always been enough for him. I don't know what I would have done if just around this time I felt really desperate I hadn't met the man with whom I'm now having this affair. He's a photographer who works for my magazine occasionally, an older man, close to fifty. He loves his wife and he made that very clear to me when we went to bed the first time in his studio. I told him that was just fine with me. And it is, that's the finest part of it all. I don't have to worry that he'll get it into his head to shake things up in my life.

"The sex is really great with him. You name it, we've tried it. And we meet three times a week, as I've told you, on my lunch hour, which is really two hours, provided I stay a little later in the evenings.

"I do feel guilty about it. There have been times I've tried to break it off, tried to go without meeting him just to see if maybe by now the urgency in my body has subsided. But I can't do it. If I skip seeing him for a week, I call him up and I'm practically shaking from my efforts to avoid him. I don't know why he doesn't get mad at me when I skip seeing him, but he doesn't; maybe it's because he's older and wiser; he understands why I've stayed away; and he just welcomes me back and we start up again. Then, when I'm in bed with him again, everything rational goes out of my head. Once I was lying on top of him and I was ready to come and the thought crossed my mind that no matter what happened, if my mother, or even my husband, were to walk through the doors right now, I wouldn't get up, wouldn't stop, and wouldn't even apologize. There's an imperative in my body that means more to me now than almost anything."

Prudence became thoughtful now and the flow of her words ceased. It gave me a chance to ask her a few questions: what was wrong in her marriage other than sexual incompatibility? What did she hope would happen? She said that nothing was wrong in her marriage and that she hoped only that she could keep her affair secret, since it would surely offend and drive away her husband, until she reached whatever age it was when the sexual urgency would dissipate as suddenly as it had arrived.

"If it started in when I was around thirty, surely it will begin to subside at some other age. I hope it does. I love my husband. We share a lot of mutual interests. I help him in his work, he helps me in mine, and now there's our son. I just think the whole trouble between us is a matter of female, or at least my, chronology. I married him at twenty-four. That's not considered a young age for marrying, and it isn't, really. Emotionally, you've been a woman for a long time; you want to share your life with someone. But what you don't know, can't know at twenty-four, is what kind of woman you're going to be sexually. If I were to marry today, I'd obviously look for a man who satisfied me in bed as well as in the head. But as I told you, even though I was experienced, and liked sex, I didn't feel sex as a bodily craving in those days. Well, it is now, and maybe if I hadn't gotten into this affair, I'd have had to leave my husband. But I don't have to now."

I found myself fascinated by the degree of marital satisfaction in this group of women. It is true that the women tended to be satisfied chiefly with only one area of their marriages—emotional or sexual. Still, I had expected a more florid and total dissatisfaction, perhaps an urge to separate. I had always believed that strong anger against a mate and a consequent but perhaps hidden desire for a new marital partner was what underlay extramarital sex—at least for women. But these women, and quite a number I talked with later, expressed preferences for their husbands over their lovers, and for their marriages over being on their own or in altogether new marriages.

I wondered whether there were many women like them today—women who seemed relatively happy—who were having extramarital affairs. Kinsey had touched on questions of marital satisfaction and dissatisfaction in his 1953 study of adulterous women, but had not used the responses to make any sort of statistical analysis on this point. But in the 1974 Bell and Peltz study, the researchers discovered that a surprising number of women with extramarital sexual experience reported high levels of emotional or sexual satisfaction in marriage. Such women did not have affairs as frequently as those who were very unhappy or very dissatisfied. Still, 20 percent of the adulterous said they were "happy most of the time." Many of this 20 percent termed either the sex in their marriages "very good" or their marriages as a whole "very good."

The fact of satisfaction with marriage—or at least with either the sex in marriage or the over-all emotional quality of marriage—did not, then, prevent a woman from having extramarital experience. It was *less* likely that such a woman would have an extramarital affair, but not *un*likely.

## (3)
# Staying Married:
## *Romance*

Most of the women I was meeting sounded extraordinarily pragmatic. They did not become deeply attached to lovers, nor did they often talk romantically, as had their counterparts in nineteenth-century fiction. It appeared that it was no longer essential for women to cite the overwhelming power of love as justification for breaking marital vows of sexual fidelity. Almost the only women who did insist on having love on their side were older women, those raised in an earlier period and with a different code. But, while such an insistence has its pretty, romantic side, its opposite face is one of turbulence and melodrama.

### Dora Rubin /
### The Long Life and Sad Death of a Fantasy

I got my initiation into the melodrama of adultery from an elderly neighbor of mine, Mrs. Rubin, with whom I used to chat in a specialty grocery store on Broadway. Most often, Mrs. Rubin was pushing a burden before her—her husband, old Mr. Rubin—who had had a stroke many months before and was only now recovering his powers of speech. A few years back, before his stroke, he had been one of the most engaging old men I'd ever known, fond of squeezing tomatoes in front of the "Do Not Touch" sign and always helping me down curbs with my baby carriage. Now I paid back, assisting his wife with the wheelchair.

Dora Rubin was tall, well-dressed, given to Chanel suits and garnet necklaces and proud to look much younger than her seventy years. She loved to talk and told me a lot about how the neighborhood had changed since she first moved here thirty years ago, before the war. She could remember the days, she said, when the building I used to live in, just a few blocks away from her house, had a huge gilt-framed mirror in the front hall and a green and gold Persian carpet. In those days the brass lamps had bright bulbs, instead of the forty watts the landlord now allowed.

"Well, we all grow older," she always ended. "Me, too. I've had a lot of walking over me, and the carpet's gone, but I'm still here." She was active in neighborhood-improvement groups, in committees to plant trees along the sidewalk, in collecting money for charities.

One day I saw her at lunch in a nearby restaurant with a man I hadn't seen before. They were whispering while eating cottage cheese and I couldn't believe my own mind when I had the fleeting thought that Mrs. Rubin was having a secret tête-à-tête. I chided myself; clearly, my book was going to my head.

But that evening Dora rang my doorbell and came bustling in, one of her heart fund cans in her hand. As soon as she had ascertained I was alone she said, "Please don't tell my husband you saw me in Teacher's Restaurant today."

"Of course not, Mrs. Rubin," I promised. And she said, "Good, because it would break his heart. But I had to go. I haven't seen the man I was eating with in longer than you've been alive, young lady. But he was the love of my life, my childhood sweetheart. You know how it is."

I hadn't even needed to bring up the subject. Actually, I don't think, or at least I didn't when I first began to interview, that I could have brought it up myself with a woman so much older than myself. A grandmotherly woman. But since

Dora had broached it herself, I knew it would be a loss not to tell her about my project. I mentioned my book and asked her if I could interview her formally about her feelings—or experiences—concerning extramarital affairs. It was her age that made me curious.

It turned out that Stephen Ott, the man she had been having lunch with, had been her childhood sweetheart when she was a young high school student living in an upstate New York town and working in her family's grocery store.

They had each married, lived long, full lives and not seen each other in close to fifty years, although somehow, through family greetings at holiday times, they had managed always to know of each other's whereabouts. It was Dora who had seen to this, never letting go. She had hoped to marry Ott, but his father, the local lawyer, had had ambitions beyond a Jewish shopkeeper's daughter. So Ott had been sent off to college to study accounting and Dora, broken-hearted, had persuaded her parents to let her go to nursing school in Manhattan.

"In those days," she told me, "being a nurse wasn't considered a good thing for a Jewish girl. It was dirty work. All bedpans and bleeding people and things girls like us shouldn't touch. My mother was horrified at the idea but my father finally saw sense to it. 'She'll marry a doctor.'

"But I was never really happy. It was true it was bedpans and dirty bleeding people and crazy long hours. I finished nursing school and started working in the hospital. I was looking for a husband, but these doctors, they were looking for a lay. You wouldn't believe it. But there they'd be in the operating room and what was on their mind? Rubbing up against the nurses. You see, they never wore underwear under their surgical gowns and they were always rubbing up, with big hard ones; it was a wonder they didn't drop their scalpels.

"But of course, I was a good-looking girl in those days. Tall, not stooped like now. I had a nice shape. I wore a size nine. I wore a size nine actually until just about ten years ago, and then I got lazy and a little heavy like you see me now, though I'm still no more than a twelve. Well, in those days, I was slender and quick and I was the belle of the hospital. But no one was out for marrying me."

It was only when she turned forty that she finally married. She had met Rubin, a refugee salesman five years older than herself, and decided it was time to settle down. His admiration for her carried her past her own conviction that no man but her childhood sweetheart could really make her happy. Carl Rubin adored her vitality, and reassuringly cared nothing at all that many men had come and gone in her life. Together, they moved into a brownstone in Manhattan's West Eighties, and did chores, sweeping the stoop through the war years when other refugees like Rubin himself favored the still-fashionable neighborhood, taking the garbage cans out and stacking them neatly in the years after the war as the poor swarmed round their doors.

From what I could tell, Dora's thirty-year marriage had been happy. She and Rubin had had no children, but they had cared for and clung to one another. But after Rubin's stroke, Dora had begun to dredge through her past during the long, silent evenings. Rubin's speech was impaired; there was television, a phonograph, and her memories. These became increasingly more sexual as the months wore on. Most of them focused around Ott, as if the rest of her life had been a blackboard on which events and men had been merely chalked, all of them eraseable, even Mr. Rubin.

She remembered, and then when she could no longer remember, she invented details of her lovemaking with Ott: impossibilities, since they had never had more than an hour or two together at any one time. But in her inventions, she had always come ten times, and he at least three; they made love all night long, not just in their parents' homes, but in romantic, outdoor settings along the banks of the Hudson.

Eventually she wrote a letter to Ott. Could he possibly come and meet her in New York?

It was that first reunion I had witnessed, the two old people so charmingly secretive. Ott's wife had died several years earlier; Dora had received notification and sent a condolence. But Ott's loneliness had not drawn him to Dora as hers had to him; he had three sons and seven grandchildren. At their lunch he had apparently treated her to photographic intimacy with them all. Dora told me how much she had enjoyed seeing her friend again, exploring his life in Kodachrome.

About two weeks later I was out on the street when I saw Ott go tremblingly up the steps of Mrs. Rubin's brownstone. His face was suntanned, an oily margarine color. Mr. Rubin was in the park with the Wednesday Jamaican lady who both cleaned the house and relieved Mrs. Rubin once a week.

Next day Mrs. Rubin barely nodded to me on the street. Nor the day after that. Inside her fluffy pink Chanel suit, her body seemed to have shrunk. There was a scowl around her mouth and her eyes looked sullen, old. Only many weeks later did she talk to me again. When she did, ringing the bell at evening just as she used to, there were no preliminaries, no heart fund ruses; her words just flowed out. She had been to bed with Stephen Ott; did I remember her telling me about him? And it had unnerved her, robbed her of something. "He was an old man," she said. "Just like my husband. He smelled bad. Smelled old. And he couldn't come into me." She seemed quite distracted and kept talking a long time.

I think I wasn't really surprised when, a few nights later, there were the animal-screeches of ambulance sirens drawing to a stop in front of the Rubins' brownstone. Some neighbors claimed later that they were sure it was Mr. Rubin, that he'd had another stroke. But the stretcher-bearers came out with a pale white female figure wearing a quilted pink robe and pink puff slippers—her costume carefully arranged before her act went on. She had taken close to fifty Nembutal, saved up from her nursing days. Mr. Rubin had found her and had managed to crawl down the stairs to the phone and in his very halting speech call an ambulance. He was whiter than she. I felt, looking at him, that her attempt at suicide had been unutterably selfish; there would be no one to keep him alive if she died. He would go to a nursing home for sure and he wouldn't survive it very long, I suspected. I felt inordinately angry with Dora and only managed to forgive her— and then just barely—when I learned that her stomach had been pumped, and that after a period of convalescence, she and Rubin had moved down to Florida.

I thought about her a lot afterwards. It was early spring and I was interviewing dozens of women. As I talked with them I noticed, as I have mentioned, how few of them bedecked their extramarital sexual experiences with the elaborate window dressing of romance. I found I felt relieved. I blamed Dora's suicide attempt and the danger in which she had placed both herself and Mr. Rubin on the enormous romantic investment she had brought to her extramarital encounter. When she had been disappointed in it, she felt she had lost not only a prospective sexual partner but a lifelong love object as well. It had made her inconsolable.

I was sorry she could not have had more perspective. Only a few years before, Masters and Johnson had tried to provide some by detailing the lengthy timetable of women's sexuality. They had reported that women over fifty, or even over seventy, sometimes felt moved to develop extramarital relationships. Such women's still-active sex drive, they said, is

> influenced by the factor of male attrition. When available, the male marital partner is an average of four years older than the female partner. Many of the older husbands in this age group are suffering from the multiple physical disabilities of advancing senescence which make

sexual activity for these men either unattractive or impossible. Thus, the wives who well might be interested in some regularity of heterosexual expression are denied this opportunity due to their partner's physical infirmities. It also is obvious that extramarital sexual partners essentially are unavailable to the women in this age group.

But, of course, although they could have been describing Dora, she herself might not have recognized herself in the words. She had wanted sex because she was in love.

Younger women rarely talked of love. Love was the justification for extramarital sex in earlier eras, but today there were different justifications: self-exploration; satisfying sexual curiosity; warding off depression. These were present in brief, riskless sexual encounters from which love and romance were by necessity excluded.

# (4)
# Staying Married:
## *Brief Encounters*

"Why was it all so complicated?" asks the married heroine of Erica Jong's *Fear of Flying* in a moment of satiric bitterness over the difficulties inherent in adultery for women. "Why did you have to risk your whole life for one measly zipless fuck?"

Brief, riskless extramarital encounters, the kind that bring pleasure to the participants but no harm to unknowing family members, are an old and even venerable pursuit of men. For women the pursuit is newfangled, but even so its history goes back at least as far as its expression in fiction in Kate Chopin's 1904 story "The Storm." Today it dominates what I found to be the most common kind of female extramarital adventuring—seize-the-day brief encounters, one-night stands, vacation adultery.

These experiences occurred in marriages that were described to me as good, as well as in those termed bad or difficult. Some women I spoke with told me they found such experiences thoroughly enjoyable. But it was more common to hear that brief sexual encounters, while riskless, were not altogether pleasurable, that their reality fell short of fantasy. All sorts of things went wrong. The men some of the women had chosen—or the men who chose them—proved inconsiderate or inadequate. The women discovered that secret illicit sex, counter to our society's mythology, was not an

aphrodisiac but an inhibitor. Or they found themselves thinking of their husbands at the very moment of intercourse when,
with their husbands, they were fantasizing lovers.

I found that the women I spoke with stressed the funny
or ironic aspects of their affairs. They would smile self-
deprecatingly at their own antics, or make me laugh by
comically imitating the faces of overly sober or overly hasty
lovers. I concluded that even when an extramarital encounter had not been altogether pleasurable, many women
tended to be pleased with themselves for having had the experience. In part, this was because they felt daring. But it was
also because they seemed to come away from their experiences
reassured of the wisdom of their marital choices. The less
pleasurable an extramarital encounter, the more a woman was
convinced that her own marriage, even if it was rough going,
represented a safe harbor.

Some of the women were planners. They spent both time
and effort divising unusual techniques for ending up in bed
—briefly—with someone they barely knew or didn't yet know.
One woman accomplished it by the imaginative roundabout
scheme of sharing her entire life for a day with a foreigner
anxious to learn American routine. Another had a letter-writ-
ing campaign for meeting out-of-town strangers. But for the
most part, the brief encounter was not a premeditated one. It
happened. It was over. It had more to do with spontaneous
adventure than with manipulation. Writing in *The Encyclopedia of Sexual Behavior,* psychotherapist Robert A.
Harper has described such adultery as "a supplement to more
generalized flight-from-reality devices, such as motion pic-
tures, radio, television, ataractic drugs, and alcohol."

## Jeannette Giddings /
## If My Husband Only Knew

Jeanette Giddings, a suburban housewife, age thirty-six,
mother of two, told me, "I married at twenty-two. My hus-

band is a teacher and for the first years of our marriage we lived in the city, but then, when the children were of school age, we moved out. We have our fights, but they're nothing special. The usual stuff. He's bossy and very meticulous and I'm not the best housekeeper in the world. He sometimes complains that I've let my figure go since we married, or he gets annoyed with me because I'm not making use of my education. I was going to be a teacher, too. We met in college. But I like staying home. I can't see what's so great about a job. It's true I spend a lot of time daydreaming. But what's so bad about that? Anyway, these are just little things; little quarrels; they happen in every marriage.

"One of my favorite daydreams is about old boyfriends coming back. I'll bet it's universal. I always fantasized about that sort of thing. But I always stopped short of actually doing anything about the fantasy. I even, you might say, have made sure nothing along those lines could ever happen by keeping myself in a physical condition that isn't very inviting. As my husband never fails to remind me, I am overweight—I weigh in at one-sixty-five—and I don't pay the right attention to how I dress. So the fact that I ever had any sort of an affair is really quite surprising, even to me.

"It happened only once. It was a short while after we'd moved to the suburbs. I still hadn't quite adjusted to life there, hadn't yet made very many friends, and one time in the spring I took my children and we came back to New York and spent a week staying with friends who lived in Greenwich Village. We went out one day to see one of those art shows they have there; sidewalk displays of jewelry and leatherwork and paintings. My friends stopped to talk to a man they knew, an artist who was doing pastel portraits. I didn't talk to him, but a few days later, I saw him again and he recognized me. I *am* a little hard to miss.

"This time we chatted. One of my kids was fiddling with his chalks and I swatted her, but this guy was so nice about it. He said, 'Your kid must like drawing.' He invited us up to see his studio. I said no, but then, we went anyway. And while we were there, he said why didn't I come back that night without the kids, and I said no, and then I said okay.

"I went back and we went to bed. He was not particularly great in bed, but I dug it. My reaction was very strong, out of proportion. He was someone very talented and he was someone who wasn't my husband. But I couldn't come. I was very excited, but just hovering on the edge of my climax. He came, and he was masturbating me, and still I was just hanging there. And then I closed my eyes and imagined he was my husband and that was what did it. I came.

"There was never any question of our getting together again. I was on my way back upstate the next day. He said he was about to get married to some woman who was in Paris but was coming home the next week. We exchanged life histories but not addresses. I went home feeling surprisingly good about it, and for a long time afterwards, whenever my husband would get angry with me over some household trivia, I'd sit there and just smile to myself and I'd think, if he only knew."

## Rita Hemp /
### In Those Days I Never Had Orgasms

Rita Hemp, a suburban housewife, age twenty-eight, mother of one, said, "My husband and I get on very well. I like everything about marriage. I like having someone to go out to dinner with and to go to the movies with and to worry about me when I've got the flu and to fuss over when he's having work troubles. I always felt this way about being married, but in the first two years I had a sex problem and sometimes I wondered if I should have gotten married before solving it.

"In those days I never had orgasms, and in fact I didn't start having them until I had my baby two years ago. No matter what my husband and I tried, I didn't. So one of the things I tried was another man. I was working then as a reporter on a magazine and sometimes I had to go out of town to cover stories. This one time there was a correspondent from an Italian magazine covering the same story. We got to talking and eventually we got onto the subject of sex and he said to me did I know that, according to statistics he had read, some huge percentage of American women didn't have orgasms. He sounded surprised, unbelieving.

"I don't know what got into me. Usually I'm very reserved, even stand-offish with men I don't know very well. Maybe it was being away from home. Anyway, I said, 'What's so odd? I don't have them either.' He came on after that with lots of European macho stuff. If I didn't have them, I must be sleeping with the wrong man. He could make me have them. So I went to bed with him, just to see.

"Well, of course I didn't have an orgasm with him either. It was no big blow to me. I'd only half-expected it might happen. But he was deflated and irritated. In fact, he insisted I was lying. He said, 'Don't tell me you didn't. I could feel the contractions.'

" 'Well, I didn't,' I said. I laughed. But it was no joke. After that I figured European women must be the world's biggest liars. Otherwise why would these European men think they knew what an orgasm felt like. Now that I have them, I know the man can't always tell.

"I went home from Chicago annoyed but content. At least my husband believed me. If I wasn't going to have orgasms, I wanted to not have them in the comfort of my own bed and with a man who believed what I had to say about my own body. I decided to make do. My husband was more upset about my not having orgasms than I was. I just figured sex wasn't everything in marriage, but since it wasn't everything outside of it either, I might as well enjoy what I had. Of course, there's no telling what could have happened, if eventually I hadn't started having orgasms. Maybe I would have tried another man again. Maybe my husband would have gotten fed up with me and tried another woman. But it never came to that since after the baby—not right after—about a year after, I started having them—not all the time, but often enough."

## Amanda Greenough /
## If He'd Looked, He'd Have Seen No Lipstick

Amanda Greenough, a suburban college instructor, age twenty-seven, mother of one, said, "All my life I always had this thing about older men. Or they had a thing about me. In college there was one professor who was crazy about me. He used to take me to the theatre. He said I was a brilliant student but unsophisticated and that I needed more exposure to thoughts and trends. He took over my education, like a private tutor. And he always made passes at me, but I always put him off. I had a very moralistic upbringing and he was a married man twice my age. I kept myself aloof. I suppose you could say I mostly live by principles. I consider personal happiness a libertine luxury. But I'm human, too, and there are times I wish I was like other people I know. Freer.

"I married right after college. My husband was at school with me and he and I are very much alike. We intend to raise a big family. It won't stop me from having a full life. Even before I got pregnant, we planned that I would continue graduate school, no matter what, even if we had triplets. And that's what I've done. My husband is a painter and he works at home in a studio we built, and we alternate the baby-sitting.

"I love my husband very much. I love making love with him. We did it before we got married, which was hard for me. It didn't seem altogether right. We'd done everything else, even had oral sex. But intercourse was something else. I know it sounds unbelievable, but there are still women who feel this way about sex—at least in the Midwest, where I grew up. I used to talk about my feelings with some of the women

I knew at school. They all felt it was all right to have inter-course with a man if you loved him. And I did love Tim. And I was sick of being odd woman out. So we had inter-course, and it was fine; I loved him just as much afterwards, and he loved me just as much, and we got married about a month after graduation.

"The only extramarital affair I ever had was three years ago, during graduate school. It was with a professor of mine. I told you older men had this thing for me. Or maybe it's that professors go into their line of work because they figure that way they can surround themselves with pretty young women who look up to them, or have to pretend they do. Now that I'm teaching I can see what power it gives you.

"The professor I had the affair with was just like the one I didn't have one with in college. He would take me to lunch to further my education. I was marking papers for an under-graduate class of his, and he set up a regular lunch schedule so he could direct me in the work.

"Once when his wife was away we had our lunch up at his apartment. He said we had to meet there because he was ex-pecting an important phone call. During lunch, he started stroking my leg under the table. Just like that. He did a whole number about how young and bright and unique I was; he'd never met another student as perceptive. All my life this kind of thing was happening to me. This time I decided to see what would happen if I went along with it. I couldn't see any harm in it. My husband would never know. My teacher's wife would never know. I had married women friends who had done this sort of thing, but I'm always the last in any group to give up convention. So I said to myself, 'Why not, just this once?' and got into bed. I walked to it. He didn't have to snuggle me over to it. I said, 'Okay, Let's do it.'

"It was okay, but afterwards I felt angry. I didn't like the expertise with which he cleaned up after me. I was still lying on the bed while he was checking to see if I'd left lipstick marks on the water glass or any hairs on the pillow slip. What annoyed me most was that if he'd really looked at me, he'd have noticed that I never wore lipstick. I decided he was deceitful and the whole thing made me feel dirty. I felt that what had been a spontaneous adventure for me was a customary and sneaky event for him. And it made me despise him. If he went in for this sort of thing frequently, why did he stay married? He wanted me to meet him there the next week, but I said no. That was the only extramarital adventure I ever had. I might have another some day, but it's been three years since that happened and the occasion just hasn't arisen."

## *Madelaine Leffert /*
## *Everything Seemed So Frivolous in the Sun*

Madelaine Leffert, New York City owner-manager of an import gift shop with her husband, age forty-one, mother of three, reported, "My husband and I have what has to be a model marriage. We not only spend a lot of time together evenings and weekends, but about six years ago I went into the business with him and began helping him run our shop. At first we thought this might make for tensions between us, but actually we handle it very well. We really like each other.

"We almost never fight. There are one or two gripes between us, but they're little things. I can't think of any. Oh yes, there was the matter of the lock. I wanted to put a lock on our bedroom door. All these years we've always felt uncomfortable about making love until after the children are asleep, and as they've gotten older they go to sleep later and later and we have so little privacy. I thought of a lock, but my husband objected because he felt that if there was an emergency during the night or even if one of the children had a stomachache, it wouldn't be right for them not to be able to reach us quickly. I do think he places the children's needs ahead of ours a lot of the time. But you really can't fault a man for that.

"The only extramarital experience I ever had was when I went on a vacation trip to Jamaica about five years ago with my children. My husband was to fly down and meet us on the weekend. On the plane going down I got to talking with a handsome black businessman from Kingston. To my surprise, he rode over to see me and the kids at our Montego Beach hotel two days later. I went to bed with him that night. Everyone around the place had seemed so free, so loose and frivolous in the sun. Even the water was sexual. The kids were occupied and I felt free. So that night I went to bed with him. I liked this man a lot. In a peculiar way he reminded me of my husband. It was the way he fussed not only over me but the kids. He brought them toy steel drums.

"In bed, he came very quickly and I didn't, but he didn't know, and he congratulated me on my orgasm. Then he began confiding in me about how much he wanted a wife. He'd had one, but she had left him. His apartment in Kingston was half-furnished. He wanted someone to pick curtains for it. He himself hadn't the time or the taste. He wanted someone to help him pick his ties. He asked me if I liked the one he'd worn on the plane. I was touched by all this, but it set me adrift. He was just like my husband, but black. I had hoped for adventure."

## Betty Riesling / I Love the Game of Seduction

Betty Riesling, New York City librarian, age thirty-two, mother of two, said, "I'm not very happy with my husband, and playing around gives me something to take my mind off my troubles. I think that when the children are a little older, I'm going to leave him. But for now, I can't afford to. My husband is always borrowing money and failing to pay back. We've had to borrow from my parents more times than you could believe, and he never even tries to pay them back, though he knows my dad is nearing retirement. If it wasn't for the fact that I was working, we'd really be in trouble.

"My husband is very inventive; he studied business management in college and he's started more businesses than you can shake a stick at. But none of them has taken off. Once he was going to sell miniature alarm clocks; you could wear them and set them if you had an appointment to remember. For a while he was getting mummy beads out of Egypt and making necklaces, but paying for someone to go over there and buy them proved terribly costly. For a while he was friends with the man who was promoting the idea of raising minks in your own home, by caging them into your bathtub. Thank God he stayed out of that one.

"The kids think my husband is the best father in the world, because he is so imaginative. He's also very easygoing. He'll let them get away with anything. I couldn't possibly disillusion them, so I'm just holding on until they're a little older, when maybe they'll see my point of view too. In the meantime, I keep myself occupied by having affairs. Nothing too serious. I wouldn't want anything serious until I was ready to make a break.

"I never see the same man more than once and I never let these things keep me away from my children. But I love the whole game of planning seductions. I never run out of ways of finding men. Some I just get talking to at the library where I work. Sometimes it's a neighbor. If a guy around here helps me home with packages, I always ask him up for a drink, and one thing leads to another; you know, everyone's on the search. Sometimes I write letters to guys I want to meet. Like if I read an article in some professional publication, I write to the author and tell him how much I liked the article and if he's ever in New York could he contact me so that we could discuss the fine points. It's amazing how many academic types will respond to this. I've had five one-night stands that began through some sort of correspondence."

## Maggie Berk /
## I Became My Old Self Again

Maggie Berk, a suburban housewife, age thirty-four, mother of three, told me, "When my husband and I started see-ing each other I'd already had a lot of deep sexual relation-ships. I'd started having sex when I was sixteen. When I was still in college I almost married a French actor. I'd spent my junior year abroad, studying pantomime in France and really getting into the life there. I fell in love there and would have married except I couldn't see leaving my friends and family forever, living in a foreign country, being an outsider. I broke off the love affair, but I always remembered those days in France as the happiest in my life, even though after I came home I had exciting love affairs. One was with an assistant district attorney. Another was with a dress manufacturer who used to arrive for our dates with a box full of clothes for me each time. Not just dresses, but shoes in my size to match them, and expensive stockings and the most gorgeous under-things. I'd pick what outfit I wanted, and we'd go out, and I'd wear the rest of the clothes on other nights with other men.

"I met Jerry when I was twenty-three, and I wasn't entirely sure I wanted to get married. Jerry seemed a little pale to me after some of the men I'd met. He wanted to settle down, raise kids, have a big house. That wasn't really my style. I had planned to be an actress. But I felt safe with Jerry. He was very protective. He fixed up my apartment for me practically the first week we met. He put in a new lock because he was worried that my building wasn't safe. And he built book-shelves for me. He really looked after me. And in those days, he'd take phone calls from me in his office no matter how

busy he was, even if he had to be called out from a conference. So I said yes. I bought the whole package. A husband
with an office job. Kids. A house in the suburbs. But marriage
changed Jerry. He wasn't *there* for me so much. Now when I
called, his secretary would say, 'I'm sorry, Mr. Berk is in conference. Can he call you back?' And he'd keep me waiting.
For phone calls, even for sex. And eventually I started doing
the same to him. That's just one of the facts of marriage
mothers don't let their daughters in on.

"All the years when the kids were little and I had my hands
full with them I would dream about my past and wish I had
a few sexy high jinks in my life right then. I always wanted
to have an affair, just a little something to keep my spirits up.
But life was serious now, and I was a responsible person. A
mother. In fact, it got so that I was more responsible than
Jerry. He would go off to work and leave me with all sorts of
problems at home and never bother his head about any of
them. And just on the days the kids had given me the most
trouble, the days I was most tired out from running after
them, on those days he'd want to make love. But on the days
I wanted to, sure enough he'd want to stay up late watching
television or he'd drag me off to some party that went on
and on until I was exhausted. It got so that we were never
on the same schedule about anything.

"About a year ago I found out that Jerry had had an affair.
He left a note on his desk, right out on top, from a woman
who signed herself 'Forever, your Mary.' I was surprised there
was no envelope marked S.W.A.K. It got me furious. There
are two Marys in his office. I told him that if he didn't tell
me which one it was and just what was going on, I'd call up
each one of them until I found out. He said it was the typist
Mary, and that it had been nothing, just a fling.

"After that, I really felt enraged. Here I was, all tied down
with the kids, and he was out playing around. When we'd
met, I'd been the frivolous person, and he'd been the down-
to-earth, responsible one. I'd not only wasted my life on him,

but we'd changed places so that he was the one having all the fun. We had a huge fight, a screaming fight, right in front of the children. The end of it was, I went off to France for a week. It was Jerry's idea, not mine. I don't think he really meant for me to do it. He'd suggested it while we were fighting. 'You're always complaining about your lost youth! Go find it! Go! I'll pay for your trip, just to get you out of here!'

"We'd had that sort of showdown before. In fact, he'd said the same thing a couple of times, but I'd never taken him up on it. This time I did. I said, 'Fine.' And a week later I left for France.

"I went to all the places I had loved when I was young and full of hope. I hung around the Left Bank, went to museums and restaurants, sat all afternoon in La Coupole. I saw de Beauvoir and Sartre there. She was reading *L'Humanité* to him and he was eating oysters. When I first got to Paris I was planning to look up my old boyfriend, but I figured he was probably married or fat, and after just a couple of days I realized that I didn't really care about him. It was Paris that had turned me on, even in those long-ago days. And it did it again. I felt young again. And when you feel young, you meet people. The third day I was there I met a Swedish newspaperman who was staying in my hotel and we started doing our touring together. We rented a car and saw Versailles. We picnicked and ate and drank together. And we went to bed together, high on aquavit. I was my old self again. I told him I was married. He told me he was. We didn't feel sad when we said good-bye. I hadn't had the affair because of him. And I imagine he hadn't had it because of me. We'd had it because of them—his wife, my husband. But I was looking forward to seeing Jerry by then. In a way I felt grateful to him, though of course I wasn't planning on telling him anything about what had happened.

"But I suppose letting him know was irresistible, because a few weeks after I was home I discovered I was pregnant. There was no knowing for sure whose kid it would be. So I told Jerry about the man in France. He was wonderful about it. I had an abortion. Jerry helped me decide where and he came with me, and actually the experience brought us closer. He said I must have been taking revenge on him and I said, 'Yes? For what?' and he said, 'For forever Mary,' and I said 'No, for forever till death do us part,' and he said 'Well, for that, it's small enough revenge, I guess,' and we ended up better friends than we'd been in years. I admit it's helped that I've gone back to acting school in the city and I meet Jerry after work three days a week. We also agreed that if his secretary said to me, 'I'm sorry, Mr. Berk is in conference,' I was to say to her, 'Tell Mr. Berk it's Miss Lovelace.' "

## Sukey Dobbs /
## It's Taken Me So Long to Appreciate Just Good Sex

Sukey Dobbs, a midwestern public relations specialist, age thirty-four, with no children, told me, "I've had a few brief affairs. I had one with a colleague about three weeks ago. It was so lovely. It's taken me so long to appreciate just sex. People say that women don't get sexy until they're over thirty, that it's something physiological, but really what it is is that it takes years to get rid of all your hang-ups. It took me eight years to realize that although I like the sex in my marriage and love my husband, I like variety too. It didn't really become possible for me, however, until a few years ago when I started the job I have now. This job involves a small amount of traveling, and sometimes I get lonely on trips away from home. If there's someone around who seems easy and uncomplicated—usually that's a married man—I try to make something happen. It's only when I'm out of town.

"It's often somebody I might not like if I got to know him too well. But there's a lot of excitement in knowing I'm just going to see him this one time, or maybe twice, and never again. Casual sex affairs add another dimension to sex. They contribute to making it good because the man is really a kind of fantasy figure. I just don't know who he is. I can create whatever I want out of it. I'm not saying I like promiscuity. I don't. I wouldn't want to go screwing around a lot. It's just something I do when I feel like it and somebody comes along. But those two things don't happen at the same time too often.

"The first time they happened I thought there was something wrong with me. I went to a marriage counselor, a man. I said, 'What's the matter with me? I make love with my husband four or five times a week. I'm absolutely content with him. What's the matter with me?' I felt ashamed, and it was very important to me that my husband not find out.

"I talked to this counselor three, maybe four months. We talked about my childhood, my marriage, my job. But we concluded there was nothing wrong with me or my marriage. I just like variety. He said there were men that were that way, so why shouldn't there be women? I said no other woman I ever knew was this way. He said maybe they are and don't tell anyone.

"I don't tell people. In fact, I try very hard for it to be someone far away. I feel it would hurt my husband if this came out. I'm talking about how other people would look at him. They'd think there was something wrong with him, and they'd think less of him. I wouldn't want that, just for a fling. But as long as it is safe, what's the harm?"

## Kay Mordechai /
### It Was Fun and Educational

Kay Mordechai, suburban housewife and poet, age forty-two, mother of four, related, "I had an Argentinian friend from my college days who used to send me interesting people. I mean she sent them if they were passing through and wanted to get to know an American family. We'd make dinner, entertain them. It was fun for us, fun and educational for the children. One time one of my friend's friends called during a period my husband was out of town. He's out of town a lot for professional meetings, and although he always used to take me with him, lately he feels it's too expensive. I didn't exactly like this Argentinian when he called because instead of saying, 'My name is Ramón,' he said, 'This is Dr. Ruíz.' He was a psychiatrist. Very stiff on the phone. But when he arrived, I was surprised. He was only about twenty-eight years old and not as formal as I'd expected. It must have been having to speak English over a telephone that made him sound that way.

"After dinner was over and the kids had gone to bed we sat and talked for a while. He was only going to be around for a day or two because he was flying to a meeting in Boston. I was trying to give him what presumably he'd come for, a glimpse into my suburban American way of life, when I got this wonderful idea. I thought, he's come here because he wants to know how his American counterparts live. Well, suppose instead of talking, I show him. Suppose I let him share my entire life for a day. He could do everything I do, go everyplace I go. Like to the supermarket. To the kids' school. Even to my therapy hour. I think it was the thought of my therapy hour that triggered the whole experiment. Ramón knew all about classical therapy, the Freudian stuff, but he'd never seen one of our freewheeling California-type therapists in action. I had been describing mine to him and he'd expressed interest in how and whether it worked.

"At first I didn't say anything about sex, and that didn't happen until the next day. But it must have been there in the back of my mind. This guy was very appealing and even his accent turned me on. But at first I was just thinking of chores.

"So he got up with me real early for breakfast and helped me dress the kids. And we drove the kids to school and I let him take the little one into her classroom so he could see the teacher and the open schoolroom thing. Then we did the marketing. He'd never wheeled a grocery cart before.

And then we went to my therapy. I think he hadn't really believed the night before that a therapist would actually let him listen in on the hour. But of course, mine said it was okay. So I talked and he listened. I really believe I said exactly what I would have said whether he'd been there or not. I did my usual stuff. Anxieties over the kids. Anxieties about how come my husband and I seem to have grown a little distant, a little too independent of one another. Anger at growing old. My therapist never wants to hear childhood stuff. It's the here and now he cares about. I did talk about how stimulating it was to have Ramón sharing my life, but I'd have said that even if he wasn't there.

"That night he came to the poetry class I was taking. He met my classmates and commented on the poems just like everyone else. And then we came home and went to bed together. We'd agreed during the afternoon to add that experience. It wasn't a wild sexual attraction on either of our parts. It was just that we thought it would be delightful and a little daring.

"There was some discomfort. At one point he wanted to back out. He said, 'If we sleep together, won't you expect me to love you forever?' I said, 'No, only tonight.' It was lots of fun and I felt proud of myself. Anyway, the next morning we had breakfast and he caught his plane. I never heard from him again. But I always felt that if ever my husband and I were to divorce, I'd look up Ramón. That day made us like good old friends."

# (5)
# Staying Married:
## *Adulterous Personalities and Adultery-Provoking Marriage*

Despite the many pages of psychological and sociological literature devoted to extramarital sex, there are in fact only two theories about what makes people adulterous. One is that they are adulterous by nature—either by virtue of human nature itself (this from sexual utopians who consider monogamy a departure from a biological norm) or by virtue of their individual nature (this from sexual conservatives who consider monogamy the norm and see departures from it as the result of personality quirks). The other theory about what makes people adulterous is that they are so by virtue of their marriages—their situations. Impressive voices and formidable arguments have been raised on both sides, with Strindberg stating the nature argument the most succinctly. He wrote, ". . . some people are born monogamous, that is, faithful, which is not a virtue but a quality, while others are born polygamous, that is, unfaithful."

Most members of the psychological professions are divided as to whether nature or situation produces adulterous behavior. Many psychologists and psychiatrists believe that people are adulterous because they were conditioned by childhood experience to be unable to form deep commitments or because they are so immature that they can acknowledge no limit to their needs or can acquire no perspective on what realistically to expect from marriage. Others stress the situational as the cause of adultery and believe that people are adulterous because they live in adultery-provoking marriages —those in which interpersonal intimacy has become disturbed. Dr. Leon Salzman, the psychoanalyst who has written frequently on the psychiatric and clinical aspects of extramarital sex says, for example, "Infidelity may be part of a neurotic or psychotic development, but more often it represents a rational and comprehensible piece of behavior in the so-called normal person."

I found that many women I spoke with wanted to ponder the question of whether their personalities or their marriages had led them to adultery. Usually, they were women who felt bad about themselves for having had extramarital sexual experiences, and who had even attempted to change either their personalities or their marriages so that they might cease being adulterous. To change personality, they sought individual psychological counseling; to change their marriages, they sought either the repair of marriage available through marital counseling or the termination of marriage available through legal means.

The question of personality versus situation was most interesting to me when it cropped up in interviews with women who had renounced marriages in which interpersonal intimacy was disturbed and who had undertaken new—presumably more satisfactory—intimate relationships with men. I always asked whether they were still adulterous and if so, why, and if not, why not. The stories of two such women are presented here. One believes she has an adulterous nature even though she is no longer adulterous; to change her behavior, she provided herself with a socially-approved form of loving more than one man. The other believes she was adulterous only because of her marital situation and that, indeed, one can tell in advance which kinds of marriages will lead to adultery: among her clues are sexual incompatability; financial insecurity; and divorce-phobia.

Approaching the personality or situation question through

individual lives can't possibly provide a universally applicable answer. But perhaps this debate is best left answered by individual lives; the generalizations have too many exceptions.

## *Irene Brakhage / Two Men to Love*

Irene Brakhage had been married twice and had been adulterous in both her marriages. The first time around she had used extramarital sex to help her find a rescuer who would untie her from a marriage in which she felt chained. The second time around, married at last to the man who had taken her out of that first unhappy marriage, she had continued to use it because, she said, her second husband had taken too long about marrying her and had thus provoked her anger. "Use" was her expression. "Being a product of my times," she said, "I used extramarital sex as a weapon. I didn't have the guts to tell either of my husbands what was wrong when things they did made me unhappy. I simply would have lovers. And then, when my husbands would continue to behave in ways that troubled me, I would sit back and let this sphinxlike expression come over me and say to them silently, without real words, 'So there!' That was my revenge. Affairs were the flowers that bloomed in my deserts."

I would have assumed that with a pattern so ingrained, Irene would have remained adulterous her entire life. But no, she had finally given up affairs, and not because she was no longer beautiful, no longer enticing. She was forty-five now, but she had given up affairs when she reached thirty-one. What had made this happen? How was it that a woman who had relied on extramarital sex as a weapon for survival, could change and become monogamous? Irene tried to explain it to me over a meal in an Italian restaurant where no waiters turned their heads, no lunching executives stopped to stare at a woman who had once thought of herself, or so she told it, as Cleopatra and Scarlett O'Hara rolled into one, a Vivien Leigh with a small-town New England accent.

"I married my first husband because I had an affair when I was seventeen with a boy I couldn't marry, a boy who didn't care much about me, and when my family found out about it, my father laid a whole whore trip on me. I lived in a small town. My father was convinced that I was going to be a whore, that no man would *ever* marry me, so I knew I couldn't ever save face unless I heard my wedding bells ring. These kids who talk about the generation gap today, what do they know? There's no generation gap today. Their fight was fought by people like me, twenty, twenty-five years ago. Those were the days when if you slept with a boy before you were married, you were considered trash. But the awful part about those days was that the wounds you got from other people's opinions of you didn't just hurt and make you bleed outside. You got internal hemorrhaging. You got to take it all into your inside. So I thought I *was* trash, was a whore.

"Of course I wanted a husband. What else was there for a woman in those days? So I set about proving my father wrong. I became as seductive as could be, and I wooed the next boy who came along and got married by the time I was nineteen. But I think I never got over the idea that I was whorish, and I decided that if that was the case, I was not just going to have all the disadvantages of being a whore but some of the benefits too. I would be a courtesan and have men falling at my feet my entire life. Maybe part of it was to show my father how wrong he and his whole old-fashioned world were about just what it was men wanted in women."

I asked Irene about that long-ago marriage. It was twenty-five years ago, 1947. Some sociologists contend that adultery among women is on the increase today because married women have more opportunity—being out in the working world—to meet men with whom to have affairs. Twenty-five years ago, at home all day in a small Connecticut town, Irene had no difficulty meeting men. Necessity was the mother of opportunity for her.

"I met men everywhere. I was very dramatic-looking. I had

long black hair and I made up my eyes to look exotic, foreign. I weighed only ninety-two pounds and I used to wear chiffon dresses in very clinging styles. Mostly black dresses. Black was considered sophisticated then, at least on young girls, and just a little bit wicked. I was always giving out signals. So if I was on a train, I'd meet a man. Or if I walked in the street, I'd meet one." She giggled, a high, girlish, flirtatious laugh. In recounting her memories, she had become youthful again and I could imagine her thin and delicate and childishly wicked.

"Were they married men?" I asked.

"No. As a matter of fact, in those days I avoided married men. They were always young men, unattached."

"Did you meet with them at your house while your husband was at work?" I asked.

"No," Irene said, "I saw them at hotels. Never motels, either. I'd make them take suites with big opulent bathrooms. And we always called room service and had white meat chicken sandwiches, seventy-five cents extra, thick as paperbound books. And sometimes even champagne.

"I didn't do one-night stands. I never did that, if I could help it. I was out looking. Looking for romance and adventure, on the one hand, but, after three or four years in my marriage, for another husband too. My first husband was irresponsible. He spent whatever he made, and he gambled a lot. My folks had to support us. Since occasionally I'd had offers of marriage from some of the men I'd slept with, I began to realize I could probably find my next husband while still with the first one."

This is indeed what happened, although the process took longer than Irene had anticipated. It began on a night she was visiting a female friend in the city and went with her friend to a late night jazz club. While there, Irene was introduced to a friend of the friend, a "very handsome, very smart-assed, very young poetry lover who had just gotten divorced."

She didn't like Gus at first. "He kept correcting my grammar." But he said to her, when the music ended, "Do you want to watch the sun come up?" So they rode to the river and watched the dawn and they talked about poetry and when she offered herself to him in the front seat of his Oldsmobile convertible, he told her, "You're not my physical type. I like ingenuous faces. Not Egyptian princesses. Not ladies with make-up." Irene had been crushed and saddened. She was twenty-three and now, at last, here was a man who did behave exactly as her father had said men would—a man who turned her down because of her sexual sophistication. She could get nothing out of Gus in terms of a future appointment. He didn't want to go one night to Lewisohn Stadium. Not with her. He didn't want to see her quaint little Connecticut hometown. He did mention in passing that he liked hand-knitted socks, and Irene had noticed he was wearing a pair of store-bought argyles. The socks were the only thing she could fasten on as a way of having anything whatsoever to do with him in the future.

"I went home and I bought yarn and I started knitting. I knitted him twenty-eight pairs of socks. My then-husband found the first three pairs and assumed they were for him and got all mushy and thanked me and I screamed, 'They're for my brother!' and got them back. And when I had twenty-eight pairs, I took them to New York and looked up Gus."

He was touched by the hand-knitted argyles and by the simplicity of her dress the day she came to see him. He went to bed with her in his ground-floor garden apartment, and she didn't leave there until almost two weeks later. "He cancelled all his appointments and we spent eleven days together. In bed, mostly. We really had terrific sex. But we talked more poetry too, and he corrected my grammar, and once I got drunk and I told him my father had said I would always be a whore and he slapped my face and I thought, 'Okay. That's it. The first time any man hits me, it's the last time,' but as if he was reading my thoughts, Gus said, 'I did that to give you the punishment you go around begging for. And now that you've got it, it's going to stand for all of it, all you ever wanted. You won't ever need any more, because you've had it.' And then, he held me, and he said, 'Look, Irene. It's one thing for a woman to be chaste when she isn't beautiful. But when a woman looks as good as you, it isn't all her fault."

Irene called her husband from Gus's apartment and told him she was never coming back. She moved into her own tiny apartment and got a job as a travel agency representative and got divorced and saw a lot of Gus.

But he didn't marry her. It was, after all, just as her father had said. "The relationship went on, but Gus wasn't the marrying kind. He was very attractive, very comfortable, and he didn't want to get married. I tried to get interested in my career. I figured it was crazy to count on Gus. I was getting on in my twenties. I figured that one day Gus was going to up and marry some eighteen-year-old girl and that I would be left, neurotic and morbidly dependent, like one of Tennessee Williams' heroines. So I decided I'd better make sure I had other guys waiting in the wings for me, just in case things with Gus didn't work out.

"I began to take up skiing. I'd leave Gus on weekends and go do my own thing. And of course as soon as I started to move away, Gus started to miss me and got afraid that I would find somebody else. He proposed to me in a dark movie. I got angry and I said, 'I don't think I want to get married. I really love what I'm doing, and I sort of like the way I'm living now.' He said, 'Forget it then!' But quick as a wink I said, 'Well, I suppose you don't want to waste the best years of my life?' And we hugged in the movie and we got married two weeks later."

Having gotten what she had worked so hard to get, Irene had thought at first that she could finally give up always keeping one man in the wings while her main act was on stage. But to her own surprise, she couldn't. Gus had kept her waiting too long, was how she put it to herself at first, and she resented him now almost as much as she had her first husband. She couldn't be sure of him even though he had married her. She had to worry about her future. And so little by little, she began the same pattern of seduction she had used earlier.

"I was older now. About twenty-nine or thirty. Now the men I met were married men. I had longer affairs. Two were intense, sustained relationships. We met during lunch a lot. Sometimes in the evenings. I got quite bold about one of them. It was a real love affair, and I wasn't sure which way I was going. I didn't really want to leave Gus. It wasn't that I'd stopped loving him. I just felt I could love more than one man. I also felt I needed to, because I always needed shoring up. The only thing I was ever sure of about myself was that I was good-looking. Nothing else. I had no confidence in myself as a person of intelligence. Whatever intellectual veneer I had was polished onto me by Gus. I didn't even really have confidence in myself as a lover. So I went thrashing about, always providing extras for myself. And one night I stayed out all night.

"It's one thing when you come home at four in the morning and you are drunk. You can always say you were with the girls, and you had to wait for one of them to drive you home because you were afraid of even taking a taxi by yourself so late. But it was another to stay out all night. Gus packed his bags and left. You see, I got what I had always expected I'd get."

She just let Gus go. She felt she deserved what had happened. She says she was never so miserable in her whole life and that she went without make-up for the first time in fifteen years and that one weekend she took forty aspirin in the hopes of ending her life. She couldn't ask Gus to come back to her. She couldn't even try. She felt like nobody, a person who had vanished.

But Irene always managed to have men protecting her, advising her, cherishing her for her very self-doubts. One of her lovers began to urge her to make at least a stab at regaining Gus. Who knows? Perhaps it was because he did not want the responsibility of this now drawn-faced, pitiful woman on *his* hands, but he said to her, "Get Gus back. You can still get him back. And this time just make up your mind to stick with him. Otherwise, you'll be a three-time loser in the divorce court. I know your type. You're never going to find any man better than Gus." Irene recalls that this lover, to whom she was to be infinitely grateful, took out his wallet, gave her a hundred dollars, and said, "Go buy a bottle of champagne and some caviar and call up Gus." She relishes that part of her story; it was the last time she used one man to gain another.

"I did what he suggested. I called Gus up and I said, 'Let's not talk about the past. Just come home tonight. Let's fuck our heads off and not talk.' And it worked; he came over; we spent the night in bed; and in the morning he was going to leave and I said, 'Try me; just try me this once more.' He said he didn't know if he could ever trust me again, but he agreed to try."

This time Irene determined to have only one man. She wanted to change. She had, finally, gotten the punishment she had expected all her life. She had almost lost Gus, and she loved him, even if she couldn't love herself. She wanted to keep her word.

"Still," said Irene when I interviewed her in the restaurant, "I don't really think I could have kept my word, given my past. Don't forget, we were all brought up on romance in those days. I wanted to be Cleopatra and Scarlett O'Hara and all those wonderful ladies in the movies. It's hard to be romantic in marriage, hard to be romantic when somebody's got a cold and a red nose and you're worried about money and you hate your mother-in-law."

"So what happened?" I asked. "How did you keep your word?"

"I got pregnant," she said flatly.

"That was it? That was all it took?" I was incredulous.

And Irene laughed, with the sprightly seductive giggle she had used when she spoke of her lovers, and she said, "It was a boy. I fell madly in love with my son. Maybe if it had been a girl, it would have been different. But now I would always have two men to love, and to love me." Her son is fourteen now, and only once during these fourteen years has Irene had an extramarital affair. "It was only once," she said, "once when Gus was very sick, and I felt all alone in the world again. Otherwise, I've been a faithful storybook wife, loyal as Penelope to my husband and my son."

## Shirley Randolph / You Can Tell in Advance

Shirley Randolph, an actress I met through a friend who runs a theatre, was adulterous during her thirteen-year marriage but, divorced and living for four years as if married to a fellow actor, had not had any extraneous affairs or been tempted to do so. "It is true," she said, "that this new relationship with Ridge is only four years old, and that I didn't have an affair in my marriage until after my husband and I had been together about that length of time. But I can tell you with absolute certainty it won't happen this time around. I won't have affairs. Neither will Ridge. You can tell in advance which kinds of relationships are going to include playing around. They are the ones with people who are afraid to leave each other."

We were sitting in Shirley's apartment, an elegant East Side duplex purchased by her former husband for Shirley and their four children right before the divorce. Occasionally, Shirley made disparaging remarks about some of the expensive furnishings in the apartment. "I cared more about material objects in those days," she said, sitting casually, sandals tucked under her, on a plush white sofa.

What bothered Shirley about her possessions was that she felt they reminded her constantly of how her husband's success and prestige as a furniture corporation executive had tied her to him for long, strenuous years of marriage.

Shirley had been married when she was twenty-one and she was a virgin when she got married. "I'd had the usual struggle in the back seats of cars" she said, "but in my day—I was married in 1956—you had to avoid sex when you were tempted by it because otherwise you might not be marriageable. You also got married, in my circle, to someone you thought would be a success. I knew from the minute I met Simon—he was at college with me—that he was going to be successful and that I was going to have an easy ride. These things were drummed into me in Queens in 1956. Marriage was an economic investment. I was only twenty-one but I felt so old then. I was awfully glad to have found a husband like Simon."

But her gladness had evaporated rapidly. "My honeymoon was a nightmare, an absolute, utter nightmare," she said: "We were both of us naive and very uptight. All the excitement we had felt beforehand just seemed to disintegrate under the pressure of *having* to make love. The last thing we wanted was to be alone with each other. While we had good, affectionate feelings for each other, we didn't know what to do with them. Sex seemed to be something we just *had* to do, had to plow forward and do; it was really horrible.

"That first night was in the Plaza, and we made it, if that's what you want to call it. It was very painful. I wasn't excited at all, so of course it was painful. But the sexual thing really didn't ever improve. I felt passion in stops and starts. Sometimes something would happen and I'd get excited but I never really became orgasmic until after we divorced. If I had been screwing before I married I might have had a better chance in marriage. Or even if I'd let Simon do a hand-job on me. But in my circle you didn't do that. In my circle the idea was that you had to be penetrated and have an orgasm during penetration and that's what we kept trying to accomplish for years and years."

After only four months, Shirley had begun to suspect that

neither she nor Simon could stand their marriage. But she could think of no solution. She began having fantasies about other men and sometimes she would have secret lunches or early evening drinks with friends of Simon's or the husbands of friends of hers. Once she almost went to bed with one of them, but she had stopped herself, fearful that somehow knowledge of the liaison might get back to Simon. Four years later, she was sorry she had not had the encounter, for Simon came home one night and told her he'd been having an affair and wanted to separate. Shirley pleaded with him not to do so; she was, she said, terrified of economic insecurity. "I pleaded with him and he said it wasn't the affair that was making him want to leave me. In fact he had broken it off. He said it was me, our marriage. I couldn't see what to do about it, and we decided on a trial separation."

They stayed apart for four months and tried dating and marriage counseling and finally Shirley tried conception. "It was classic, I guess," she said. "One weekend we left the kids with a housekeeper and went off to a motel to see whether there was anything between us that was at all salvageable. And that weekend I got pregnant. That was what we salvaged. Six more years. We stayed together another six years until Simon had a big affair which broke us up for good."

After the first separation and their reunion, Shirley also had affairs. "Two small ones. One with an old boyfriend; one with a therapist I was seeing. And one big one, with an actor. I never told Simon about my affairs, whereas he insisted on telling me about his. It's something men do; they have to tell, because they always need either to be forgiven for them or admired because of them. I kept mine secret, even the big one, which went on close to two years. By that time I'd decided to study acting so I could at least pretend I had a little independence. But independence doesn't spring out of a fear of losing security. You just walk into water up to your knees, turn around, and come right back. I did a couple of commercials, and several times I was offered big parts out of town.

But I had a great fear of not being with Simon, so every time a chance came along, I'd turn it down."

Her "big" affair with the actor had started while she was acting in an off-Broadway show. "This guy and I were working together," Shirley explained. "That's what made it so good, made me feel so good. We would rehearse in the afternoons, and then get together in his apartment before a show; we had a lot of time, especially in the summer when Simon was out in the country with the kids on weekends.

"I felt all the things an affair makes you feel. Beautiful again. Less afraid of growing old. I'd visit this boyfriend in his apartment. In reality it was a dirty actor's pad in the Village, but I'd come out of there feeling glowing all over, like we'd just been to the beach. There are many places that people search for their egos and unfortunately, one of the popular places is in somebody else's eyes. We all know it *shouldn't* be that way. You shouldn't have to depend on someone else to make you feel good about yourself. You should be able to arrive at self-love yourself. But it just doesn't work that way. There's no great self-image in changing dirty diapers and keeping the house, and sometimes the only thing a woman's got to her image is her body, and the only rewards she can get are with it or for it."

It was hard to believe that Shirley, a striking-looking redhead with high cheekbones and pale skin, had ever had a poor self-image, and yet perhaps, as she said, she had believed only in her body and her beauty and they hadn't been enough. I was finding that many women complained of their need to establish their worth, or re-establish it, no matter how attractive or even how competent they appeared to me.

Shirley, who had been quite animated earlier, reflected this by sounding depressed and flat as she approached in her story the break-up of her affair. "But then, I did what I was raised to do. Simon got transferred to the West Coast and I just said good-bye to my lover. Just like that. I felt very bad about leaving him, but I had never expected it could last; that hadn't been my intention. We had always known one day it would end, and so it did."

Out West her life was worse than before. She spent her time furnishing a house, working doggedly on it. She said, "It's always seemed to me that when my life is crumbling, when inside I'm dying, that's when I have the most possessions and the most elaborate facade. I lived up to everything I was supposed to live up to. I met and entertained all Simon's associates and made friends with mommies so the kids would have friends. And then towards the end of that year, Simon started going off on frequent business trips. As I've said, he could never quite keep it a secret when he had a girlfriend. I was pretty certain he had one now but I didn't know who she was. I told a few of my friends my suspicions and they made inquiries. Finally, at a party, one of my friends produced her. 'I've figured out who Simon's seeing,' my friend said, 'and if you want to take a look, I'll have her over to a party.' I got pretty drunk before the party. But I went. As soon as I arrived, my friend pointed out this young girl to me, a girl who couldn't have been much more than nineteen. I remember going up to her and saying, 'My name is Mrs. Randolph.' And I remember her looking at me a little nervously and then saying pathetically, 'How are the children?' It was touching.

"Anyhow, then there was another young girl. And then another. And then finally there was one Simon said he wanted to marry. I felt terrible, just as I'd always known I would. Not about him. I don't think I'd ever cared about him, or that he'd ever cared about me. I had just cared about staying married. And once we divorced, I could see why I'd cared so much about that. Divorce was worse than my worst fantasies of divorce. When you're left, you feel horrible for a long time. You've been left. You're just no good.

"But I survived it and surviving it was the best thing that ever happened to me in my life. It taught me that if I could live through that, I could live through anything. I knew I'd never be afraid of anything again. And one piece of courage stood out above all the others. I knew I'd never again live in a situation with a man where I let him play around because that alternative seemed better than his leaving me or where I would play around because it seemed safer than leaving him.

"Lots of things have happened to me since then. For one thing, I met Ridge and fell in love. For another, I finally have become successful as an actress. Forgive me if I take an economic view. The truth is, money is even more important than people ever admit. I'm no longer scared about money. Simon gives me lots of money for the kids. I make money for myself. So I'm hardly dependent at all on what Ridge makes. It's made me into a new person. It's made me someone who would never again be willing to sustain a relationship that was a lie.

"I met Ridge after more than a year on my own, a lonely, freaky, desperate year. But a year in which I saw a lot of men. I picked Ridge because we have a great sexual relationship. We tried it out for eight months before we moved in together. And I picked him because he's sweet and sensitive and loving. Since I've been with him I've never thought of another man, which you have to admit is really a sign of how special what we have is, given the life of an actress. But I'll tell you something. If I did start dreaming about someone else, it would mean I wasn't getting everything I needed from Ridge and if that happened, I'd just leave. I'd do that because it takes two to tangle and if I was thinking about someone else, chances are he'd be too, and I might as well just end it or else one day he would."

Shirley Randolph had touched on one generalization about women's affairs that I found accurate. Affairs, when they started, were usually undertaken not to disrupt but to preserve marriage by women who were, at least initially, somewhat phobic about divorce. Often they hoped to stave if off through extramarital sex. Nevertheless, a surprising number of divorced women told me that they had had extramarital sexual affairs prior to making conscious decisions to divorce, or prior to having their husbands decide to divorce. It appeared that even though an affair did not arise as a step in the direction of divorce, it nevertheless often led there.

# (6)
# Breaking Up:
## *Deciding to Be Alone*

Affairs catapult questions of divorce. This is true despite the fact that most women do not intend to abandon their marriages when they first turn to extramarital sex. Yet as I was to discover, even the briefest of affairs could cause immediate changes in life situations, abrupt separations, dramatic divorces. It was always difficult for me—or for the participants—to tell why this was so; to decide whether an affair pinpointed a marriage's deficiencies and thereby caused divorce, or whether a deficient marriage already hurtling toward divorce paused inevitably at an affair.

I have arranged the reports I heard from once-adulterous now-divorced women into three chapters. The first two deal with women who themselves decided to end their marriages after some exposure to extramarital sexual experience, either to be on their own, or to realign with their lovers. The third deals with women who wanted to continue their marriages but whose husbands decided on divorce.

Among those who decided to end their marriages were a handful of women whose lovers had been catalysts but not goals. These women had used extramarital sex as an almost ritualistic precursor to divorce, a rite of passage that established that they were sexually or emotionally desirable. Even living for a short time in quarrelsome or neglectful marriages could cause women to doubt their desirability, and although they might contemplate breaking up such marriages, they hesitated, fearing that no man would ever again find them appealing. Winning the affection of lovers, or feeling affectionate once again toward new men when they had felt only anger or resignation toward their husbands, was a sign to such women of their sexual and psychological capacities. It gave them courage to undertake new life situations for themselves —to leave their marriages—but not necessarily to be with their lovers.

These women tended to consider their lovers way stations, but not the end of their emotional or sexual routes. They felt that because they had chosen men while they were still married, they had chosen under duress. When they divorced or separated, they did not long realign with their lovers. Typically, their affairs ended as soon as their marriages did. Dramatically reversing the fairy tale view, lovers lost their glamour overnight and princes turned into frogs. Extramarital sex proved, for such women, to have been a stepping stone, a pathway out of turbulent or difficult marriages.

### *Carol Battersby /*
### *Stop Teaching. Have a Baby. It'll All Be Okay.*

One of the first women I talked with whose affair and marriage had ended almost simultaneously was Carol Battersby, who lived in a small, midwestern city. A twenty-four-year-old schoolteacher, she had, just three months before we spoke, taken flight from both her year-long affair with a fellow teacher and her three-year-old marriage to a law student.

We talked in her apartment, three rooms in a private house on a quiet, tree-shaded street. She was sharing the rooms now with a young man she had met only a month ago, but with whom she was having, she said, "the best relationship of my life." I found her very enthusiastic about the role her extramarital lover had played, even though she seemed no longer even to like him. "When I think how I might have missed this new relationship," she said, "I bless the affair I had, even though it was really pretty lousy. I bless it because I don't see how—without it—I'd ever have had the courage to start out on my own again."

She had gotten married at twenty-one, she explained: "It was a typical right-out-of-college marriage and two years later I started the love affair. The guy taught with me. At the time we started, his wife had just had a baby and I'm sure he just really wanted to screw somebody. I was attracted to him. Not just to his body but to his mind too. I mean, it didn't happen like, 'Hi! What's your name? Let's screw?' At least, it didn't seem that way to me. Maybe it would to you."

"How *did* it happen?" I asked.

"It was at school. That was the wild thing. In a closet at school. It was a supply room kind of thing. There was space to lie down on the floor. It was a totally physical, brute sort of thing. I went home after and took a shower; I felt really dirty. But at the same time I knew I had thought about it and wanted it for weeks and weeks before. Still, it was crazy. I mean, to start a relationship just like that on the floor. I wish it had been a little bit more glamorous and comfortable, but what the hell."

Carol refused to get bogged down in what she called "the guilt trip" because, she said, "I was there. I was there for the first six months and now I'm someplace else." What had happened was that during the first six months of her relationship with the fellow teacher, she had tried to glamorize him. "He told a lot of funny stories. I told myself how entertaining he was. But you know, he was just a really heavy come-on type of dude. Guilt makes you exaggerate a lover's good points or overlook his bad ones."

What had her marriage been like, I wanted to know. Carol said, "Sex was lacking. That was one thing. But that's only a symptom of other things that were lacking. One thing I could say about myself as a sexual person goes way back to when I was in high school. I began having intercourse when

I was a junior, and then I went away to college, and there were lots of true loves between the beginning and the end. But then I ended up marrying the first guy I'd ever been to bed with. My husband had lived down the street from me in high school and he was my first. What I think is that when you start screwing you feel guilty, no matter what age you first start. I felt guilty, not about the later experiences, but about that first early one. So I ended up marrying him. It wiped away my guilt, but it didn't do anything at all for our relationship.

"This turned out to be a dud, a blank. I don't know what changed between the beginning and the end, but after we were married a year we were down to screwing maybe once a month. I didn't exactly count, but around the time I was expecting my period I'd look up and think to myself, 'Jesus, the last time, wasn't that just before my last period? Or was it just after?' "

I wanted to know if she and her husband had talked about her sexual deprivation. "Yeah," she said, "but he had all these million excuses. He was too tired was the biggest one. He was going to law school, and he's no great brain, and he had to keep up and he had to study and anyway, after a while I just didn't care. I masturbated. He locked himself up in the kitchen to study and I locked myself up in the bedroom and I got cleverer and cleverer about masturbating, trying different things, different textures, trying wet washcloths and leather gloves and stuff. You know, varying it. I couldn't have cared less after a while whether he approached me or not."

For about six months her affair with the fellow teacher delighted her. "I was never so energetic in my life. I mean, wow! Like I just functioned on very few hours of sleep because I'd think about him all night and wake up each morning and say, 'Wow! Do I get to see the dude today or not?' And actually, it did a hell of a lot of good for my marital situation. In terms of living together, I think my husband and I were much happier. I'd still come home, fix good dinners. And I got along better with my husband during those months."

In this period Carol was meeting her lover at her house in the late afternoons and sometimes at his, once his wife had returned to work. But after a while, she had begun to grow restless. "When I think back to then, to what my intentions were, I guess I really didn't have any at first except to go on doing it as long as I could. You have to understand my background. I come from a family of churchgoing Presbyterians and divorce was the worst thing I could do to my parents. Divorce was unheard of. You just don't get divorced. You know, you work it out or you sit there miserable for the rest of your life. So at first I was trying to work it out. Whenever I'd let on to my mother that things weren't just as rosy between my husband and me as she liked to imagine, she'd come back at me with the solution: 'Stop teaching. Have a baby. It'll all be okay once you have children.' "

In her efforts to work things out, Carol had continued to see her lover, but found that she wanted more from him than he was prepared to give. "In the beginning just talking to him in the corridor for a second was just great. Like we'd stop for a minute and chat, and he'd say, 'I think I can get away tomorrow,' but then the next day at noon he'd tell me, 'Yeah, well my wife is home today and I can't think of an excuse for getting back late.' I felt like, 'You sonofabitch! You can't think of an excuse! You just don't have enough balls to do it!' And once I started getting angry, it started getting less and less fun."

I asked, "How did it affect your sexual relations with him?"

Carol said, "Badly. I got into this thing where I began feeling, 'You're just coming here to get in bed with me, and like that's cool, but why can't we do some other things too? Like eat lunch or at least talk more or something.' It wasn't like I wanted him to buy me gifts or anything, but I wanted him to spend time with me as a person as well as a body in bed."

Around this time Carol decided to broach with her husband the idea of separation. "I think I had finally realized all this wasn't worth it. And somehow, just from doing it, I'd gotten rid of the idea I wouldn't be able to find someone else pretty quick. That was a thing that had really frightened me. But now I figured, if this guy was breaking his ass just to meet me for a couple of quick hours, I must be pretty good. Something like that.

"I got into a lot of heavy stuff with my husband. Like, 'We're going to work on this; let's go to a marriage counselor.' And we did; we were in limbo for a number of months. But I think I already knew what I wanted to do because one day I said, 'Look, I'm going to leave in three months when the term is over.' And that's what I did."

### Rose Marie Corelli /
### It's Always Oneself When One Says "The Kids"

Perhaps, I thought after interviewing Carol Battersby, deciding to be on one's own with neither husband nor lover for insurance is possible only for the young woman or the woman without children. But when I met Rose Marie Corelli, a thirty-seven-year-old editor with two young children, I realized that even older women and mothers were as capable as Carol had been of viewing their affairs simply as life-preservers thrown down to rescue them from icy or storm-tossed marriages. Once ashore, they let go. Rose Marie, who was recommended to me by a professional colleague, said, "I had two affairs while married, the first one brief and unrewarding, the second one lovely, a joyous experience. I've never felt guilty about either one of them, which is strange because I had a very religious upbringing and I am still quite religious. Not in the conventional sense. I don't go to church. But I believe in good and bad, in right and wrong, in punishment for our sins. But the sin for me was staying married, because by that act I was forgetting that joy existed in the world. I was denying, to myself and all those around me, that life had value.

"I stayed married years longer than I should have because I had two little children. Whenever I'd think of ending my marriage I'd say, the kids; the kids. But I did end it, after the second affair. I came to realize that the kids were going to be okay. And, as you've seen, they are. Kids don't go around blaming you for taking them out of a marriage, even when they love their father, if they know that *you* know that what you're doing is right. And what's right for a woman—for any human being—is to live with the knowledge and expectation of joy.

"It took the affair for me to get that again. My marriage was placid, even companionable. But it was also a form of violence. I was slowly suiciding. My husband seemed to have stopped liking my body. He didn't want to get close to it, to explore it. And he tried to keep me at a physical distance, too. I don't mean there was no sex. Obviously, we had sex. But it became rare, occasional, and tentative. Sometimes I thought of us like creatures in a science-fiction movie, two enormous disembodied brains, his a little bigger than mine. We talked a lot. He was poetic, an analyzer. But neither of us had any substance.

"From longing for his touch I went to feeling a revulsion toward it. I wanted to leave him but my friends and family and the voice inside me said, 'the kids.' It was only after I had the second affair that I began to realize that when one says, 'the kids,' it's always oneself one means. It's always oneself who is the primary and central kid, oneself who feels too vulnerable and helpless and scared to face life all alone. I began to perceive that you can be more alone with a husband than you are by yourself, and that your kids can be more alone with you and your husband than they are with just you when the 'you' inside marriage is dying.

"I must have known it was dying for a long time, but when you think back to these things they come dressed up as revelations, fancy realizations. My dissatisfaction hit me one summer when we were in France. We always traveled in the summers. I was working free-lance then. My husband was an academic, and we took the whole summer and went to glamorous places. Jamaica. Mexico. France. I had been poor as a kid and the traveling was always like dreams come true. But that summer in France, while we were purchasing spices at an outdoor market, I remember looking up at the big full trees overhead and thinking with a monumental sense of dread, "This is what I've got. Everything I ever dreamed of. But it's all I'm ever going to have. And it's not enough."

I had my first affair shortly after that. There was a house in the town in which we were staying which was occupied by a household of interesting English people. One of them, the father of five children, most of whom were in and around during the summer, was the most elegant individual, extremely charming, extremely handsome. When he professed love and lust for me in equal measure, I went to bed with him. But it was hardly a world-shattering or even a momentous experience. I didn't feel guilty, as I've told you. But I didn't feel any better. Just more dullness and more dread. I was frozen, positively rigid in bed. He never came back for any more.

"During that summer I'd also had some bantering with one of his sons, a nineteen-year-old who was going to attend college next year in California. He too came on with me, but I never considered him. I was thirty-four. But I talked with him a lot. He was astonishing. He'd climbed Mount Everest with the sherpas; had won the chess award; had hitch-hiked halfway around the world when he was sixteen. He was brilliant and full of enthusiasm.

"Just before my husband and I went back home in the fall, Reggie, the young man, asked if he could spend a week with us in New York before his school started. We said sure, and one rainy September afternoon he arrived. My husband was at work. The kids were at school. Somehow, without our

really planning anything, we just ended up in bed. It made
Reggie wild with delight. I was suddenly one of his enthu-
siasms. He thought of me as a first love. Said he'd adored me
all summer. It was infectious. I began to feel so good about
his pleasure.

"He stayed with us two weeks and then he went off to
college. In those weeks, I spent a lot of time in bed with him.
It was still hot, and I've never really liked the heat, but I
remember how magnificently slippery and sweaty we were.
I can feel it still. It's become part of my consciousness and I
can summon up at will how joyous I felt to be sticky and
smelly and trammeled at last. It was like awakening from
the dead.

"I never tried to stop him from going off to school. I knew
it was an impossible relationship. He had wild ideas. Was
into drugs. I couldn't lean on him. But when he was gone I
began to realize that I had been happier in that almost mind-
less two weeks than I had been with my companionable
husband for years. I began to consider a life on my own. I
would take the kids. I would get a job. Somehow we would
survive. And as you can see, we have. I'm almost never sorry.
How can you be sorry if you were suiciding and changed
your mind in the middle because it hurt too much and
miraculously someone arrived and pumped the poison out
of you?"

## Gail O'Connor / Breaking the Crutch

Gail O'Connor, a forty-one-year-old fashion coordinator, had
decided when she was thirty-eight to force herself and her
three children out of the magnetic field of her marriage. The
magnet had been her lover, not her husband. He had helped
her overlook the flaws in her marriage. When she decided
to separate, she broke off with both men.

"I was married for fourteen years. After about four or five
of those years, I started thinking that other men were in-

teresting. But the possibility of really doing anything about this was something that didn't occur to me for a number of years after that. I would meet men I was attracted to and I would think, 'Wouldn't it be nice to have a new experience?' and I would feel some sort of nostalgia for it. But I figured I would never be able to again.

"Then, finally, I did have an affair. It was with a man for whom I was working. It took him a long time to beat down my resistance. He said that if he had had to sit across the lunch table from me once more, he was going to grab me right in the restaurant. It's a standing joke with us that it took forty-eight lunches to break down my resistance.

"My marriage was going downhill at the time and I think this relationship helped me to keep my sanity. The marriage was a mistake. My husband should have married a nice, quiet housebody Irish girl from the Bronx instead of a live-wire from Brooklyn. I kept thinking that it would all work out. But he was a very hostile guy, very demanding. He felt very threatened by me, by my working, and he was very angry most of the time. Still, because of my background, which is Irish-Catholic, I felt I had to stay married.

"When I met the man I had the affair with, I had one child, a boy. Then, after seeing him for a time, I had my second child, another boy, and then the third, a girl. The children were another reason for staying with my husband. And there were other factors.

"My husband lost his job and I just didn't want to leave him when he was low. And then, my mother was quite ill. So I saw this man on and off in hotel rooms, on business trips we took, for about five years. Then I realized that I could no longer stay married. I just couldn't tolerate my husband. But I didn't leave him because of the affair. In fact, when I decided to separate, I broke off the affair because I didn't want to use it as a crutch. I knew I'd be limping but it seemed best.

"I just wouldn't have wanted to marry the man I had the

affair with. He was fatherly and kind and sympathetic, but he would have been a mistake for me too. And it's very strange. He still comes back. I broke off with him about three months before I asked my husband for a divorce, which is three years ago, and at least once every year I get a call from my ex-lover. I hear from him every year, especially around holidays, and this past December he called me and he wanted to have dinner. And I know that he'd start up with me again tomorrow. But I don't want it. It was good for me when I was married, but it isn't what I'm looking for now. You need different things from a lover when you're married than you do when he's going to be the central man in your life."

## Gwen Tully /
## Only Crazies Would Have Come Along

What was the process that enabled a woman married for many years and for many years pushing at the walls of her marriage to lean ever so lightly on a lover and then almost at once bring down the marriage? It was hard to capture. Even when one woman, Gwen Tully, gave me the diary in which she had detailed some aspects of her flight out of marriage, it was difficult to get inside the process, to understand her sudden grasping of independence. I found I admired it without understanding it.

> August 26, 1971
>
> It's the middle of the night. I am going to sit down and then I am going to try to forget it all. It can't really be so important. Why am I torturing myself with it? Just an hour in bed with a man. Comical, really. I was holding my breath the whole time, afraid Everett would get home early. He had gone to pick up the kids from camp. Comical, all the torture over a penis going in and out a few times (well, more than a few; I liked that part). Probably it wouldn't seem so terrible if Carl hadn't been Everett's friend, if we hadn't spent so much time this

year *en famille.* I want to put it in perspective. I haven't been able to sleep the night through since that afternoon. I spend what seems like six hours trying to sleep, then manage an hour or two. Not even that sometimes. I wonder how much longer I can bear this. Unfortunately, probably an infinite time. I have some sort of inner strength. I feel I might be better off without it. I have a fantastic capacity for suffering.

I want to run. But where? Out of myself, that's for sure. Shed myself. Sleeping offers no relief for the first time in my life. When I wake up my heart is pounding fiercely.

It can't be just because of that single hour. It's that I'm afraid, afraid of facing the here and now. Afraid of five more months like the last ones, with apathy eating deeper and deeper into me. I know I still love Everett. So how could I have done this? Because I believe I am growing old. Because gather ye rosebuds while ye may. No, I'm not so sure I do still love him. We always quarrelled like cats and dogs about everything. I love certain aspects of him, and I love his love for me. But he's been so tense and withdrawn and absent, vacated. A structure, not a person. I needed to feel *with* someone in someone's arms. Which is how come Carl. This says nothing and I'm going to try to sleep now.

August 27, 1971

Carl called this morning. He said that if it was true I'd felt flattered, and wasn't angry (how old-fashioned he is; or maybe all young men are old-fashioned; they haven't learned yet that we court them) then could he see me again. He suggested his place. I'm not sure and I told him I'd think about it. It gives me a lift, thinking about it. But I can't see what's the point. He leaves in mid-September to start his research fellowship. Suppose I grew attached to him, he'd just be going away. But why should I grow attached? I'm a married woman with two children, heading for thirty-five and he's a mere thirty. Why isn't he married anyhow? Must be something wrong with him. When we got married, Ev was twenty-four.

September 7, 1971

I think I've finally had enough. I am so thoroughly angry and disgusted, not just sad and tired like most of the time, but genuinely furious. I am so angry with Everett. He's tricky. On the one hand he's the soul of gentleness. There's never anything one can get angry with him *about*. And yet the diffidence he treats me with has made me so horribly insecure. What a boring weekend it was. If I say, "What's on your mind?" he says, "Nothing." If I say, "Talk to me," he says, "I have nothing to talk about." If I say, "I'm going out of my mind from boredom," he says, "Maybe next year you could get a job." I don't want a job. I want a man.

I feel so much anger toward him. Sex seems like a trap and a trick. I feel he uses my being hard-up as a way of controlling me. Perhaps that's why, after all, I did sleep with Carl. And will again.

September 8, 1971

How funny Carl's apartment was. A pad. Just a big bed that filled the whole bedroom, and bookshelves laid out on bricks, and a kitchen with a bathtub in it. We took a bath togteher. I felt clean. I feel clean about this whole thing. Not dirty. I haven't been near another man besides Everett in over ten years, and where's the harm in a couple of afternoons?

September 9, 1971

Phyllis said today she hopes Aunt Miranda's baby is a boy so she can marry him. I said, "But you'll be eight years older than him." She said, "So what?" She is so precious; so fresh and new.

September 10, 1971

Carl called and we had a big discussion. Should we
get together once more before he goes? He wants to very
badly. I don't get it. I don't see what he sees in me.
Maybe he just couldn't get started with someone his
own age when he knew he was going away so soon. Anyway, what's the harm? After next week he'll be gone
and no one will know. Except you, Diary. I haven't
written in a diary since I was fourteen. Oh, the confessions I used to make then. I stopped the time my mother
found one of my diaries while I was away at camp and
came tearing up the Taconic and wanted to take me
home and send me to a psychiatrist all because I'd
written I'd been doing "it" with some pimply dummy
whose name I can't even recall. I told her "it" was
petting, which it was but she was still crying bucketsful.
I never confided in a diary again. When I finally did
grow up and go to a therapist he said I'd probably left
the diary around just in order to get caught. I don't
believe that. It was hidden in the bottom of a huge box
of records. Am I writing this one to get caught? I keep
you hidden in the laundryroom; steamy you are. Everett
never goes downstairs; God forbid he should bother his
philosophy with a touch of Dash. No, I don't want to
get caught. I won't get caught. Maybe I'll catch *him.*
Maybe the reason he's been so distant is that he's got
someone on the side. Somewhere in the house is a coun-
terpart of my diary: his. Filled with confession and
undoubtedly more high-toned than mine. Her white
flesh. Her blond pubis, her moans and groans and
frowns and gowns. I'm sure Everett must write a better
diary. Would I care if he had someone else? Only if he
fell in love. Men are so much more susceptible to love
than women, in my opinion. It's they who make declarations while coming. "I love you." Carl said it to me last

time. I said, "Cross your heart and hope to die?" But I
was faking, playing that it mattered.

September 14, 1971

Said good-bye to Carl. I had managed to get the whole
afternoon. We screwed twice and I came twice, each
time. "Only twice?" he said. I told him it was four times
more than with Everett over the past six months. A lie,
but Carl has a weak ego. I protect him. I'm mothering.
Maybe that's what's behind it all. He's so slight, so
timid. So philosophical. Like Everett, really. Another
intellectual. I wouldn't mind a gardener, a plumber
sometime. Still, Carl touches me. I feel so important
with him. I haven't felt important to Everett in years.
It's as if the last five years he's had nothing on his mind
but writing journal articles that no one ever reads in
order to make money that we never spend together because he's so busy writing more journal articles. Dinner
is always at 7:00 P.M. Sex is always at midnight. Maybe
I will get a job. Just so we can change our bedtime hour.
Am I sad that Carl is going? Not really. I've felt uneasy
about lying to get time in the city. Even when I pull it
off without a hitch I feel bad, as if maybe Everett isn't
even paying much attention. But whatever is wrong with
my life, I have to solve it on my own.

September 23, 1971

I had a letter from Carl today which he sent me care
of Miranda. What a letter! He said he was convinced we
were destined for one another, that he'd never been with
another woman who had given herself to him in bed as
fully and joyously as I did, and that he knew it meant
I loved him. As for himself, he said he knew now that
he loved me, that it had been a mistake for him to have
gone away, and that he wanted me seriously to consider
informing Everett of what had transpired between us

and coming out to live with him. Is he crazy? What about my children?

September 29, 1971

I wrote Carl he was crazy, that all that giving was just the way I screwed. That lots of women screwed that way, as if their hearts were in it. And that besides, I was the busy mother of two. Today, Miranda gave me another letter from him, this one more insistent than the last. He said I had to come out there, that he couldn't live without me, and that if I wouldn't come, he was going to quit his fellowship and come back to New York. He said he'd always meant for me to bring the children, and that surely it was worse for them to grow up in a loveless household than in the atmosphere he was planning to make for the four of us. And he ended by saying he didn't want me to sleep with Everett anymore. He sounded either insanely possessive or really in love. Is what he feels love? Is being loved as good as loving?

The letters kept coming and Gwen kept discouraging Carl, but it was as if, she told me, she herself did not exist. Only his image of their love existed. He insisted she tell her husband. He threatened that if she didn't, he would tell her husband himself. And for a long few weeks she began to waver, wondering if perhaps his definiteness and love made a lot more sense than her own mocking attitude toward what had occurred between them. There was a diary entry early in November in which she wrote:

One thing is sure, I can't love Everett at all anymore. I don't think I love Carl either. But all this love talk of his, the letters, oh God, the letters, have made Everett and the dryness of our life seem like a desert. Maybe it was always a desert. But once there were waterholes here and there. A film we'd see together and only we would share an opinion, different from everyone else's, different from the critics, our own sharp, brilliant view.

Or an insight into a friend. But we hardly even talk anymore. Perhaps Carl is right. Another thing that's sure is that I really want to see him, want to live in his atmosphere at least for a bit, for a while, to see if it's all sheer fantasy. I have written him that it is impossible for me to come out to him. That's part of the blindness in him; his idea that one can disrupt the life of two small children to go careening after love. But if he still feels the way he does about me when he returns in the spring, I will see about moving out, about making a stab at a temporary separation from Everett.

Carl just called Miranda's house and told her to call me. He's quitting his fellowship and coming back to New York. I am too nervous to write anymore.

Gwen left her husband shortly after Carl's return to New York. She decided she had to explore the relationship with Carl. He had turned her head. She told Everett what had happened, asked for a temporary separation, and moved, with the children, to a sublet city apartment. Everett was bitter and bruised but agreed to the separation and promised to help support the children. They went to a city school; Gwen got a part-time job in a nursery school; at night she saw Carl constantly. He wanted to move in with her at once but she fended off that arrangement.

She describes that period as hellish. Carl kept threatening suicide; she herself was terribly confused. He kept telling her she loved him but she remained unsure. She started psychotherapy, started making city friends, started going out on dates. After only two months she decided that she most certainly did not love Carl but that, despite appearances, she herself had been responsible for what had happened between them, that she would never have inspired his enthusiasm for her if it hadn't been that in some way she had already been up for emotional grabs. She then broke off both her marriage and her affair with Carl.

I read her diary, which she had dropped off with me, then visited her one day in the rather dreary, six-room West Side apartment she and her children now occupied. The boiler in the building had broken down that day and we sat in coats and gloves. "Surely you're sorry?" I kept asking, but Gwen insisted she was not.

"Carl was a catalyst," she said. "He was wrong and so was I. I didn't love him, but I *was* giving a great deal. In bed. In our conversations together. Giving it just because I had it all to give and Everett wasn't taking anything from me. Hadn't been for years. But I wasn't giving it because I loved Carl. He was so young, so childish, so solipsistic, and while all of that touched me, moved me, really *moved* me—made me leave my home and all—he wasn't the kind of man for me and I always knew it. Thank God I always knew it. I think a marriage with Carl would have gone sour in a year. I don't want to be someone's mother. But although I'm lonely now, I'm not sorry at how things have turned out. I'm not the kind of woman who has affairs casually. I wouldn't have slept with Carl if life with Everett hadn't become so dreary. And at least now, I'm on my own again and there's a chance, a thin gossamer chance if you will, that I'll find a man I can love. I couldn't have if I'd just stayed with Everett. Only crazies, babies like Carl would have come along."

# (7)
# Breaking Up:
## *Deciding to Realign*

It took, I think, a certain strong-mindedness and realism for adulterous women who wanted their marriages to break up to accomplish their separations without immediately substituting lovers for husbands. Certainly realignment was the more frequent urge and many women went directly from their husbands' to their lovers' orbits. But they did not always revolve there happily. All too often they had chosen partners whom they did not know well or deeply.

This happened because of the very nature of adultery. Women who have seen men only under conditions of secrecy can rarely be certain that their attachments are not the result of the compression of emotional and sexual exchange into brief, bittersweet moments. They often suspect that the men they have chosen value them precisely because of their lack of availability or are themselves in some way emotionally unavailable. Often they make definite negative estimations of their lovers, yet even so desire realignment. They say they are in love and are compelled to act.

Once in a while a married woman does accurately select a lover who is for her a potentially compatible mate after marriage, despite the impediments adultery places in the way. But even under these circumstances, obstacles to the realignment are rampant. It is difficult to speed from one relationship to another with no detours or accidents in between.

### Beverly Sneden /
### Most People Mourn the Death of Their
### Marriages

Beverly Sneden had left her husband and moved in with her lover. I met her while doing some research for an article I was planning on mental health clinics. She ran one. She was a psychologist, very assertive, very direct, asking me as many questions as I asked her. I liked the forthrightness of her manner, and I began talking to her about my work. The article, I explained, was something I would turn to in the near future. Right now I was finishing a book on women who had extramarital relations.

It was a fascinating subject, Beverly said supportively. Almost all her female patients had had extramarital experiences or at least extramarital fantasies. Had what I found confirmed her impression, that extramarital sex was highly prevalent among women?

I said, yes, I had found a great deal of it, but that one thing surprised me. There seemed to be so few extramarital affairs that terminated happily, or at least happily in the old-time romantic sense; few lovers chose one another, overcame obstacles, and ended up living contentedly together.

Beverly said, "Yes. But then, you'd better interview me. I was married ten years, in love with my next-door neighbor for seven of those years, had an affair with him for one year, and now both he and I have left our spouses and are living together. We've taken a house."

"How long have you been living together?" I asked.

"Six months," she said. "And I am happy, busy, and overflowing with love. Even my kids feel good about it. They love Nick too. He was almost like a father to them, and they love having him in their own family now. It softens any rage they might feel about being separated from their own father."

We agreed on an interview date. We were both very busy and couldn't choose a time sooner than a month from that initial meeting. We each wrote it down. Five o'clock. At my office.

A week before our interview date, Beverly called me and began speaking very agitatedly. "I don't think you'll want to interview me," she said.

"Why not?"

"It's not a love story. It's just another one of those things you found over and over again. He's moving out."

"How do you feel?"

"I'm breaking in two. I feel I can't breathe. That I'm choking. I'm going to need medication. I can't even drag myself to work. I've been in bed for three days. He told me on the weekend and he's packed already."

I thought, that's different, or at least, if other women I'd spoken to had felt this way, they hadn't spelled it out for me. They had all seemed so controlled about the end of their affairs. Of course the end of their affairs had all been more distant by the time I spoke with them.

I told Beverly that I wanted to interview her anyway, even if her story hadn't had a happy ending. "If you can bear to tell me," I said. She said, "Yes, of course. And if I'm still here, still among the living."

And so we met a week later in my office. It was summer and the air conditioning was on. Doors closed, windowless, the room began to seem stifling to me, as if I too might choke on Beverly's anguish. I saw now the opposite side of the coin of her forthrightness. Even though she was taking tranquilizers, she was clamorous and histrionic. Her pain had to be shared. She was, I supposed, of the school that holds that emotions should not be restrained or they will rise up and taunt at some later time. Still, I wished for her sake she had gotten them more under control. It seemed frightening to me to watch a woman I had found so capable and interested in things outside herself only a month ago lost now in the sensations of her own depression. What troubled me most was that she seemed to want to mock herself, to demean herself.

She told me first that she didn't want to shock me but that there was one part of her story she felt might do so. I said, "I've heard everything." "Not this," she said.

What it was was the way she courted her neighbor, the way she first pried her way into his heart. Even he had never been told. "I've had the hots for this guy as far back as I can remember," she said. "His wife was a good friend of mine. And three years ago the women in my neighborhood formed a consciousness-raising group. I had prior knowledge of the dissolution of his life with his wife, of precisely what she wouldn't give him at the table and in conversation, and what she would no longer do in bed. And I used it all. Oh, how I used it. But I never felt guilty, and I don't now. Because I loved him."

Beverly had married her husband ten years ago, after an active young womanhood that had included many sexual and emotional relationships. She was, then as now, tall, buxom, dark-skinned and crowned with a head of curly, thick black hair.

"What was wrong with your marriage?" I asked.

"It's much easier to tell you what was right," she said. "To tell you what was right will take thirty seconds. There was nothing right. To tell you what was wrong will bore you by taking forever."

"Did you know you weren't suited before you married?" I asked.

"Yes. I knew my husband and I had nothing, but I tried to make up for it in my head. I was twenty-six years old and tired of living alone. I had fucked everything that walks, breathes or crawls—oaktrees, avocados. I couldn't pay my Bloomingdale's bills. I didn't want to work anymore. Instead of going to a shrink, which I should have done then—I only did that three years later—I went to Puerto Rico to a conference. I got out of the taxi from the airport, and in front of the hotel in which the meetings would be held there was this man, this solid, not bad-looking substantial guy just standing in front of the building. He was a chemist, on vacation alone. And we began to see each other and we saw each other for a year and we got married."

I said, "Yes, that was what was wrong about you, but what about him?"

She said, "He was a man who was in every sense of the word a loner. He did not need people and I do. He views his life as a structure and I view mine as a process. He was unavailable. He could not communicate. But I didn't care. I was going to make a home for myself, a family for myself. You see, this was 1964."

"You mean, 'way back then'?"

"Yes," she said. "It was a different world. For me, at least, it was a different world. My mother had died when I was a little kid, and I was raised by my grandparents, and I was tired, so tired of living without a family of my own. I just decided I'd make one. Perhaps it's different today and women of twenty-six who aren't married no longer feel so useless. But I doubt it."

She and her husband had. raised three children, and she had continued to work. The children played with the children of the next-door neighbors, Nick and Ramona. Beverly gradually grew intensely attached to both of her neighbors. Unlike her husband, Nick and Ramona were talkative, intellectual, alert—her psychological equals. They amused her, looked after her, masked the disappointment she felt in her marital choice once she had admitted it to her consciousness.

Nick and Ramona were more worldly, more sophisticated than Beverly. They had traveled, lived abroad. Beverly took up their hobbies. She studied Italian cooking and learned about wines and read all of Nick's favorite books. Both he and Ramona were journalists and current events were very important to them. As a psychologist, Beverly had insights to offer, and the three of them broadened each other. Nick loved to ride and Beverly, terrified of horses, took lessons and got on a horse for the first time and rode as if she were fearless. She was in therapy and her therapist urged her to make the best of her life since she had chosen it.

Then three years ago the women in Beverly's neighborhood started their consciousness-raising group and both Beverly and Ramona decided to participate. The group grew intimate and Ramona said things about her marriage she had never said even in years of friendship with Beverly. She began to confess boredom with Nick, boredom with marriage, the desire for personal self-fulfillment. Nick was sexually demanding and Ramona was turning off. Some women in the group supported her staunchly: the sex trips men laid on women were too heavy; wives were entitled, even obligated, to refuse sex when they were not turned on. Ramona also confided that she found Nick's perpetual conversation somewhat battering; it gave her no time to think her own thoughts. When she wanted to work on a story at night, he was in and out of her study with observations on what he had just read, just heard announced on the television, just witnessed at the supermarket.

It was Nick's very obtrusiveness that Beverly liked. He was so different from her own morose husband. "So in the group I began making notes in my head," she said. "I kept mental notes of just what Nick was no longer being supplied, and when, and how, and where. It was all very Machiavellian. I used the group. I used Ramona. I even manipulated her. I took a position basically foreign to myself. 'Yes,' I would say, 'yes, even the most well-meaning men are limiting us with their constant demands for attention.' But still, I didn't take anything away from Ramona. I just fit in, just went along with something that was already happening in Ramona's head. I didn't smash anything. I just picked up the pieces. What I took was no longer in use."

Ramona had not discussed with Nick her growing disenchantment. But increasingly there were marital squabbles. Finally, Ramona reported to the group that she had told Nick she didn't want to sleep with him for a while, not till she cleared her head. Beverly began to be actively seductive. "To this day he doesn't know the schedule by which he was seduced. I mean, he was hit. With both barrels. In places where he had no way of knowing that I knew he was vulnerable. It's really not cricket, but I had to do it. I had loved him for years. She didn't want him; I did. I felt our destinies were linked. I did everything humanly possible to get his love, and it's terrifying to think of all that effort gone to waste now. Perhaps it was because the relationship was intrinsically dishonest, but I actually don't think so."

Beverly began picking Nick up in the city after their work days had ended. "It was the nature of my husband that if I called at five o'clock and said, 'I won't be home until about eleven,' he asked no questions. He always operated by denial. I mean he blotted out things he didn't want to know. All the possibilities of what I might be doing, he blotted out in his head, and I just went about my business. As to Ramona, she thought Nick was staying away to keep out of her hair and give her breathing space. So we were able to work out a fairly regular schedule.

"I'd gotten Nick interested in therapy and he had group therapy on Wednesday nights. I'd meet him after the group, and we'd go to an apartment we were lent by a friend. On Thursday nights Nick had a private session with his therapist. We always met after that too, for lovemaking. And then we'd meet a third night to have dinner or see a movie before going to the apartment. We used to pray for snow that winter, but only for Wednesday or Thursday snows, like kids praying for their Monopoly pieces to land on just one certain space. And twice, I remember, it did snow on one of our nights and we got the kind of big heavy snowstorms that entitle you to call home and say, 'I'd think it'd be best if I didn't drive home tonight. The roads look bad and there's no way of knowing how long it will take.' How I prayed for snow. And those two snowy nights were the happiest nights of my life. I didn't care if the world got covered up and blotted out with snow, as long as he and I were buried in its softness together.

"Late in February we both asked for divorces. My husband moved out right afterwards. Nick took a little longer. Ramona was agreeable, but at first she wanted him to have the kids. Then she reneged. He wouldn't have minded. He loves his kids, all kids; it's part of how wonderful he is. But she decided in the end to keep them, and he took an apartment in the city. Now we had my place to meet in, and he dropped in whenever he felt like it. Noontime, evenings. His need for me was enormous. He was really scared. Living alone, missing his kids, not knowing what was going to happen to him. He needed me to be with him day and night.

"And then, at the end of March, we rented a home together. We wanted to start out in a new place, with no old associations. We were very happy. At least, I was, and I assumed he was. We did all the things we'd always done, talked about all the things we'd always talked about, but now it was in *our* house together. He was transferring his love for his kids to mine, and they were transferring their love of their father to him, and I was never so good at my life or my job. That's the way it was for six months. That's the way it still was last month, when you and I first met and I told you yes, there were love stories and happy endings."

"How did it all go wrong so fast?" I asked.

Beverly said, "I suppose it started to go wrong earlier, but that I had refused to notice the evidence. About two months ago, Nick had begun saying things like, 'Maybe we were too hasty, moving in *together*. Maybe we should have taken some time for adjustment.' I had said, 'But you love me, don't you?' and he had said, 'Yes, yes, but it's all so fast.' He'd known Ramona since he was twenty, married her when he was twenty-four, broken up with her at thirty-four, and moved right in with me. He had never had the kind of free, cruising sexual experiences that men relish and require for decision-making. I pointed out that the point of those experiences was to fall in love, and that if he was already in love, they were beside the point. But he was insistent. So I backed off a little, gave him some rein. I understood how he felt, and actually, back then, I didn't feel at all threatened. I knew it would be a better relationship if Nick got a chance to do some exploring. So we had agreed that on Wednesdays and Thursdays, he would stay late in the city, presumably to date other women and see for himself how he felt about me. I could do this, you see, because I was utterly secure in the power of my own love and respect for him."

That had been the situation until I first met Beverly. But two weeks ago Nick had gone to the Caribbean on a vacation alone. He had called Beverly four out of the five nights he was gone. But when he came back he had announced to her that he could no longer live with her, that perhaps he had used her to help him get out of his marriage and that he did not want to live his life with her. At least not right now.

Beverly had pleaded, sobbed, fallen apart. As she came to this part of her story, she was as distraught as she had been a week ago when she called me. "I don't know how I will survive this. I am living on tranquilizers. I need two Seconal at night. I loved him for seven years!"

And then she stopped her mourning for a moment, and was—and I could see that she would be again—her professional self, not wallowing but seeking. "Have you noticed I never say anything about missing my husband? Most people mourn the death of their marriages. Not me. I never mourned it once. But I guess everyone has to pay their dues. You can't expect to get out of marriage scot-free. There's always something to mourn."

"Perhaps Nick will come back," I said, hoping to comfort her.

"No," she said, rejecting my superficial palliative. "Even if he does, it'll be years from now. He'll be different. I'll be different." And then she was dismal again. "My kids ask me all the time where Nick is. They don't ask where their Daddy is. They know where Daddy is. They go to see him every weekend. But they never see Nick anymore. And that hurts them so much. They want to know why he doesn't like them anymore. Why they can't play with his kids anymore. You know, this is really divorce. You are never as divorced from a man you married as from one you loved but never even married."

## Ann Simpson /
## It Wasn't Just a Case of "Her or Me"

I felt dismayed by my interview with Beverly. Was this always the end of affairs, then? Did no one who entered an affair while married realign and live happily with her once-extra-marital lover? Were extramarital experimentation and love-seeking always merely peripheral to women's lives or always doomed to failure? But of course, some women did end up living contentedly with their lovers. I found a few of them eventually.

There was Ann Simpson in Dayton. A friend in New York was a childhood friend of hers. "She and Steve have been happy together for six years now," said the friend. "But it was rough going in the beginning. A lot of the people they knew took sides against them, and they almost had to move, but they stayed put and it all blew over. One thing neighbors can't resist is a happy peaceful home alongside them. And they tend to forget soon enough how it got put together."

The Simpson house on a sidewalkless sunny street was indeed peaceful and also impeccably neat. I was surprised, since I'd heard the Simpsons had six children, two of Steve's and three of Ann's and one between them. "Well, of course, Steve's are off in college," Ann explained. "And when they're back, they live with their mother. So all we do is keep an empty bedroom for them for the nights they come to visit.

For years they didn't even come. They were so angry at their father. But they do come now sometimes."

Ann was tall and awkward and forty-five. I thought it inconceivable that she had ever seduced another woman's husband. She looked more like a woman who always won her prizes at covered casserole suppers. "If anyone had told either of us that we would have ended up in an extramarital affair, and then married," she said, "I'm sure we would have been shocked. Steve's a solid family man and I was raised as a strict Baptist and there's a lot of Baptist still in me."

But they had done both. They had met at the art museum where both were delivering children to Saturday morning classes. They had become friends, introduced their spouses to one another and only ever so gradually become intimate, driving away, after delivering the children, to a small motel out on the highway. Ann brought flowers and homebaked cookies to the motel room.

"We talked about our families and our responsibilities to them a lot before we went to bed. In fact, I think we tried to avoid physical contact at first. Steve more than me. He had cut out on his wife a couple of times in twenty years. Maybe twice or three times. They were very brief things, not bothering anybody. But with me he knew it was going to be different. And he was scared of that. His wife was a teacher and a church lady and very popular around here. But Steve had married her a long time ago, right after the war. And things had changed between them in twenty years. You never really know about somebody else's marriage, but I believed him. His marriage had become just one of these polite things, where the closeness had been frayed many years ago. And mine never even had much closeness. My ex-husband was a man with a violent temper, as likely to overturn the dinner dishes if the meat came out well done as to finish a meal without an incident.

"Steve and I never spent more than two hours a week with

each other before we asked for divorces. But those two hours were more precious to me than the whole of the days and nights that preceded them. Once he got sick and I felt my own life draining out of me. He'd had a mild heart attack. I couldn't visit him in the hospital, couldn't even send word. Suppose he had died?

"It was when he recovered that we decided that whatever people around here would think of us, we had to end our marriages and be together. I was thirty-nine. I knew I might be divorcing only to marry a man who might be an invalid, who might even die on me. But none of that made any difference. We would at least have whatever time we could."

It had been very hard on Steve's wife. Forty-six at the time, she had just been getting ready to settle down with Steve to the relaxed life of people whose children have noisily grown and quietly parted. She wanted to go to Europe with Steve when he recovered. When he told her his plans she tried to kill herself, driving their car careening and screeching into an abandoned barn. But she lived, coming through her collision with only minor injuries. Ann felt troubled about relating this. "People around here took her side against me. They think I acted blindly. But I didn't. I understand how much she hates me, and why she kept the children from visiting Steve all those years. It could have been me, when I'd reached her age; women shouldn't have to spend their last years alone. But it wasn't just a case of 'her or me.' There was Steve, too, and he needed another chance, a chance with me."

I stayed overnight at their house. When Steve came home from work, he embraced Ann heartily and only then turned to be introduced. I had a moment in which I observed them, him unaware of my presence, cuddling his great gawky wife. Yes, it ended in this kind of realignment sometimes.

I was glad I had finally come across Ann Simpson. Later I met a few others like her. Yet only a few. I often wondered how it was possible that out of close to seventy women, I interviewed only four or five who had chosen their extramarital lovers with sufficient care and concern that a good life in the future was possible with them. Would I have found many more who had ended up together, and happily together, had I doubled my sample, talked to a hundred and forty women? Tripled it and talked to two hundred and ten? Or was it just inevitable that extramarital sexual relations had to end bumpily? There was so much to collide against. Still, the urge to end a marriage and be with a particular lover could be overwhelming. The fact that sometimes such arrangements worked—no matter how rarely—would provide sufficient fuel to make such voyages at least possible destinations.

## *Barbara Bendiner /*
## *I Decided, Let Them Laugh*

I was considering all this when I went out reluctantly one stormy February night to meet Barbara Bendiner in a Third Avenue bar and grill. It was one of those nights when you get soaked to the skin just stepping out from under a canopy and into a taxi. But I had been trying to obtain an interview with Barbara for over a year. From the time I first heard of her situation I had been curious.

"She is fifty," said the friends who had first told me about her, a husband and wife who had known Barbara for close to twenty years. "And the man she's been seeing for the last five years is only twenty-six. And there are other incongruities. She's very conventional and he's a poet and he's black."

"What does she look like?" I had asked, seeking the expected component of beauty or extreme youthfulness.

"Rather ordinary," said the wife.

"Fairly well-preserved," said the husband.

The wife, a gentle, perceptive woman, had said, "On Barbara's part the relationship strikes me as somewhat masochistic. For one thing, she's helping to support this man."

The husband, and it was surprising from him, had said,

"But what's wrong with that? You wouldn't call it the same —call it masochism—if it was a man and not a woman sleeping with someone younger and contributing to his lover's support."

The wife said, "No, but you can't compare the two. Not yet."

How curious I became about Barbara. But a year went by before the interview was arranged. My friends had hesitated, unsure of whether or not Barbara would talk to a stranger. From time to time we would discuss it, and they would mean to ask her, and then draw back. Finally they introduced us at a lunch at their house in the suburbs and Barbara said yes, she would get together with me. There was something, actually, that she wanted to ask me.

Barbara had chosen to be interviewed in a noisy, dark café on Third Avenue. It was a place she and Keith, her lover, hung out in on nights they came into the city. She had been planning to bring him along, she told me when she arrived, but he had had a wisdom tooth pulled today and was home with a bad ache in his gums and she herself would have to drive back soon to look after him. She mused for a while on how babyish men are, how unable to care for themselves. "If they get a cold they won't even go out and buy a box of tea for themselves. I have to do all Keith's marketing or he'd starve to death."

While she was talking I was, I must admit, staring at her. Wasn't she an embodiment of a poignant fantasy, the older woman able to appeal to and hold a younger man? She did seem younger than fifty, if I didn't look closely. She had the kind of pale skin that I associate with youth; freckles and passing blushes of pink. And she was dressed like a schoolgirl, in a turtleneck sweater and a wide wool skirt. A little peaked cap hid her forehead, and it was only later, when she removed the cap, that I saw that her face was at all wrinkled.

"About how long have you been married?" I asked.

"Since 1942," she said.

"Let me subtract. That's more than thirty years. You know it doesn't look possible. You look so young."

She said, "I was twelve at the time."

"You must have been!"

"I was about seventeen or eighteen," she said.

"Does that youthful look run in your family?" I asked.

"I guess so. But I always looked very young. When I was twenty I looked like twelve."

"Who is the young man that you're seeing?" I asked.

"He's a very close friend that I used to work with. I work in a social work agency. He came there as a clerk, about five years ago. But now he's becoming a poet, and he's studying writing. He's black. He's very black. I don't mean colorwise, although he is that too. I mean culturewise. I never knew anybody black before, not until I started to work at that agency.

"It was about five or six years ago, maybe even more. You lose track of the time. It goes so fast. It might be even six or seven years. It's a long, long time ago."

"He's also married?" I asked.

"No, he's a young man. He's the same age as the eldest of my three sons. He's only twenty-seven years old now."

"So he was just a youngster when you started out. Were you one of his very first girlfriends?"

"No. In the culture that he's in, I know it sounds crazy, but young men have girlfriends at a very early age. He told me that the first time he went to bed with a girl was when he was thirteen. So of course I was not his first. In fact, he was going with a girl when we started up. He had been going with her for a couple of years. And he continued seeing her on and off during our first years. Although we were together, he would, you know, go with somebody. Perhaps if I had been much younger, I might have minded. But I didn't. I always felt, if he goes, let him go."

"Still, you must have had a lot of insecurity about it."

"Not so much. I don't remember. I suppose I probably did. But I always felt it was the only thing I could do, that it was the only thing you can do with a man. Just say, 'Go, fine. I mean, you go right ahead.' After all, just look at me! Look at me! I'm very old."

It was at this point that she removed her cap, ruffling her shoulder-length blond hair. "In the beginning, you know, he was a kid. We talked about it. We said, 'Why? Why? Why do you love me?' It wasn't just me saying, 'Why do you love me when I'm so much older than you?' It was him saying, 'Why do you love me when I'm so much younger than you?' He sees it this other way. It's really funny. It's cuckoo. I don't mean to say that he has a low feeling about himself, either. He's got a swell image. He's well respected and he's a very fine poet. He's had various offers lately about publishing his poems.

"My answer for why I love him has always been the same. I always said, 'Because you really enjoy everything so much, and when I'm with you, I enjoy everything.'

"In the beginning when we started going together, I used to think everybody was staring. They probably were. But he always thought they were staring because of the color thing, while I always thought they were staring because of the age thing.

"Of course, he helps me pick my clothes. I love that. And he's taught me how to dress, and how to wear hats, and what colors look best on me. But no matter how much younger I look, I can never look as young as him. So I used to think people were staring, and also that they were laughing at me. But after a while, my attitude changed. I decided let them laugh, because if they knew what Keith and I had together, they'd be jealous.

"The first time we went on the Staten Island Ferry, for instance, we went back and forth eight times. He'd never been on it before, and when we went, he just wouldn't stop. From the afternoon until the evening, we went back and forth, and he was so excited, so interested in everything, the clouds, all the different colors on the water. To this day when we ride on the East River Drive he's forever pointing out this and that to me—things I'd never notice by myself. "I know it sounds crazy. I look in the mirror. I say, 'Oh, God. In five years I'll be an old lady.' But that's just the point. He makes me feel I'm getting and giving the kind of love I'd been waiting for all my life."

Their affair had started off slowly. "It just happened," said Barbara. "I didn't plan it. He was working late one day, and I was waiting around for something, and he came into my office, and I just waved to him. And we started talking. And I drove him home to the apartment he was staying in with friends, and he invited me up for a beer, and we talked some more and it happened."

At that time, and for the first two years they had sexual relations, Keith was seeing a young woman with a baby quite steadily, and Barbara and he got together only rarely. But their relationship had deepened when his other affair broke off, and they began spending a great deal of time together. "It works out that we see each other almost every day. I go over to his place all day on Sundays. But I only stay late with him one night a week. Tuesdays. The rest of the week we just get together for an hour or so after work."

I wanted to know about her husband. How did she explain her absences?

"I don't anymore. He knows about Keith and me."

"And you're still together?"

"That's the point!" she exclaimed. "He once found us together. Now almost any other man would just have walked out and said, you know, good-bye. But he didn't. Partly it was a practical consideration. You know, if you're rich, you can just walk out and go down to a hotel, or get another apartment. But when you're not rich, where do you go?

"And then, it's his personality. He's a very angry guy, and he's always very down and depressed. He's interested in nothing. Nothing. Not other women, not movies, not going places. Since he found out about Keith, we've been separated, at least in effect. He sleeps upstairs and I sleep downstairs. It's been that way the last three years. And we haven't had sex for about two years. But I guess we stay together because neither of us knows where to go next."

Barbara was growing uneasy now, and soon she had launched into her dilemma. She told me that the reason she had come to be interviewed was because she wanted my advice. Knowing what I knew of her story, and whatever other stories I had gathered, did I think it would make any sense for her to move in with Keith? Lately it had become her obsession. Her three sons were grown, so there was no longer any point in maintaining the big suburban house with its lawns and yards and sports equipment. She and her husband had begun to discuss future plans. At first, they had talked of selling the house and getting an apartment in the city. But little by little she had determined that now was the time to break from her husband, the time for her either to take her own apartment or to move in with Keith. She was heading toward the latter choice.

"Keith wants it. But I'm worried. We've been together so long that we're practically married, except for the fact that we're not living together. We take certain things for granted. You know, we take care of each other's needs. I take home his wash. Lots of times when I'm there for the night, on the Tuesdays when I'm there all night, he'll get up and take the car and drive off to Hempstead to visit friends or do whatever he wants. Or his friends will come in to visit him. They don't pay much attention to me. I'm old hat. There's no bedroom in Keith's current apartment. The bed is in the living room and I have been in that bed, you know, lying there, half-asleep, when he has come home with friends. And I just, you know, either look up and say hello or continue sleeping."

What worried Barbara was that, although two of her sons

were married and on their own now, the third, still in college, was still coming home for vacations and weekends. She and Keith would have to take an apartment big enough for the three of them. What did I think of that? she asked. Her sons knew Keith, but she'd never quite explained the relationship to them. There had been no direct conversation. What did I think would happen if now she took a place with Keith, and her youngest son came home there on weekends?

What I thought would happen was that if she were to do it, which I totally doubted she would, within a month she would be on her own in a place of her own. But this is not what happened. Barbara and Keith took an apartment together. Barbara's husband moved to the city, alone. And Barbara's youngest son stays with her and Keith on his vacations and holidays. It has been a year now. Is she happy? Is Keith happy? My friends, who see them from time to time, can make no clear evaluation of the relationship. The wife reports that Barbara seems more nervous these days, somewhat disjointed in her language, tense. But Barbara herself holds that she has finally made sense out of her life, finally done what she should have done years before. My friends worry when they see her about what will happen if Keith becomes attached to a younger woman. But whenever they allude to this possibility Barbara says, "I want whatever I can get now. In four years, I'll be a very old lady."

# (8)
# Breaking Up:
## *The Decisions of Husbands*

I met, of course, a number of women who, once-adulterous and now-divorced, had not desired the termination of their marriages. These women had never become even temporarily attached to their lovers. They had had casual affairs while hoping to preserve their marriages, and had sought adventure, self-exploration, sexual variety or temporary balm for a husband's neglect or his own extramarital adventuring. They resembled many of the women I had interviewed whose motivations for extramarital sex had been the same, and whose marriages were intact. What made one such marriage come apart while another stayed together? Usually it was a husband's decision to break up the marriage.

Had the women's extramarital experiences contributed to their husbands' decisions? I always asked this, whether or not the husbands had been made aware of their wives' affairs.

Kinsey had asked it too and had heard from a majority of the once-adulterous, now-divorced people whom he interviewed that they did not feel that their extramarital activity had been any factor leading to their divorces. But Kinsey believed that extramarital sex could set up an atmosphere of "neglect and disagreement" which could indirectly affect marriages and cause divorce. Thus he had felt constrained to comment drily about those who saw no relationship between divorce and extramarital sex, "It is to be noted, however, that these were the subjects' own estimates of the significance and, as clinicians well know, it is not unlikely that the extramarital experience had contributed to the divorces in more ways and to a greater extent than the subjects themselves realized."

My experience with interviewing women on this question was quite the opposite of Kinsey's. I met almost no one who did not attempt to find a relationship between her extramarital experience and her divorce, even though at the time of her experience that relationship had not been clear. Perhaps twenty years ago people were less willing to take subtle responsibility for divorce, or perhaps the women I met were just more psychologically-oriented.

Several who explained to me some of the more indirect ways extramarital sex may have contributed to their divorces speak in this chapter.

## *Claire Obrist /*
## *The Little Things Add Up*

I met Claire Obrist, a market research corporation executive with two children, three years after her separation from the husband to whom she had been married for twelve years. It was clear to me that she had liked him; she spoke about him with a gentleness and pride that is atypical after divorce. But, she said, she hadn't known quite how much she had liked him at the time she had started playing around, nor that in some ways she didn't like him at all.

"I didn't marry until I was twenty-seven. I had had tons of sexual experience but very few substantial relationships. I was scared. I felt I was being promiscuous, and although I'd go through periods where I'd sleep with whoever asked, I'd also go through others where I wouldn't, even when I really liked the guy. I didn't know what was going to become of me, not just because I was sleeping around, but because the world I lived in seemed so chaotic, so fluid.

"Everyone around me was jumping from new thing to new thing; my friends were forever traveling, to Europe, to Africa; one even went to New Zealand. I was a market researcher, a glorified doorbell ringer, and I had no roots. When Mickey came along and fell in love with me, I was ecstatic. He was the best-looking man I'd been out with, and the most loyal, and the deepest. He had a sense of direction in life. He was studying social work, he wanted to help people, he wanted children. And I wanted him.

"I was faithful to him for eight years, and he was to me. I quit work, had the children, was a terrific mother. But when our two kids were both in school, I went into a funk, a depression. I didn't know what to do with myself. Should I go back to school? Get a job? Raising children had been a great goal and really taken up my time while they were little, but now I had hours on my hands, and I was right back where I'd been at the beginning. Not Mickey. He was still the same, a good family man, putting me and the kids above everything, struggling to give as much to his clients as he could, making it.

"I went back to work; I was a market researcher again. But in the few years I'd been off the labor market, things had changed for women. I got promoted, became an executive in the company, and made money. I really felt good about myself. And it was around then that I started playing around. Not with my boss, but with other men I'd meet. I hadn't ever felt really sexy before, in those early days when I was screwing around, because I hadn't felt like anybody, really— just a body. But now I felt like a *good* body and one with a good head on its shoulders too. I found that I loved being flirted with, and coming up with quips that would turn guys on, and I saw nothing wrong with this. A woman needs to know she's attractive.

"My affairs were casual things. Unplanned. I had four. Maybe five. Actually, they weren't really affairs, just episodes. Sometimes Mickey would be out of town, and someone I had

to take to dinner would suggest a walk afterwards, and I'd
call the babysitter and ask if she could stay later, and I'd get
turned on during the walk and go to a hotel room with the
guy, and just feel splendid about myself afterwards. Next
morning I'd be hustling the kids off to school, packing
lunches, wiping up breakfast food, but feeling terrific. I was
proud of my kids and proud of myself for handling them and
then getting off to work and for being so various, so alive,
and so into everything.

"In the next few years I made lots of friends—women
friends as well as men—and there were things I shared with
them that I didn't share with Mickey. And sometimes I found
I just wanted to be by myself, not with Mickey or the kids
or anybody. But what was wrong with that? Marriage, I felt,
wasn't meant to be a jail, and who's to say that a married
person can't have a good friend—forget about sex—or enjoy
a movie more with, say, a girlfriend, than her husband; or
enjoy a weekend in the country all by herself and her
thoughts and not with him; or prefer going to the zoo with
the kids, and not with him along. All my friends felt this
way. And sex is not a bigger part of this need for a private
life than are any of the other things.

"But when you get right down to it, all these little things
—not just the sex—add up. Mickey divorced me after he
found out about a one-night stand I'd had. A friend was responsible, because she inadvertently asked something about
where I'd been on a night I'd said I was with her, and Mickey
kept probing, and eventually my date came out. And he
went into an icy period. Wouldn't talk to me. Shut himself
off in the bedroom. And then finally came out insisting on
divorce.

"At the time it seemed totally insane to me. He's not the
wounded-pride type, and I couldn't see why he was over-
reacting this way to his discovery of what was at best a casual
affair. I begged him and pleaded with him not to do this to
me; to us; to us and the kids. But Mickey said it wasn't the

affair that had brought him to wanting a divorce. He said
that from the moment I had turned onto flirtations and private friendships, I had turned off him. He said I never would
have needed to flirt if it hadn't meant that in some way I no
longer considered him an estimable person. He said my having intimate friendships, even with women, was a sign of
my not getting from him what I needed in terms of intimacy
and friendship. And he said these things—not the date—had
made him decide we should divorce. He had been rankling
about them for years.

"I fought against his view. It seemed so moralistic to me.
I did love him; I did want to live out my life with him; I
just wanted a few frills. I never accepted his view, and he
never accepted mine, and he left me. We're still friends, by
virtue of the children, but recently he's gotten deeply involved with another woman and I believe they're going to
get married.

"I miss Mickey. I miss him a lot, even though I have a
terrific social life. I handle the kids and my job and all of
that, and I almost got remarried last year. But I didn't feel,
even with the new man, what Mickey seems to have felt about
me, that contentment, and wanting no one else. So I didn't
marry him, because I've decided maybe Mickey is right. It
isn't affairs that come between people, but wanting them is
part of all the little things that give you a hint that the person
you've married isn't a person you want to spend most of your
time with. And those things wound that person's pride as
surely—maybe more—than sex."

I asked Claire what it was about Mickey that had made
her turn off. She still sounded so fond of him. She said,
"That's what I've never quite sorted out. I think it was his
seriousness, a certain do-gooder-ness, which sometimes made
me scoff at him—not aloud, never aloud, but inside myself.
I'm kind of a noisy person; I'm tempestuous. If I had a
tantrum and he treated me with understanding instead of
with a comparable rage, I'd think, 'He's understanding and

kind because he's afraid to be otherwise. He's uptight. I'm
the exciting one, the interesting one around here!'

"So I did put him down. He was right about that. And
maybe I would again, if he and I were together again. I put
him down when I went to the country alone, and when I
took the kids out without him, not just when I went to bed
with other men. In fact, going to bed may have been the
least of it. If I ever remarry it'll have to be to someone about
whom I have no reservations at all."

I asked whether she believed this was ever possible and
Claire said, "Sure it is. Mickey had no reservations about
me."

## *Miriam Mindell /*
## *Affairs Seemed Wiser Than Divorce*

Miriam Mindell, another once-adulterous, now-divorced
woman whom I interviewed shortly after my meeting with
Claire, was not nearly as complacent about the rupture of
her marriage, but then, it had occurred quite recently and
she was still in some shock. At the time I interviewed her she
had been separated only a few months from her husband.
After fifteen years of marriage he had, she said, "true to
cliché," fallen in love with his secretary and left his family
to realign with her.

Miriam had had affairs during their marriage but had
minimized their emotional content, believing that extramarital sex could be tolerated within marriage provided
family came first. That her husband's affair had been conducted more emotionally than hers and thus resulted in the
break-up of their marriage infuriated her.

We met for a lunchtime interview, since Miriam worked
as a film publicist and was on a very crowded schedule. She
said, "I had several affairs, most were trivial. As far as I know,
my husband only had one, this one that's broken us up. We
had a bad sex life, which is, I think, what caused the affairs,

mine and now his. Let's not beat around the bush. My husband came too quickly. All our life together he got on top of me, stuck his penis inside me, and came. Sometimes he'd masturbate me later, but that wasn't such fun. When it's always after the man comes, it feels like a chore you've both agreed to undertake, not something that's fun.

"In the last few years he read that there was therapy that could help him. He wanted to go to a therapist and see if they could do anything for him. But it was part of the treatment that we would have to go as a couple. I suppose this will sound mean to you, but I refused to go. I couldn't see the point to it, after all these years. I'd gotten used to the way things were with us, finally. I was making do with occasional affairs, and sex just didn't seem very important, in or out of marriage.

"I had my first affair years ago and I think that what happened then was very significant. It was the only really meaningful affair I ever had. I was working as a secretary at a motion picture company and that milieu was big on sex. I was working part-time then since I'd already had my first baby. All the married men were having affairs, and so was the other secretary, a Dutch woman who had been married longer than I was and who was constantly involved with somebody or other. I guess I began to figure, 'That's what people in the arts do.'

"The man with whom I finally had my first affair worked with me. He was married but his marriage was coming to an end. He was terribly lonely and he spent a lot of time at our home. It was clear that he found me attractive. He came over almost every Sunday evening. And sometimes my husband would go to bed and we'd just sit and talk. I mean, no sexual thing was involved at that point. After a while, we started going to the movies together. Then I stopped myself. I thought, 'Miriam, you are crazy! You're mixing with the wrong crowd. You better cool it. You have a child. You've been married five years. Sure, it's not a perfect marriage, but whose is? Stop it. Stop. This is the time to have a second baby, not an affair.' I gave a party and I did not invite this man. And it happened that that night my husband made love to me and I got pregnant with my second child.

"Oddly, it was only after I got pregnant—safe and sound and committed again, I guess—that I actually slept with this man. I was very pregnant by the time we did it. I was wearing a maternity bathing suit and we went away for the weekend. We went to a place in the country. I took my oldest daughter, as if I just wanted a weekend away from home, the kid and me. And he met me there. It was fun. It was pleasant except I was very sunburned besides being very pregnant. I had a blister on my nose.

"I saw him a lot the last months of my pregnancy and we talked about my divorcing and our getting together. But I thought, 'Why should I marry him? He's just like the man I'm married to. A little better in bed, that's all.' Anyway, the affair pretty much ended when my baby was born, although I did see him from time to time after that. He married somebody else and I later became very close friends with her. I didn't regret my decision. In fact, I developed a philosophy about extramarital relationships which I tried to live by.

"It was that they were a lot wiser than divorce. Intellectually and emotionally we would like to believe it possible for two people to relate only to each other—intellectually and emotionally and sexually. But we know that this is not always possible. I think that on a practical level it would be better to resist most of the impulses to have extramarital relationships because there's only a certain amount of time in the day for anything, let alone for two men or two women. However, I think every so often there comes along a relationship that's marvelous that does fill a need, whatever the need is. Or you think it does. It's okay to sample it, but you have to do it only once in a while and keep it discreet. You don't have to let it take anything away from your marriage and you certainly don't have to dissolve your marriage. That's crazy! That's going on the false assumption that there's only one right person for you, one forever. Now you figure, 'I made a mistake and I'm going to try the other one.' But the ideal adult is able to have and cope with more than one relationship; the ideal adult doesn't expect any relationship to be the be-all and end-all of his or her life.

"This isn't just my philosophy alone. I know others believe in it too. Take my ex-lover's wife. She tells me they're not having sex at all. And they haven't for several years, ever since their child was born. But everything's fine. He's a marvelous father. He makes a lot of money. Their parents have come to live in the same town with them, which is nice. But then, there's this sex thing, and she says he refuses to discuss it. I don't think he'd have had a sexual problem with me, but who knows? Maybe there would have been some other problem. As I said, whose marriage is perfect?

"I never had any regrets about my philosophy until my husband left me this spring. When he did it, when he had his first affair, he suddenly out of the blue decided he had to break up our home and live forever and ever after with this girl. I can't tell you how angry it makes me. Men are just so much more romantic than women are, I guess. But it makes me feel so terrible. Sometimes I have dreams in which I'm locked up in an elevator and my husband and his girlfriend are outside, keeping the doors shut, and I'm just riding up and down, all alone and stifling to death.

"I don't think my affairs had much to do with our divorcing. But I guess they had something to do with it in this way: they made me complacent. Because I had decided to make do with occasional better sex outside our home, I assumed my husband was doing this too. I figured that, like me, he believed that our marriage and the children mattered most and was keeping his sexual affairs discreet. But all along he was too worried about his sex problem to try any other woman but me, and as soon as he did, and as soon as she told him she loved him and how great he was in bed—

what can she know? she's only twenty-six—he was up and out of here like the flash in the pan he is."

## Jolla Marshall /
## Making Marriage Work

Miriam, fighting her bitterness with a sharp-tongued humor, seemed strong to me. We laughed when she finished her story. Jolla Marshall, a university instructor, was equally bitter but a lot less strong. She was in her early forties, tall and slightly bent at the shoulders, a weeping willow of a woman. In her case, the relationship between an extramarital affair she had had and the break-up of her marriage seemed to have lain largely in the fact that she admitted the experience to her husband at a time he may have been seeking a reason for divorce. He himself had had affairs for years.

Jolla had come to see me partly through a misunderstanding. She had heard about my book from a doctor we shared. But Jolla hadn't realized my concern was just with *women's* extramarital affairs. She thought I was writing about the more classic situation: the wandering husband. Edwin Marshall had been one, and Jolla had overlooked his interest in other women for years, staunchly upholding a woman-as-victim role. Men were outrageous and sexually unfair, but women had to put up with this. It had always been this way and always would. If women did have affairs—Jolla's had happened after eleven years of marriage—it was only when under undue provocation from men. She doubted that I would be able to find very many women who were adulterous except reactively, except when provoked by their husbands' own adultery. Indeed, she seemed to think I might be betraying sisterhood by showing that it was ever any different.

We argued strenuously. I tried to explain to Jolla a feeling I had just sorted out. It was that if women were always to be presented as victims, then I myself could no longer bear to write. I craved another image of women, wanted it enough to have sought it out. It made me less fearful and miserable. I didn't think I was betraying sisterhood to show it. I felt other women would feel, with me, that a perpetual insistence on victimization was just as much a betrayal. I told Jolla that she had pushed me forward in my thinking, in my understanding of my interest in the subject. And to my surprise, we became friends.

But that discussion came later. First, in my office, she told me,

"My husband must have been screwing around for years but I guess I didn't want to know about it. When he'd say he was working late, I'd say 'Okay, honey,' and hold dinner till whatever time he arrived. In the last few years we were married this was getting to be as late as ten or ten-thirty several nights a week. But, you know, mostly I really did think he was working late. He's a lawyer, and he'd gotten into political work, and he often had meetings at night, and people calling him at odd hours. Even on weekends in the country he'd suddenly be called back into the city for important conferences.

"He started developing a temper. He'd get angry over the slightest provocation and if I urged him to keep more regular hours he'd scream at me. Didn't I know he was working so hard for me and the kids? That sort of thing. Besides, he was clearly enjoying his work. And we were too. The kids and I. It was glamorous. I went places, met people I'd never have expected to meet. And I think that basically I was quite content with being Edwin's wife except that I knew I was restless. He was overemployed and I was underemployed. So I decided to go back to school and finish my degree. I'd stopped in the middle, as so many women of my generation did. Now I went back. It seemed to ease things between me and Edwin.

"We weren't having a very sexy marriage. But then, we'd never had. Edwin wasn't very sexual. Even in the early years he made love to me only a couple of times a week.

I had the idea this was enough for him, and in a way it was my conviction that sex wasn't too meaningful to him that made it so easy for me not to be jealous. It would have been another story if he'd wanted more than I wanted to give, if I was turning him down in bed a lot. But I wasn't. I never did that. Sex just wasn't a big thing for him.

"Well, I was a *little* jealous. I did notice that he'd become more flirtatious with women, but then, so were so many of the husbands of my friends. It seemed to me that as all the men of our circle entered their mid-thirties they became more ingratiating with women. It had to do with their confidence, their success. So if I did happen to see Edwin hugging a woman hard, or catch out of the corner of my eye his hand stroking some woman's bare arm, I put it all to his feeling that he could—and should—get away with a little more these days. He was important now and successful, so he could afford to be a little more daring. I didn't mind as long as it didn't come between us.

"During that last couple of years I had an affair. It came about quite unexpectedly. Edwin did a lot of traveling without me but one time we'd gone to London together, with the kids, for a kind of special treat when he suddenly announced he'd have to leave me for the weekend. There was a meeting in Paris and there seemed no point in taking me and the kids along just for the weekend. So we waited for him in London.

"I didn't have any friends I wanted to see so I took the kids around to the parks there and I got a babysitter for one night and went to see a show by myself. Well, it was all a fantasy sort of thing. I was feeling sorry for myself, I guess. I started talking with a man sitting next to me in the theatre. He was an American in London on business. He didn't know anyone either. At first I didn't tell him I was married, although he told me he was. In fact, he told me a lot about his life. He owned a printing shop in Chicago. He'd made more money than he'd ever expected he would and he was a little bored with his wife. He loved her, but he really dug someone like me, he said. Someone sophisticated.

"I was sympathetic. I could understand that sort of thing. I knew he was just like Edwin, but whereas for Edwin, some Mrs. Hooten-Smitten would seem sophisticated and just the right challenging bit out of reach, so for this guy, a New York political lawyer's wife had the same flare and consequent appeal. I went to bed with him and I guess I was hoping that whoever it was Edwin might occasionally spend the night with would have as much good sense as I was showing. I wouldn't fall for Mr. Miehle from Chicago, wouldn't call him up late at night, wouldn't arrive in town unexpectedly so he'd have to leave his house abruptly before his kids had gotten to show him their compositions or their new clothes.

I saw Miehle from time to time, whenever he came on business to New York. I'd meet him after my classes, have dinner and a few hours in a hotel room. I never stayed away very late and I never saw him on a night when Edwin was at home waiting for me. But it was getting to be that there weren't too many nights he was home anymore. It was meetings, conferences, business dinners night after night. I went to a lot of dinners with him, of course, and so it wasn't as if I wasn't part of his life. People were forever saying to me, "Mrs. Marshall! How proud you must be of your husband." And all this time I *was* proud. We were making it—socially, economically, and even as a couple—while all around us people were breaking up.

"So in the end Edwin had to bludgeon me with the thing. He started coming home even later. Once or twice he didn't show up until two in the morning. I'd catch people looking at me peculiarly when we went out. Did they know? I think it was those looks that finally unnerved me. I could have handled the whole thing if I'd been sure no one but Edwin and whoever his girlfriend was knew. But I was starting to feel that our friends knew too.

"I think this was what shoved me into telling Edwin, one

night, that I was willing to share him with another woman as long as she wasn't Number One. He could see her—just as I saw Miehle—but it had to be discreet, secret. We had the children to protect. And that's when the marriage came apart.

"He acted enraged when I told him about Miehle. How could I do this to him? What was the matter with me? He carried on and screamed, quite as if he'd never done anything like it himself. I suppose he was hurt, and that's why he lashed out so. But then he told me he wanted a divorce. I said it was ridiculous. He'd had affairs. Had I divorced him?

"But he was wild with anger, unreasonable. He said, what was the matter with me to put up with something like that, once I knew about it? He himself wouldn't stand for such a thing in a wife for a minute.

"I think it was all some kind of show. I think he'd decided long before that he wanted to divorce me but he hadn't quite known how to bring it about. I think that in some peculiar way he was furious with me for not having proposed divorce years ago, when he'd first started spending so much time away from home. But of course, to me divorce was a chasm, and I'd sidestepped it and clung to all sorts of ledges to avoid getting pushed into it. I clung on even when he was so mad about Miehle. I kept insisting we could still go on together, as long as we kept things discreet. But then he gave me a final push. He told me who it was he'd been seeing. She turned out to be a woman I knew quite well. That hurt a lot. But what hurt most of all was that he also told me that a number of our friends knew about him and her and had seen them together socially.

"I'd always figured I could handle the wandering husband bit, but I couldn't take the fact that his affair had been so public. I really felt demeaned. Well, it hardly mattered. For Edwin, the fact that I'd had any sort of affair was apparently as terrible as the fact that he'd had such a public one was for me.

"So we did end up getting divorced, and I'm not really

sorry about it anymore. The experience of being on my own with the children hasn't been as terrible as I'd anticipated. But I couldn't have known that then. I suppose you'll think that I was a mess in those days, that I was very masochistic. But I really don't think it was *me,* my character. It was the way I was raised. I believed in marriage, in making it work, no matter what the cost."

## Phyllis Eanes /
## A Time for Negotiating

Phyllis Eanes, a psychologist with two teen-aged children, had also tried to keep her marriage going by overlooking clues to its decay. In her situation, it was she and not her husband who was sexually active outside the marriage. She had started having affairs after she had been with her husband thirteen years in a marriage which initially had been comfortable but which, as she had grown older, had seemed competitive and confining. The affairs had created a smoke screen. The marriage had continued to deteriorate, but she had never directly expressed to her husband the aspects of their life together which made her chafe. When she finally did, she discovered that it was too late. They couldn't change life patterns that were now thoroughly ingrained. Curiously, she maintains that the fact that she was in analysis at the time of the affairs kept her from discussing their marital difficulties with her husand. Instead, she concentrated on private anxieties. Today, she practices marital counseling.

We met in her apartment, a spacious old-world place, filled with heavy antique furniture and elaborately framed oils, an apartment as elegant as Phyllis Eanes herself. She said,

"I was twenty-one when I married and my husband was twenty-five. That was twenty years ago, and we were married seventeen years altogether. I had been seeing my husband-to-be for a year and a half before we married and we had then, and continued to have, good sexual experiences together. He was the first sexual partner in my life, but I never felt curious about other men or in any way disappointed in this aspect of our life together. I was perfectly faithful to him for thirteen years of our marriage, and I don't think he ever was adulterous. Oh, possibly with a call girl once when some of his friends sort of dared him into it, but otherwise he was totally faithful. And so was I until after thirteen years.

"But there were a lot of things wrong in our marriage. He wasn't meeting my dependency needs. I should have said to him, 'Look, you promised this and this, but here I am working like a dog. I can't take time off. I'm paying all the bills. You let me down. I'm mad at you.' He expected me to work harder than him—both at my profession during the day and then in the house when I got home at night. I think it was because he was very competitive with me. When we married, I was just a little admiring girl. But I had grown up, become a mother, become a professional. He was one too —a lawyer—but I think he was afraid I might outstrip him. I should have said, 'Look, Eugene, you're too competitive. I work too, yet still you treat me like a kitchen slave.' I think he couldn't have changed his personality, but perhaps we could have negotiated much better than we ultimately did. In every marriage, there's a time for negotiating, but you can miss it if you're acting out instead.

"That's what happened to me. I was afraid to face up to him and instead I began having affairs. Mind you, I didn't know this at the time. I knew I was angry, but I thought it was mostly at my parents and myself. I had started analysis and in analysis I was bringing up a lot of self-derogatory feelings. I felt that my mother, who had had lots of men in her life, was more beautiful than me. I felt I had been awkward, a grind, ever since early childhood. It didn't occur to me that Eugene was contributing to these feelings. Analysis made me concentrate on *me,* on how I'd always felt. If Eugene would say, 'You look ugly in that dress,' I just assumed he was right, since I invariably felt ugly. It didn't register with me then that a husband is someone who thinks you're beautiful, even when you yourself doubt it, and that a husband can help to change those bad childhood feelings.

"Anyway, I started having affairs, and other men helped me see that I wasn't an ugly duckling anymore. I had three affairs, two of them short, the third one pretty long. During that time, I began to look better. I lost weight, and I learned how to put on clothes, and actually I improved as a person. I became more assured. I had more fun.

"I wanted to stay married, but I also wanted to stay feeling competent and self-assured. I tried, finally, to talk with Eugene about the things in our life that bothered me, to make demands. But it was all too far gone. We had lived so long with him as boss and me as the meek underling that he couldn't change fast enough and I had grown impatient and too independent. But it was Eugene who left. I was trying to negotiate. And I never stop daydreaming about the possibility that had I talked to Eugene earlier, and maybe gone into therapy *with* him, instead of alone, we might have accomplished something together.

"I don't like being single. I'd like to be married again. Recently I've been in a two-year-long relationship with a man I like a lot and which has many elements of a marriage. But during it I have found myself getting interested in other men again, and I have had to catch myself or I would have just started it all over again. I have had to say, 'Hey, there's something wrong and that's why I am doing this and I am working it out in this way.' What's different now is that I'm seeing several men, but I'm also very openly discussing with my primary lover what is wrong, what my disappointments are, and why I suddenly found myself attracted to other people.

"I can't speak for all women, but I wonder if it isn't true that a woman only has affairs when there's something wrong in her primary relationship. Otherwise, even if she only sleeps with a man once every two weeks, if she really loves him and if she's really satisfied with him, she's not going to have an affair. I don't think that's true for men particularly, but I have a feeling that it's true at least for middle-class women brought up the way I was."

But what about the new generation? I knew that Phyllis Eanes must be seeing younger women for marital counseling and must have come up against an ethic concerning extramarital sex that did not align with her own. What about those who insisted—even after scrutiny—that they felt no anger toward their husbands, only a biological tickle? What about those who had agreements with their husbands that permitted extramarital sex? Phyllis said, "It's difficult. One hardly knows where to begin with them. One must ask oneself exactly where they are different from oneself, and exactly where they are the same."

# Part III

*Interviewing: Experimental Marriage*

# (1)
# Staying Married:
## *Accommodators*

More and more often as I continued interviewing, I was to meet women whose adulteries were known to their husbands. They told me they lived in open marriages or that they were trying out new marital alternatives or alternate marital lifestyles. Many new formulas for marital behavior were embraced under these headings, but invariably one ingredient was that the women had pacts with their husbands specifying that sex with partners outside the marriages was to be sanctioned. Some of the women I interviewed who had opted for experimenting in this way with marriage were quite young and had agreed upon open adultery before or very soon after they were wed; others were older and their pacts concerning extramarital sex had evolved only after long years of marriage.

The kinds of adulteries which these women had agreed upon ranged from those to be experienced during group sex or mate swapping in which the partner participated, to those to be experienced in private sexual encounters, known about but not participated in by their spouses. Often, while extramarital sex was itself considered permissible, there were limitations placed upon the prominence such sex could have in the couples' marriages. Most common was a time limitation. A wife or husband had a spouse's permission to have extramarital sex only while the marital partner was away on business; only during vacations; or, with a precision resembling college course scheduling, only Tuesdays and Thursdays, only Mondays and Wednesdays. If a regular schedule was not observed, one spouse was usually required to give the other certain days' notice before making or keeping an appointment for extramarital sex. There were also content limitations, but these were more vague. A spouse might reserve the right to ask his or her partner to discontinue an extramarital relationship if it became emotionally threatening or if it encroached upon sexual, economic or companionship patterns.

The women I met who were engaged in open extramarital sex were idealistic and evangelistic. They considered their method superior to the practice of monogamy, which they felt was limiting and anti-hedonistic. And they also considered it superior to the method followed by couples in traditional marriages who kept their adulteries secret from their partners. They stressed that while open extramarital sex was technically adultery, it was not infidelity—not a betrayal of a trust. Consequently it offered two great advantages over secret adultery. One was that it removed the burden of guilt toward a spouse. The other was that it was more convenient, and therefore permitted the practitioners greater choice, enjoyment, and relaxation. On the question of whether being open about adultery could potentially wound a spouse's spirit, these women were emphatic: the old notion that what one doesn't know can't hurt was wrong; they preferred the new adage that it is only what one does know that can't hurt.

In my preliminary discussions with women in experimental marriages, I thought they sounded remarkably alike. But when I came to interview them in depth, I found that despite superficial similarities, they fell into two distinct categories. One group were instigators of experimental marriage. It was they and not their husbands who had originally desired additional sexual partners. The second group were accommodators. They had acquiesced to their husbands' wishes for such partners in an effort either to please the men or to forestall the mens' desires to break up the marriages. Open extramarital sex was a pacifier they mouthed or one they extended. It was not really food for them.

## Amelia Furman /
## My Husband Would Be the Perfect Lover

I became sensitive to this distinction when I interviewed Amelia Furman, mother of two, wife of a very successful real estate manager, and a recent convert to open extramarital sex. At times it seemed almost a religion for her. She was ecstatic about the changes in her sex life with her husband that had resulted from their making a compact for open adultery. But Amelia was clearly an accommodator to open adultery, not a true believer.

We met at her house, a mammoth columned building with wide lawns and a dock that reached down to the waters of the Long Island Sound. It was here we sat to talk. It was a Tuesday night in late spring and the water was calm, un-ruffled by the motorboats that would churn and contaminate it later in the season.

Amelia, a chubby, pleasant blond of thirty-seven, began by telling me how far she had come, not just materially—which I could see—but sexually. She had grown up, she told me, in a far less prestigious Long Island suburb and been raised with the strict morals of the fifties. She had married the handsomest man in her college class, but they had fought their way through most of their sixteen-year marriage.

"First of all," said Amelia, "I think I married Sylvan for all the wrong reasons. I wanted to shock my parents. Sylvan came from a very poor family in Brooklyn. He was a scholar-ship student, obviously very ambitious, but also very un-predictable. He was very sensual and a bit wild. These qual-ities made him attractive to me, but I really didn't cherish them in those days. It's only been lately that I have come to see the light about Sylvan, come to see how very special he is.

In those early days, once we were married and the fun of trying to dismay my parents was accomplished, I just kept trying to change Sylvan.

"I thought he was oversexed. He thought I was undersexed. I was always trying to limit him. If he wanted to read dirty books to me, I'd react with shock. If he even wanted to take a bath with me, I'd get angry. Can you imagine? Just a homey little nude bath together, and I'd react like what he had suggested was something to call the police about."

He was, she said, "an orgyist, a sexual astronaut, an explorer," and she had been repelled by his morality. But very recently, because of events she promised to describe, she had had an enormous reversal in her thinking. She had come around to his way of thinking. She had become sexually emancipated. They had recently formulated their marriage on a new open plan. Each of them had Tuesdays and Thursdays to pursue other relationships, and the effect of this had been to cause a sexual recrudescence between them.

They had, for example, just two months ago bought a tiny vibrator from a discreet sex shop in the city, and they used it now to enhance their trips across the Fifty-ninth Street Bridge. "This thing," explained Amelia, "is smaller than a Tampax. We used to hate driving home at night; it depressed us. But not any more. Now we sit in the car with my coat over me, so the drivers of big trucks can't look in. I turn on the vibrator and Sylvan gets all excited from just watching me. Sometimes he pulls it away and then starts it up again, to tease me. We have lots of fun.

"This is something I never could have done before, you understand. And it's the kind of thing Sylvan always wanted of me. I was as sexually cowardly as you can imagine. Instead of honestly saying, 'Well, how do I really feel about this idea?' I'd always say, 'Well, it's different and it's strange and it makes me uncomfortable. So let's have none of it.' I'd complain and yell a lot, and I'd read into all Sylvan's sexual wishes that he was bizarre. And then he began making fewer demands on me. I took this to mean that he had come around to my way of thinking, but now I know it only meant that he was turning to other things, other people. I suppose on some level I even suspected this. I did have the feeling we were growing very distant. But on the surface everything was calm, so I pretended to myself it was all okay. And around that time I got pregnant, and I had my two kids right in a row and I was oblivious. Not happy, but not unhappy either."

Amelia had a rapid way of speaking, but I noticed that in between sentences she always looked closely at me to ascertain my reactions. It gave me the sense that she was rehearsing something, reciting a speech just barely committed to memory. Her style made me nervous. She told me, for example, "I believed in the idea that you got married forever and ever and that if you separated you'd be completely broken-hearted and destroyed." Then, pausing, she looked at me for confirmation but said, "You know, that *myth*." The first sentence sounded authentic. The second sounded forced. I believed that Amelia still believed in the idea, not the myth.

When their second baby was about a year old, she now went on, "I finally learned that what Sylvan was into was orgies. There was this guy, who used to run orgies and was forever calling Sylvan up and neither of them let on to me what it was about, and then finally one time Sylvan told me and said, 'Do you want to go?' Of course I was appalled. Not only did I refuse to go, I begged him not to. I carried on. I screamed, 'If you loved me, you wouldn't do this.' So then he made a clean breast of a whole lot of things he'd been doing over the past years; not just orgies but different women, women in his office, old friends of ours from school. I ranted and raved and thought I was going to have a nervous breakdown. I told him I'd kill him and got a kitchen knife.

"It took a long time but Sylvan calmed me down. He said none of it had been important to him; no one person. And he swore he'd change, give it all up. But then—it's funny talking about it now, because when I say this, it all sounds absolutely terrible, in terms of working toward anything meaningful between two people—even then he wasn't honest.

"It sounded as if he was honest, but he wasn't. He was very apologetic. He kept bringing home gifts for me, always in pairs, one for my soul, one for my body. If I got Yeats' poems I also got Revlon body lotion. If I got a record, I got a cashmere sweater. I was flattered and I relaxed. I just assumed my ranting and raving had, you know, changed him. But really, it hadn't. Because maybe it was five years after that, there was a night we were meeting in his office just before going to the theatre. He'd been out of town on a business trip and he suggested, very romantically, I thought, that the night he came back, we meet in his office, screw on the rug, and go on to see a play. I was flattered, got all dressed up and arrived in his office all cheerful and excited. But I was early and he was late. I was sitting behind the desk waiting for him, and after a while I opened a drawer, and the drawer was full of letters with Italian stamps. I didn't guess what was in them. I just opened one up, and it started out, "Lover," and just then I heard Sylvan coming in and I didn't have any pockets in my dress so I thrust the letters down my bra and as he came to embrace me I yelled, 'I have to go to the bathroom' and I ran out and I read the four or five letters I had grabbed. And I was shocked."

The letters were all from a woman the Furmans used to know, a neighbor who had moved with her husband to Italy. They were love letters. Amelia didn't say anything to Sylvan when she came back from the bathroom. "Of course," she related, "I didn't let him screw me on the office rug. I said I'd just gotten my period unexpectedly. We went to the theatre, and out to dinner afterwards, and although I was shivering all night, like in shock, I didn't let on I knew anything."

The next day she decided to talk to Sylvan about it. His reaction was that it was somehow her fault; if she hadn't looked in his drawer, everything would have been fine. Amelia was upset by his response, but even more by her conviction that from the tone of the letters, "It sounded as if this affair wasn't just for sex; it sounded as if he had told this woman he loved her. The problem is that the kind of woman that always gets to him is the slim, intellectual, Gloria Steinem-type. They're bright and sensitive, so he ends up talking to them, which is more of a problem for me than if he just slept with them.

"Well, we went through a whole thing. At one point, he wanted to leave me. But when it came to making a move, he couldn't or wouldn't. He said I had to be the one to do it. I said I couldn't, not if he still loved me. I said I wouldn't, if he swore he loved me.

"And he did swear. He told me he just had to write to this woman in Italy the way he did in order to keep her attached. And I decided to accept that.

"It was after that, which was about a year ago, that Sylvan said that since we were staying together, he felt it would be a good idea if we put our marriage on more honest grounds. He said that ever since I'd known him there had always been these sudden surprises, these shocks for me, and that if we were to have a really decent marriage, we'd have to be open with each other. He suggested that each of us have a couple of nights a week, no questions asked."

Amelia had agreed to this. She had talked it out with Sylvan and accepted his theory that an open marriage would bring them closer, and cause their marriage to grow rather than decay further. Sylvan insisted it had to be something they both did. He didn't just want her permission for *his* affairs. This presented a problem since in her youth Amelia had never had any boyfriends except for Sylvan and she certainly had no one lined up right then. But she had made up her mind that she wanted to try for a new climate in their marriage, and she no longer believed it would come by her efforts to tame Sylvan. So she told Sylvan that in principle the nights out were okay with her, but that she didn't know anyone. "He said he could fix me up," she explained. "But he didn't have to because just a few months later I met this terrific guy, an auto racer, a ski champion, one of those people who can do everything. He was Hungarian and really gorgeous.

"I met this man at a party at my cousin's. I'm sure that if I'd met him six months earlier he never would have so much as smiled at me. But there's something about being available, about knowing you're available, that communicates itself to men, and before I knew what was happening, he was playing with my fingers in my cousin's pantry, turning my wedding ring and rubbing his thumb along it.

"We made a date and I felt marvelously daring. It was around that time that my sex life with Sylvan began to improve so enormously. I felt so flamboyant, so seductive, so turned on. And I knew that Sylvan liked me more, wanted me more. As to my Hungarian, that was something else. The first date we had, he came and picked me up here and we got into his beautiful sports car to drive to his apartment and I lit a cigarette and he said, 'Please use the ashtray.' So I began wondering what am I doing here with this guy that I thought was such a swinger? Then when we got to his place, before we went in he wiped his feet on the mat outside. And after that he actually changed to a smoking jacket. At this point I was trying not to laugh, which was really hard when he said, 'Would you like a drink?' and came out with a silver tray with fifteen different kinds of aperitifs.

"Then we went to bed. And I thought, 'What a bore this guy is.' There were silly things happening, not kinky things, but just things like sticking his cock in and out, no big deal, but I guess the Hungarians do it that way. He believed in straight intercourse with the man on top. And clean! I mean he was always running up and washing—with soap and water —and I shocked him because he'd say, after every time he came, 'Don't you want to go and wash?' and I'd say, 'No.' He made me feel like I was his grandmother, kind of, which was strange.

"It taught me how good Sylvan was, and how lucky I was to have Sylvan, and I didn't want to spend any more nights with this guy. So I broke it off. I told him and Sylvan that someone else had come along who was more interesting to me, and that was that."

It had gotten dark over the water and I found myself shivering, at once both cold and uneasy over Amelia's story. I realized it was a Tuesday night and wondered what she had told Sylvan she was doing tonight. When I asked, she said, "He thinks I'm out. I do keep up a little pretense over the thing. I don't want him to think there's no one. When he's going out, I go to the theatre a lot. I see old girlfriends in the city. Sometimes I buy myself a piece of jewelry and leave it on the dresser a while, hoping he'll notice it and wonder if it was a gift."

I think Amelia could feel, even in the darkness, my dismay, for next she said, "Well, what am I to do? Most men don't appeal to me; or I don't appeal to them. Which is why Sylvan is so unusual. He's honest and really sensual, which is why I like him. He'd be the perfect kind of person for me to play around with. I told him once that if we ever get divorced, the one thing he has to promise to do is come and sleep with me because he really is just fun to sleep with."

I went home feeling embarrassed and troubled for Amelia. I couldn't help feeling that she was doing patchwork on an old-fashioned marriage, stitching experimental designs onto fraying conventional patterns. What she made would not wash; the threads would come loose. It seemed to me that marriage itself had gone topsy-turvy. Where once wives lied to conceal their lovers, now there were wives lying to conceal their lovers' absence. If Amelia's was an "open" marriage, what would a prison be like?

## *Cleo and Paul Amber /*
## *We Had a Discussion and Chose Open Marriage*

Acquiescent extramarital sex wasn't limited to already established and already tenuous marriages. I encountered it in a brand-new marriage too, and had the opportunity to interview both partners, the husband and the wife. Cleo Amber was studying sociology with a professor I knew and had volunteered to be interviewed when he mentioned to his seminar that I was interested in talking with women who were having extramarital affairs.

Just before the day of the actual interview, she telephoned to say that her husband would like to be included too since theirs was an experimental relationship in which each had extramarital affairs with the knowledge and approval of the other. I said that I hadn't been talking to men, that it might disrupt the pattern of my book, but then I figured, why not? Surely it would be more informative to talk to both.

I interviewed them at their tiny three-room apartment, a fifth-floor roost in a walk-up building largely occupied by students. I spoke with each of the Ambers separately, Cleo first, then Paul.

Cleo, who was twenty-four, was full-breasted, small-waisted, round in the hips, a beautiful young woman with cascading chestnut curls. She hoped to have children one day soon, but in the meantime, lavished a great deal of petting and love on three scrawny gray and white kittens and their large black mother who purred continuously on Cleo's lap. She began by explaining to me why she and Paul had decided two years ago on an experimental marriage.

"The thing is," she said, "that it's sort of like Paul and I never ever have to part if someone else should come into the picture. I mean that's one of the main reasons that people separate. After five or six or ten years of marriage, along comes somebody new. There's something exciting about somebody new. It's a new body, it's a new person, and they see you as a new body and a new person. And I think that's what causes people to break up. Someone new comes along and you cannot get involved with this new person without somehow ending your marriage. But this way that Paul and I have, it's sort of comforting. We can always keep our thing, which is really warm and intimate. We're so close. We're best friends. But we can still get involved with other people when the occasion arises."

I asked her what kind of relationship with other men she was having right now. "Well," said Cleo, "I don't spend much time at this. It's not like when I was a twenty-one-year-old child and every guy in the street looked interesting. I'm very busy these days. I'm working toward my M.A. in sociology, and I have a pretty demanding job as a group worker with children. So actually I rarely see other men. I only do it occasionally. I'm involved in an intermittent relationship with a guy who lives in Tampa, who I used to date several years ago. But it's not who I'm seeing that's important. It's the fact that this openness is there between Paul and me."

I asked, "How does your friend in Tampa feel about the relationship you have with Paul? Does he mind? Does he feel at all like a second fiddle?"

Cleo said, "It's a very, very special situation. He was overseas in the South Pacific for two years and he contracted malaria. He's very ill right now, and all his energies are invested in his recovery. So it's not really a question of, well, you know, not a question really of sex. It's just a question of I go and I see him."

I said, "You're just being supportive and nice to him?"

"Right," Cleo said. "Right. I go down to Tampa and I stay for a few days every few months."

I said, "I guess you don't care for him in the same way that you care for Paul?"

"No," said Cleo, becoming somehow defensive. "I happen to love this other man. But it has nothing to do with the way I love Paul. One of the things that I have learned is that you can love people in different ways. Some of the qualities that I love in Paul, Ernie does not have and there are important qualities that Ernie has that Paul does not have. One has nothing to do with the other."

"Does the fact that either of you is seeing someone else cause jealousies between you and Paul?" I asked.

"There are twinges of jealousy," Cleo said thoughtfully. "But I think that when you weigh the advantages against the disadvantages, the advantages far outweigh the others. But, if you're talking about jealousy, I'll admit I'm a little bit jealous because Paul is involved in this relationship with a woman named Janine and he loves this woman. He sleeps with her and talks to her on the phone quite a bit. And because he is involved so intimately with Janine, he sometimes tells her certain things that he doesn't tell me. For example, he had a relationship with another woman, Lisa, and I was dying to find out about it, but Paul didn't want to discuss it with me. Well, last night Janine called and he talked to her for a long time and I got the feeling from the conversation that he was discussing the situation about Lisa with Janine. And that's the kind of jealousy that I feel." She stopped and looked warily at the tape recorder. "It's nothing," she said. "It's not a sexual kind of jealousy."

I said, "You mean you're not jealous that he makes love with her?"

Cleo said, "Right. It's just that I would like to know everything about his life. I find him interesting. And I do know everything about his life but the one thing that he's ever really withheld from me was that thing with Lisa. And you know, I'd sort of like to find out."

"Does he feel any jealousy about you and Ernie?" I asked.

"Not really," she said. "Well, there might be a certain amount but not of a disruptive kind. Jealousy really doesn't cause trouble between us. We sort of know that the jealousy is there. We even talk about the jealousy. It can't cause trouble when it's open. You know?"

I said I wasn't sure and that this was the big question about experimental marriages. "If an affair happens and a spouse doesn't know about it, maybe *that* doesn't cause trouble," I said. "I'm not sure about this way."

"Oh, the old-fashioned way *does* cause trouble," Cleo said.

"That's where you're wrong. There's no such thing as not knowing about it. All these older men who are running around, their wives know. Their wives know, at least deep down. And that would absolutely *kill* me. Like if Paul was sneaking around, then I'd imagine that the other woman was the most gorgeous thing that was ever created on the face of the earth."

I said, "You know what Janine and Lisa look like then? You've met them?"

"No, I've never met Janine or Lisa but Paul has assured me that neither of them is more attractive than I am. Paul's met Ernie, though. Ernie was here. Well, the reason that Ernie was here was that Paul went away to London for about three weeks, and I was getting lonely. Separate vacations are part of our arrangement. The idea is, you feel more excited about your husband or wife when they're not always underfoot, when you have private experiences to come home and share with them. But I was getting a bit lonely, and I called Ernie, and he decided to come to New York and stay with me till Paul came home. I knew approximately when Paul was due home, but what happened was he came back two days early, and Ernie was still here. And then, I don't know, maybe I was really a little angry about the separate vacation bit, but I got this fantasy thing in my mind that since we had this open kind of marriage we could take it a little step further, and Ernie could stay here a few days even while Paul was here. But of course, that was childish. It didn't work out."

I asked, "What went wrong?"

She said, "It was crazy. Ernie was sleeping in here, on the couch, and Paul had been away for three weeks and he had this terrific sexual need for me, and he said the whole point of going away was that he could come back to me all turned on and we could fuck like crazy, like in the first days we met, so he was mad that Ernie was here. I was going back and forth between the living room and the bedroom, and it got crazy. Paul said I was punishing him for something I'd given my word I wanted to do as much he did, and I decided he was right, so I finally asked Ernie to leave."

"So now you see Ernie only occasionally?"

"Yeah, once every two or three months."

"You see Ernie less frequently than Paul sees Janine?"

"I don't know. Yeah. Yeah. At one point Paul was seeing Janine about two nights a week. He was out an awful lot. And that was too much."

"And you told him?"

"I did tell him. Yeah. We discussed it. It was just too much. He's cut down some. But he can't cut it all the way down, or else we'd be back in one of those closed relationships and I'd be worried about what I don't know. I like the fact that I don't have to fear that we will ever have to part because somebody new comes into the picture, that we can incorporate new people and still have our thing. I find a certain amount of security in that. I see everybody around us getting divorced and you know, I find a certain amount of security in the fact that it won't happen to us."

Paul had been in the kitchen with the door shut the whole time I was talking to Cleo. Now I went and spoke with him. He was twenty-eight, short, and darkly handsome. An ingratiating man, he had made coffee for me while I was with Cleo, and he served it to me now, pouring a cup for himself. He did not offer to take any outside to Cleo and I could see how even in minor matters this man guarded the principle of separate experiences.

"How did you and Cleo meet?" I asked. I'd forgotten to ask her that. Paul said, "Right here. We met exactly downstairs in this building. She was sharing an apartment for the summer with a girlfriend, and I was already living here, and at the end of the summer we got married and she moved right in here."

"How did your pact concerning extramarital sex come about?" I asked. "Was it something you decided on before you got married, or did it evolve?"

"Before," Paul said. "We had a discussion and we decided upon an open marriage. One that could involve a lot of outside sex."

"Did you put any barriers or restrictions on just what was open?"

Paul said, "Yes. The restrictions are that we have to tell each other who we're going out with, and when we're going to be out. You know it isn't just like I say, 'I'm going to go out tonight with Janine.' We agree upon an evening in advance, and Cleo knows about it and that's the way it works. Cleo knows that such and so evening I'm not coming back, and she knows who I'll be with, as opposed to, you know, her just wondering if I'm coming back or who I'm with."

"She knows you'll be back the next day?"

"Right. The same with her. It works both ways."

"At the point that you got together, was there any other woman in your life? Or were you just anticipating there might be?"

"Yes, there was someone. There was a woman named Lisa I'd been seeing for a while before I met Cleo. I'd had a fantastic sexual relationship with her, better than it ever was or got to be with Cleo, and I really didn't want to give her up altogether although I knew she wasn't someone I could live with. And I wanted a woman to live with. I saw Lisa for a while after Cleo and I got together, but eventually that relationship broke up. But Cleo and I kept the arrangement. It's based on theory, not on personalities."

"Is it working well in your opinion?" I asked.

"Yes," he said, "although there is a certain price involved. A certain, you know, higher level of insecurity. I think the benefits outweigh this, though. The benefits, the way I see them, are that by being in other relationships we have a chance to explore ourselves, and also a chance to have good friends outside of just our relationship, as opposed to stagnating in a monogamous relationship which gets worse and worse every year."

"What's your sense of commitment to Cleo?" I asked. "I mean, do you anticipate remaining married to Cleo?"

Paul said, "For as long as it's good, we stay with each other, but presumably having other relationships will make it stay good longer."

I asked him about Janine, the woman he was seeing. "How frequently do you see her? Is she more available than you?"

"Oh, it varies. Sometimes I'll see her every week, other times a month may go by or something like that."

"You call her?"

"Yes. We're always in touch on the phone. She has a steady guy too. She's been seeing him since childhood, really. He lives in New Paltz. So she's pretty tied down. She's about a year away from getting a Ph.D. in art history and studying takes up most of her time, and the time she's got she likes to go to New Paltz. So if anything, I'm freer than she is."

"When you see her do you spend most of your time making love or do you do social things together?"

"Oh, we do a lot of things. We may just sit and talk. It's not predominantly sex. The main thing of the relationship is more the friendship. Before Janine and after Lisa there was another woman I was seeing in a relationship that was more primarily sexual. It didn't work out. She called me a lot and Cleo would be here, and that put a certain limitation on the conversation. And she got a little anxious. See, she didn't have a steady boyfriend and so she felt the limitations more. Janine's better for me because she has to study, and she has her hands full already just in terms of getting her work done."

Paul seemed a little annoyed that I had referred to his marriage with a name, as an experimental marriage. Now he told me that he didn't think that his and Cleo's relationship was at all typical of what other people they knew were doing, and had, therefore, not to be named, not yet.

"This is something very new," he said. "We're explorers. Most of our friends who are married are all monogamous. Even most of Janine's friends in her New York Radical Feminist's Group are monogamous too. So I don't think anything has really changed much from the past generation to this one. And it's time for a change. But nothing changes. For example, there are a lot of restaurants in this neighborhood, Chinese restaurants especially, and it's very, very infrequent in any of them to see a woman pay the bill. Usually the guy gets up and pays the bill. It's the same when it comes to parties. Recently Janine and I went to a party one of her feminist friends was giving and this feminist friend did all the cooking and all the party shit. Her boyfriend didn't do anything. The average liberated woman is having relationships that are only liberated verbally rather than in actual content or action.

"In that sense what I'm doing for Cleo is really liberating her. I don't go in for a lot of talk. I'm action-oriented. Sometimes Cleo is disappointed in how we live. She only sees this guy of hers, Ernie, once in a while, and he's been sick, so the sex isn't that great with him. But I tell her forget about Ernie and get yourself something good. You're free to get whatever you want.

"I wish Cleo didn't feel disappointed. I know what we're doing isn't easy, but I also know it's necessary for me. My parents were married for thirty years and then just a few years ago, they got divorced. I don't think it was my parents' divorce that made me develop my philosophy. It had an impact of course, but that was just part of it. I just think that monogamy leads to breaking up over other people, and that this way, well, it may hurt a little, but it won't hurt as much as breaking up, and that's what I told Cleo from the beginning, and I think she agrees with me."

I remember feeling convinced, after speaking with the Ambers and Amelia Furman, that experimental marriages with compacts for open adultery were more advantageous to men than to women. The wives had settled for lovers who were second-best or even second-rate, while the husbands had sounded more gratified in their choices. This seemed logical to me. Men would of course, I thought, have an easier time finding desirable partners willing to share their sexual attentions, since our tradition lends itself toward such sharing of the male but not of the female. This would explain the wives' disappointments.

But I was wrong in seeing the advantages of open adultery as so sex-related. The advantages, the *spoils* so to speak, went not to the men but to the instigators, whether male or female. The person proposing open extramarital sex was invariably the partner who had a sex or love object already in mind at the time the arrangement was first agreed upon. The accommodator settled for whoever he or she could find, or waited for opportunity to provide.

# (2)
# Staying Married:
## *Instigators*

Women who instigated open extramarital sex were dynamically different from those who accommodated. They tended to be more radical and to view their sexual activities as political action. The most emphatic I met was Pamela Lewisohn.

## *Pamela Lewisohn /*
## *I Don't Believe in Casual Sex*

Pamela was late to lunch on the day of our appointed interview. When I arrived at the expensive French restaurant Pamela had selected, the woman at the antique front desk informed me that my lunch guest had telephoned and left me a message explaining that her dog was in labor and that consequently she was going to be delayed. Nine puppies had already been born, she had said, but she was going to have to wait around a while longer to see if there was to be a tenth. The entire restaurant staff was concerned. Not only the front desk woman, but the hatcheck girl, a captain, and a waiter had become involved. Each reassured me my lunch guest would be along soon.

I was not surprised by Pamela's advance men and women. Her life is a series of emergencies, contingencies, urgencies. She goes nowhere, does nothing, without involving extras in all her choices and decisions.

When she did arrive in the restaurant, all heads turned. Her clothing was not spectacular; she is too much a believer in women's liberation for sexy or expensive clothing. But she cannot help being dramatic. She has wavy, rust red hair down to her waist, wide emerald eyes, pale skin, long slender arms and legs. At the table alongside us, three garrulous businessmen were eating; they became more and more subdued, more and more interested in our conversation. They could not hear us, but they were trying. They leaned forward and attemped to advise us about the wine. They joked about Pamela's *poulet en croute*. She was pleasant to them, her green eyes squinting, appraising them. Then she heard one of them say to another, "Don't you know a woman can never be sure whether you're telling a joke or laughing at her?" Pamela was finished with them after that. "Fucking sexists," she said. No matter how they smiled and sat forward and angled for attention afterwards, she would not even look at them. I was to remain continually aware of them, but Pamela had shut them out of her perception.

This meeting at the restaurant was our second interview. A year before, I had interviewed Pamela in her office about an affair she had been having with an academic colleague. That situation had been special enough: shared evenings obtained through permission of both their spouses; planned events with both their sets of children. Now Pamela is in a new relationship, one more to her liking. She is spending half of the week with her husband and the children; the other half of the week with her new lover. Again, there are set visitations with the children. It is like a separation agreement. She calls it a love agreement.

I had originally heard about Pamela from two sources. The first was a historian who taught in the same university as Pamela and knew about my book; she had given me Pamela's phone number. "You should talk to someone like Pamela," her fellow historian had said. "I doubt there are many like her, but perhaps you can read the future in her." The second person was the woman whose husband was having the affair with Pamela. "What is odd about her," this woman said, "is that she insisted on discussing the whole thing with me beforehand, on obtaining my permission."

"Did you give it?" I asked.

"Did I really have a choice?" this woman said. "Just because she said I had a choice, did that mean I had one? But there was more to my saying yes than that. Pamela caught me right in my lib-rad principles. I had no choice, not because they would necessarily have gone ahead without my approval —I'm not sure my husband would have—but because I was hoisted by my own principles of not restricting other people's destinies."

Pamela had explained that experience this way. "I told Jake's wife that I was a feminist, that I was *really* into the women's movement, and that I didn't want to fuck over another woman. Still, I was terribly turned on by Jake. I had met him at a party, and I know this sounds corny, but I had fallen absolutely, incredibly, staggeringly in love with him. For two years I did nothing about this. He was *married*. I was too, but I knew I could get Kevin to agree to the affair. Still, I didn't want to fuck over Jake's wife. When I was a single college student I'd had innumerable affairs with married men, and I'd seen how easily they grew attached to young women who didn't require anything of them, who adored them simply because they were older. I had seen how they began to treat their wives with contempt just because they now had houses filled with kids with snotty handkerchiefs and wet diapers; I'd seen how they wanted to start life over again. But start over again how? If any of them started over with me I'd quickly enough give him more kids with snotty noses and wet diapers. I told the men this. I felt closer to their wives than to any of these guys. And I felt close to Jake's wife. I had no intention of stealing her husband. So in the beginning I avoided the whole sex question. I proposed that since I loved her husband, the four of us spend a lot of time together, nonsexual time. Weekends. Vacations. I said, 'As long as we don't fuck, it's going to be okay.' For me, fucking is a very heavy thing."

She remembers with indignation that Jake's wife considered her childish. "She said I was a titillator; a tease and a titillator. She said, 'People can fuck without being involved. I don't mind the fucking; it's the build-up I mind. Fucking is just a physical thing. Why does it have to be so weighted?' "

Jake's wife had said this in the middle of a four-way discussion the two couples were having, an arbitration session to straighten out what their position would be on Pamela's infatuation with Jake. Jake's wife had gone on to add, "It's not so unique. Everyone does it. You act as if you were the only woman in the world to want to take a lover. It really isn't that special." To demonstrate, Jake's wife took Pamela's husband to bed. It was a tutorial act, meant to instruct Pamela that sex, even extramarital sex, could be trivial, happenstance.

"I wanted to trivialize it," Jake's wife explained to me, "because Pamela had made her attraction into a timebomb, with all of us dancing nervously around it waiting for it to go off. In her mind, restraining from sex with Jake would simply indicate on the day she finally bedded that their attraction to each other had cosmic importance, that it had proved bigger than all of us. I wanted her to come down off that fevered Lawrentian peak, to see that it is in the nature of the beast to sexualize. I'd had consternation in the past over the difficulties of contenting oneself with one limiting set of circumstances, with one partner and one life as it is lived with him or her for all our days. I wanted Pamela to see how ultimately ordinary this consternation was, how it belonged to every woman, not her alone."

But Pamela is incapable of being merely life-size. Once free to sexualize her relationship with Jake, she became fierce about her terms; she wanted not sporadic encounters; not just occasional weekends. "I need," she told the three of them, "two nights a week—one of them in my house, so the kids can get to know him too; lunch once a week; and a full weekend together twice a month. I don't believe in casual sex."

Pamela says she never had any intention of ending up with Jake. "My husband is much more solid than Jake. Jake is a loner. He withdraws. Everybody who knows him says that he never quite comes out of himself, that he's very internal. This may have been what made me love him. I found him so thoughtful, so brilliant. But it would have made for a lousy marriage. So I just wanted him *in addition* to my life. He was sexually fantastic for me. But so is my husband. I wanted them both. I know this sounds greedy, but I wanted it all. It's only very recently that women have been able to talk about this, but I think you'll hear it more and more. I had fantasies of Jake's moving in, but I never had fantasies of my husband's moving out."

The encounter times Pamela wanted were negotiated and the affair got underway. But it did not work. Pamela and her husband are in their late twenties; Jake and his wife are in their late thirties. As Jake's wife said, "Pamela is just sufficiently younger, sufficiently political and idealistic to be against secrecy, to want to live her life in a new way. In a way, I respect that in her. But for us, it couldn't work. Both my husband and myself had had occasional affairs in the past. But we kept them secret from each other. There's something about telling that is injurious. Pamela doesn't buy that but to me it's basic. When you tell your spouse about your affairs, you wound him or her. Perhaps Pamela wore Jake out. But perhaps he stopped their affair because he didn't want to go on injuring me. For all I know, when Jake broke off with her he went on to some secret affair. But that's okay. There's consideration—even love—in secrecy."

Pamela's affair with Jake had ended just before my first interview with her. She had closed that conversation by saying, "I know that what I want is to love two people. My husband and someone else. And I don't want that other person to be a casual part of my life or a hidden part of my life. I want *both* the people I love to be presences. I'm looking for that other person now and if I find him, we'll talk again."

At the restaurant she told me about the new man. He, like her husband, was young enough to be on her side about an open relationship. While Jake had found the inevitable meetings and TV-watching with Kevin uncomfortable, her new man took this in his stride. They had drawn up a contract for their relationship which specified that they have three nights a week together, at least one of those in her house with her children (Kevin was in an affair that got him out of the house one night a week); lunch twice a week; and two weekends a month, one with, one without her children.

"I haven't yet resolved how much of this the children are to know," Pamela said. "I don't, for example, let them see us in bed together. But I don't see what's wrong with their knowing there's another man in their mother's life, another person besides their father with whom she likes to spend time. It's conceivable, at least, that such knowledge could be helpful for them, give them security, especially since they're female. I certainly don't see why people make an automatic assumption that relationships like these have to hurt children. They haven't happened often enough yet to be studied, so how does anyone know?"

Her new lover is a doctor and has a classy future. Pamela has therefore opened negotiations with him concerning money. She feels this is the one area in which married women who have lovers are most retrogressive. "They're afraid to ask for money. But why shouldn't they, particularly if the man has it? If they married him, they'd expect some financial sharing. If one conducts an extramarital affair like a half-marriage, then there should be financial arrangements to cover the situation." She is currently looking into legal precedents.

"The sex is fantastic," she says, predictably. "Part of what makes it fantastic is that no children are around most of the time. We can screw anytime we want, without having to worry about kids crawling into the bed. We can get up in the middle of the night and make zabaglione and drink champagne. We can listen to music as loud as we want it. We see the children, as I told you, so they're not unaware of what's going on. The thing isn't shrouded in mystery. But if a woman has children—and I like children, always wanted them—what she needs in order to stay married are some of the very advantages that separation or divorce give her, at least if she's middle-class.

"The middle-class husband who separates or divorces usually agrees to have the children several nights a month or sometimes several a week. This gives the wife free fucking time. I don't see why society can't head toward this kind of freedom within marriage."

But there is, Pamela now tells me, one disadvantage to the new relationship. Her lover is recently separated from a wife who left him for another man. Pamela foresees that this may make complications. Her lover has already begun demanding more of her time than she is prepared to give. They have discussed the fact that "exclusive possession" is dangerous to love, but still he seems to want it and has urged her to leave her husband.

I ask her what she will do if her lover decides he cannot tolerate the arrangement she has established and decides instead to choose a full-time woman. "I'll look for someone else," she says easily. "I'm not going to exchange one nuclear family for another. It's my absolute belief that people who leave their spouses for other spouses are absolutely doomed. This is particularly true when a man has to leave his children. Men are so fucking maudlin about children it makes me nauseous. But even when they don't leave their children, when they take on *your* children, it's a mess. Now they've got children who aren't even theirs who are climbing into the bed with shit dripping out of their diapers and who never leave you alone and you can't fuck in the morning because they're running around, and all the financial hassle—well, in practical terms it just strikes me as impossible. So I don't care how long it takes me, I'm going to find a man somewhere who sees it the same way I do."

I never knew quite what to make of Pamela. She was a self-dramatizer, a type I ordinarily dislike because their productions are rarely worth sitting through. But Pamela's show was sparkling. I didn't believe she would ever be able to achieve the arrangement she wanted. Somehow, she was too abstract, too intellectual. She did not, I suspected, really fall in love, but rather, plotted what love must be. Nevertheless, I always felt a begrudging admiration for her and even for her emphasis upon the economics of extramarital love. It is not altogether new, any more than is the so-called "open" marriage. In 1716, Lady Mary Wortley Montagu described her experiences in Constantinople in a letter to a woman friend; she was astonished, she remarked, at how many of the Turkish women with whom she socialized and dined not only had lovers, but had lovers who were known to their husbands. " 'Tis the established custom for every lady to have two husbands," she wrote, "one that bears the name, and another that performs the duties. And these engagements are so well known, that it would be a downright affront, and publicly resented, if you invited a woman of quality to dinner, without at the same time inviting her two attendants of lover and husband, between whom she always sits in state with great gravity."

But the thing that most surprised Lady Mary was the economic base of these relationships. She reported that these "sub-marriages" generally lasted as long as twenty years, "and the lady often commands the poor lover's estate even to the utter ruin of his family . . . a man makes but an ill figure that is not in some commerce of this nature; and a woman looks out for a lover as soon as she's married, as part of her equipage, without which she could not be genteel; and the first article of the treaty is establishing the pension, which remains to the lady though the gallant should prove inconstant . . ." The pension, thought Lady Mary, might actually make for constancy, and indeed, was not considered a base concern when a woman took a lover. "I really know several women of the first quality, whose pensions are as well known as their annual rents, and yet nobody esteems them the less; on the contrary, their discretion would be called in question, if they should be suspected to be mistresses for nothing. . . ."

I have no idea whether what Lady Mary reported was an accurate description of Turkish high society at the start of the eighteenth century, but I do know that the sexual modes she ascribed to her Turkish friends could well have been applied to Pamela. I also know that I found it rather refreshing to hear Pamela's pragmatic appraisal of the economic and sexual benefits of open extramarital relationships. She sounded down-to-earth. Other women involved in open adultery had talked of gifts like "growth" and "marital closeness" and had seemed distressingly fey.

## Patricia and David Dorsky / There Are All Different Kinds of Loves

Patricia Dorsky was another woman who was more keen on having a sexually experimental marriage than was her husband. He seemed merely to go along with her extramarital needs, although he had actually been instrumental in helping her define them. I interviewed both of the Dorskys, Patricia first. We got together in her office; she works as an administrator for a family-owned dress company and so, although she is only twenty-four, had a large and airy private room in which we sat quite comfortably on a leather couch, our feet up on an enormous coffee table. We had started out with her behind her desk and me in a chair facing her, but she had politely, in practical executive-fashion, suggested we move to the couch where there would be no wooden barrier between us. When she got up to move, I saw she was startlingly thin, with the vulnerable awkward grace of a wistful animal I had seen somewhere, an antelope perhaps, or the unicorn of the tapestries.

"I've been living with my husband for five years, but we've only been married for three," she said to start.

"Where did you meet him? Were you in college?"

"Yes, we were both in California. I was there on a lark and he was there getting an advanced degree in music and we lived together out there almost immediately upon meeting. We met in the parking lot of a supermarket and I went home and spent the night with him. We spent the night in bed and it was really good and we decided to pursue this rich area as long as we could. I moved in the day after I met him and we've been together ever since.

"We had a lot of problems with his family. I am not Jewish, and his family is. They acted as if they were going to disown him if we got married, so the first two years we didn't. We didn't feel any need to. But then my mother was moving out to Chicago, and she had a nice little apartment which was dirt cheap, and my mother wanted to give it to us but she was a little reluctant, not that she had any objections to our living together, but because of the neighbors. So one day, while we were walking around the city, I said to David, 'Why don't we get married and solve all our housing problems?' Several weeks after that we did get married.

"David and I have a very free relationship in which there aren't any policies. I mean we never sat down and said, 'Okay, you're free to do this but not that and I'm going to do this or that.' We just play things by ear. Nothing about other men or women happened until I was going through a period when I was very depressed. I'm a very depressive type. I get to feeling unattractive and rotten and stupid. When that happens I don't even want to go outside. Forget about walking in the park. I mean I don't particularly want to do anything.

"So David was going to parties that our friends gave all alone. He met a girl he liked at one and they became friends. They spent a lot of time together, mostly listening to Wagnerian music. I hate Wagner and I wouldn't go anyplace where Wagner's music was playing. One time, at one musical party, David met a friend of this girl, a depressed Czechoslovakian anesthesiologist. And he said to me, 'You would really like Jan.' He told me several times about this man but I wasn't interested beyond hearing about him. Then one day I agreed to go to a party that this anesthesiologist was having and I met him, and David was right, I liked him. I liked the way he looked. The evening progressed and he and I talked and we were both attracted to each other. I don't remember all the details. There was a lot of drinking going on and Jan and I spent a lot of time talking. And we just hit it off incredibly.

"Let me think now. What happened? How did it happen that everyone left and it was just David and Jan and me still there? I can't quite remember, but I know it was very late and everyone left and I was drunk and I still didn't want to go home. Then David fell asleep on the couch and Jan and I got into his bed and fooled around and then we made it. It was almost dawn when I woke David up and we went home. On the subway, I told him what had happened and he just said, 'Yeah. Okay.' "

"That was it?" I asked.

"Yes," she said. "No trouble on David's end. So I got the idea he mightn't mind if I got together with Jan again. It had cheered me up, being with Jan. So I suggested this to David. I told him I had liked making love with Jan, but it was nothing special, nothing like between him and me, so that while I'd very much like to do it again, if he didn't want me to, I'd just skip it. I told him I didn't think it should make him jealous or uneasy, since we obviously had such a very special relationship, and that I wouldn't feel jealous or uneasy if he screwed some other woman, if he had been making love, for instance, with the music-loving girl. Provided, of course, it wasn't an overly emotional thing. And David said okay, fine.

"No. There was no trouble on David's end. The only trouble I had was with Jan. You have to remember that Jan is a foreigner. He doesn't understand America particularly and especially our morals. Everything is too out in the open for him. When I phoned him and said I wanted to see him again he acted peculiar. He said he'd liked it with me, but that he figured the only reason I wanted to go to bed with him was because David and I were having troubles. He said he felt I was using him. I told him that that was not the case, and explained to him that there was nothing wrong between me and David but that there are all different kinds of loves, and all different kinds of feelings. I told him I thought we should go ahead with it and that David knew all about it and had said, 'Okay. Fine,' and all that. And Jan said, 'Well, I don't believe you.'

"I was exasperated. I really wanted him, and he was letting all these scruples get in the way. A few days later, Jan called our house and asked to talk to David. So David got on the phone and they made arrangements and they met one day for coffee. Jan said, 'You don't love her.' And David kept saying, 'No. I didn't say that. I do.' And Jan said, 'Well, how can you love her and say okay about me?' And David said, 'Because I think she needs this.' And Jan said, 'But she's not a library book. You can't just lend her out.' And David said, 'I'm not lending her out. In the first place, I don't own her, so how could I lend her? If she wants to be with you, I don't object. I don't see how it will interfere with my relationship with her.'

"What it came down to was that Jan was seeking David's permission. It was very odd. He kept saying, 'How can that be? How can this be?' And David was getting exasperated because it was taking on ridiculous proportions. He told Jan this, so Jan decided to try and understand it all and I've been seeing him for the last six months."

"Did he finally become comfortable about it?" I asked.

"He accepts it for a while and then for a while he can't. Several times he's called me up and said, 'I can't handle this. I don't want half of you. I want either all of you or I don't want any of you.' And I've said to him, 'Well, okay. But I think that's stupid. I really think that's stupid.' He asks me how I feel about David and I say, 'I love David very much. I have no intention of leaving David.' But lately he seems to have stopped doing this. At this point, now, he hasn't started this stuff for quite a long time. I think he's finally decided that he's learning new ways and he's willing to accept that people do things differently."

"When do you see him?" I asked.

"It depends. We don't have a schedule. Pretty much whenever one of us feels like it. Sometimes three times a week. Sometimes once a week. Sometimes four times a week. We speak to each other every day. We have since January. Sometimes I go over there at night after work and spend the night there. Once in a while I've spent the weekend. I don't particularly care for doing that. I like my own bed. I don't like being out of my own setting. I enjoy Jan sexually. I'm new to Jan and so that makes it feel special with him, whereas David might say I'm special in bed, but after all this time I'm not really."

"What is it about Jan that appeals to you?" I asked.

"Well, the first thing that appealed to me were his looks. I like his kind of suntanned looks. Then, he's older—past thirty—and he's got a very intriguing accent. I like that too. But mostly it's his demeanor. He's like me, sort of depressed and melancholy, and I like that. David is so different. David is a very good-natured person. If he hated you, he would not let on. He would still be polite to you. I could never have married someone like Jan. He would never have been able to accept me on my own terms. I don't think anybody but David could. As I told you, I'm very difficult to live with. I get depressed often. I have a tendency to be very bitchy. When I'm upset about something, I have the very bad habit of attacking the person closest to me, which is David, and I don't think most people could handle that, but David does. I mean, it doesn't even affect our relationship. David and I are sort of soul-mates. He just accepts me, I mean on any level, and I don't think I could ever meet anyone else who does that."

David himself was not involved in any other relationship. His friendship with the girl who had introduced the Dorskys to Jan had ended. "He spent a weekend with her," Patricia said. "One time they went skiing and it ended up in bed, but that was it. David didn't want to pursue her. He had no interest in her in that context. I mean, he felt that it ruined their friendship to get involved sexually. At last account, he told me that he didn't want to bother with anyone extra.

"He said it wasn't worth the aggravation. Of course, if someone came along, I'm sure that he could get interested. But he's very self-sufficient. He's teaching music now, but he doesn't really like teaching. He likes being alone and writing music. He loves books and records and if you put him in a room with books and records and closed the door and slid a meal under every day, he mightn't want any more than that. He's a calm person who can always amuse himself."

"How do you account for his lack of jealousy?" I asked.

"I don't know. I don't account for it. I'm just grateful for it. In the beginning I thought that he just *thought* he wouldn't be jealous, and I kept saying to him, 'Are you sure you're not jealous?' And he would say, 'I'm not.' And now I've decided he really isn't. He's not the type who can hide anything from anybody. I mean he is actually incapable of lying. So the only explanation I can offer is that he really isn't jealous because he knows that our relationship is some-

thing that can't be touched by anyone else. He knows that
I don't like people terribly much and that it's rare for me
to meet someone that I want to be involved with. And that's
why he thinks that therefore I should pursue it when it happens. Now whether he would approve of me doing this on a
regular basis with different men, I have no idea. But then,
that's not my nature."

I was very curious to meet David. Patricia had told me
she was sure he would want to speak with me and explain his
own feelings about sharing his wife with Jan in an experimental marriage. But on the day of the interview I had arranged with David, Patricia called me and said he'd changed
his mind. She said it was not because he didn't want to talk
about it but because he was very busy that day. I said I was
very sorry and hoped we could do it another time, and Patricia said, "Well, look. Just come by at the time you said
anyway. I'll call him back and tell him to see you regardless."
I said, "I wouldn't want to go there if he's busy, or if he
really doesn't want to talk with me."
"No," she said firmly. "It'll be okay. He'll do it."
I went to their apartment, an orderly three rooms in a
well-kept East Side brownstone. The Dorskys had a garden,
lots of books, mountains of records. David greeted me at the
door. Patricia was home, but she was in another room. This
was to be David's own show. But it wasn't very original. He
did, indeed, repeat almost precisely the information Patricia
had given. He was not jealous. He was not having any relationship of his own. He was not, as someone who knew them
both had suggested, either homosexual or interested in getting
rid of Patricia. It was just as she had said: he thought another
relationship would be good for her at this time, and he figured nothing that ever happened with other men would ever
come between her and him. The only thing that was startlingly different between David and Patricia was the way in
which I had to pump him to get him to talk.

I asked, "How do you feel about the fact that Patricia is having a relationship with somebody else?"

He said, "I'm not basically a jealous person to begin with. If it were done behind my back, then I would be more angry than jealous."

"Has her seeing Jan changed things between you?"

"No. I knew it wouldn't."

"How did you know that?"

"I don't know. Somehow I knew it. I knew from the start that there would be something between them but that it wouldn't affect us."

"How do you account for your not being a jealous person? Can you explain it?"

"No."

"It really is unusual, I feel," I said.

"I just don't like jealousy," he said. "It's petty."

"Have you ever felt jealous?"

"Yes," he said. "I once went through a stupid jealous thing. A girl I was seeing a few years ago was seeing someone else too and I didn't know about it and I found out about it and I never want to go through that again. I was angry and it was all so stupid. I like to get on with people. I hate having to be angry."

"Do you feel the need to put any restrictions on the amount of time Patricia spends away? Could that become a problem?"

"No. It couldn't."

"Suppose you're planning to go to dinner with X and Y and that's the night she's not coming home?"

"It doesn't happen like that. I am informed that she is going to see Jan. We agreed that she would always inform me in advance."

"Do you think the kind of relationship you're having is something that is at all feasible for other people? Do you think it's something you could continue when you had children?"

He chose to answer only the second part of my question.

He said, "I don't want any children. Neither does Patricia."
He spoke these words so much more firmly than anything
else he had said, quite loudly really, that I asked him why he
felt this way. "I want to be liked, as I told you," he said.
"And children don't like their parents when they grow up."

"What, never?" I asked.

"Well," he said, "I certainly didn't like mine. I thought
they were wonderful when I was little, but when I grew up
I despised them. And I expect that happens a lot. And for
myself, I couldn't take that disappointment. I couldn't take
someone's loving me for a long time and then one day turning around and looking at me and saying, 'You're awful; I
never want to see you again,' which is what I did to my
parents."

It was my first opening into his guarded approval of Patricia. "I guess you wouldn't ever want Patricia to stop loving
you either?" I asked in a very neutral tone.

He said, "That's true," but he wouldn't or couldn't am-
plify.

I asked whether it was likely that he himself might have a
relationship with someone other than his wife, but he said
he doubted it. "Perhaps if it just happened spontaneously,"
he said. "But I wouldn't want to go out looking for it.
Patricia is a much more jealous person than I am, so it's
probably best this way. I don't find it odd, and I wish everyone else didn't always act as if it were."

"Well, it is a little odd," I said, hoping to get him to talk
more. But he wouldn't. I had to go on. "Most people feel
threatened when someone else makes love to their husband
or wife. And traditionally, men feel this even more than
women do."

"Well, I just don't feel threatened by that," he said. "I
can't imagine that."

"You can't?"

"No, I can't."

He seemed impatient to be rid of me, and I left shortly

afterwards. Talking to David had been like pulling teeth and I found I was tired, more tired than I had been after any of my other interviews. I wasn't sure whether I had failed to penetrate David's guardedness or whether he really wasn't being guarded and the answers he had given me were, after all, precise representations of how he actually felt. Okay. Fine. I walked home slowly that night, wondering if perhaps people living in experimental marriages were such foreigners to someone like me—raised on possession and exclusive love —that I could not begin to understand their language.

# (3)
# Breaking Up:
## *Gains and Losses*

Proponents of open adultery tend to be almost old-fashioned in their allegiance to the institution of marriage. They are enthusiastic about extramarital sex not just because they are hedonistic, but because in their view it helps make marriage more permanent. They argue that many if not most divorces are caused by the desire for sexual experimentation, and that therefore permitting sexual variety within the institution can have the potentially stabilizing social value of forestalling or eliminating divorce. Sociologists have defined marriage as an arrangement that promises both permanence and exclusivity. The proponents of open adultery hope to accomplish greater permanence than is customary these days by letting the exclusivity go.

But does permitting sexual experimentation within marriage forestall or eliminate divorce? Is divorce actually caused by sexual monotony? The marriages of people practising open adultery also came apart.

## *Judy Miller /*
## *Sex As the Holy Grail*

Judy Miller, whom I met at a friend's party in a sprawling suburban house in Connecticut, had had an experimental marriage that had just shut down tight. Six months ago, after

**225**

twenty-five years of marriage, her husband had left her, leaving Judy and their two teen-aged children to occupy the rambling suburban house next door to my friend. He had moved to an apartment in the city and his departure was still a raw wound for Judy. She felt betrayed. She had, she said, "tried everything, *everything* with him. Years of therapy. Years of open sex. If open sex won't keep a marriage together, what will?"

We were standing in my friend's crowded living room and Judy was talking nervously. Later we withdrew to her house next door, to her tape recorder and a borrowed tape. "My husband meant everything to me," she said. "And I can't let go, even now, even when I look at the separation papers. I've thought about this a lot. I'll tell you how to start my story. If I were writing my story, I'd start it with the day my husband finally, after a hundred stops and starts, was really on his way out of the house. He was in the bedroom, packing his shirts. And I was showering, trying to be as casual as I could be. And suddenly I came storming out of the shower, the towel wrapped around me, and, I don't know what got into me, but I was screaming at him. 'Listen, Miller,' I was screaming. 'You can't go yet. You and I still have unfinished business. It's not finished yet, you bastard. You still haven't fucked me in the ass.' "

I wasn't sure why Judy considered this statement so revealing, and I pointed this out to her. It seemed at best an ambiguous remark to me. That's when she said, "No! Don't you see? I wanted to try everything, *everything* with him. I'm a fighter. I wasn't going to let my marriage come to an end unless we tried everything to keep it together."

She had first met the man who was to be her husband just before her seventeenth and his twentieth birthday at a May Day parade, where, ardent members of the Young Communist League, they had marched side by side. "We carried signs. I don't mean the personal ones, like the dungarees of the boys, the turtleneck sweaters and dirndl skirts on the girls. I mean the actual signs. 'Youth unite. The future is yours,' and 'Books not Bombs.' And we sang, 'We shall all be free. We shall all be free, someday.' And that's how we fell in love."

They were both living at home that spring. He had dropped out of college for a term to take a job "in industry," as the Movement had directed him to do. They used to make love in his mother's living room after the grownups had gone to bed. "Women's liberation?" Judy said. "I had it all in those days. After getting out of bed at three in the morning, he'd put me on a bus and I'd go home to our apartment in the Bronx. Past empty lots and desolate corners. Boys didn't walk girls home in the Movement. We were all equal. But I know now that even then I wished for somebody, some guy who would be concerned about me, care about me enough to see I got home safely."

After two months of intimacy Matthew had asked to marry her. "I would have died if he hadn't, but I knew all along he was going to. The Movement was so puritanical. You couldn't have any self-respect if you made love to a woman and didn't marry her. She was your comrade."

So they married. Matthew went back to college. Judy got a job doing political organizing. But before a year was up she knew the marriage was in trouble. "I could never tell what was on his mind, what he really wanted of me. I was intense, confiding. He was like a tomb. At work I had a sense of being emotionally close with people; at night I came home to his silence."

Judy felt that Matthew had withdrawn from her. They rarely made love. After two months of marriage, they limited their sexual encounters to once a week.

One night, to provoke Matthew, she decided not to go to bed with him but to put her blankets on the living room couch. He said nothing. The next night was the same. In her mind, she went over the possibilities of leaving him. But on the third night, he said, "Come to bed, honey."

"I don't want to," she had said. "I'm thinking of leaving you." He had come and sat by her and very thoughtfully said, "You know, that's what I thought I wanted. I thought I wanted to get you to that point. But now that you're there, it's not what I want. If I can't make it with you, I can't make it with anyone."

After that Judy was hooked, she said. She explained that whenever he would drive her to some breaking point through silence—and sexual abstinence—he would woo her back by admitting how special he found her, or, actually, by expressing his conviction that if he didn't have *her,* he'd have nothing but failures. Never mind that she was a failure for him. Neither of them wanted to look at this. So life went on. He finished college, went to graduate school, became a psychologist. She had babies; two of them. And after a long time in which their marriage came to her to seem settled if not stimulating, he told her that he was angry with her for having years ago squelched his sexuality.

She insisted that his view had to be insane; it was her, not his sex which had been padlocked. But he maintained that he had always found her too overwhelming in her intensity, too demanding. He wanted to leave her. It would be best for both of them. He wanted to leave so that each of them would have a chance at still spending some youthful years with more compatible mates. Life was running out.

Judy had balked. She proposed that what he was going through was simply some sort of predictable mid-life crisis. He was craving sexual experience. Why couldn't they, old comrades, find sexual salvation together.

It sounded so reasonable. Matthew agreed to think about how to try. A short while later he tentatively proposed that she join him in a shared sexual experience with some friends of his, a couple of gray-haired psychotherapists somewhat older than the Millers who wore Indian necklaces and sandals and smoked pot and were into "living" and "experiencing life, no matter what the pain."

With this banal couple Judy and Matthew tried to rejuvenate their sex life. Listening to Judy's description was, for me, like twirling a kaleidoscope and seeing the pieces of a pattern suddenly split, swirl, and reassemble. With mechanical suddenness, this stolidly political couple now moved from almost total abstinence to group sex.

They went to the therapists' house, listened to jazz, turned on with pot. Judy's description of the first night was that, "Nothing happened for a long while, but then after a lot of giggling and jokes, the male therapist began caressing my arms. From across the room my husband and the therapist's wife were watching. Matthew got up and came to where we were. He began unbuttoning my blouse. The therapist was unzipping my slacks. I was both inside myself and outside myself. I was very worried about it on one level, and saying, 'What kind of madness is this?' and yet on another level I was saying, 'If it's what Matthew wants of me, why not? I'm a gutsy lady. I'm brave and special and I'd do anything for him.' The therapist and I made love on the straw-matted living room floor. "But then something terrible happened," she said. "While we were fucking, Matthew went over to the therapist's wife and lay down naked alongside her. But he couldn't get it up. He was impotent. What a scene we had then, the four of us! Matthew crying. Me holding him. Lilliana and Newton talking about the pain and experience of it all. After a long, long time they went to bed and Matthew and I fell asleep on the straw rug. But before we did, he made love to me, and it was all very deep and intense and I figured it had been worthwhile."

They continued to see this couple on a steady basis. The sex was always good for Judy, and Matthew got over his potency problem. Later they advanced their experimentation by finding different partners for one another. For her, he located an old friend who had recently divorced. For him, she too found a friend, her very best, a woman who was married and more attached to Judy than to Matthew.

For a while this arrangement did actually seem to improve their marriage. "Things were good," Judy said. "The best it was for years. I'd go out to Queens to visit this friend of Matthew's. Matthew would have my girlfriend over. When I got home he'd want to know all the details of what had happened to me: how long we'd fucked; how many times I came."

Judy wanted to know if I thought that perhaps there was something homosexual in this. I said I didn't think so, that the homosexual explanation always sounded very handy but was too universally applied. I had the feeling that Matthew must always have felt sexually inexperienced, consumed with curiosity about what was normal sex, what it was that other people did.

"Yes, I suppose so," Judy said, "since he was having no trouble making it with my friend. That turned out terribly for me. She proved to be the kind of woman who could have three orgasms in ten minutes, and she wanted to see him more and more, and I was furious, jealous. Especially since I didn't care that much for *his* friend. That relationship was exciting, but foggy. Matthew's friend liked screwing me, but he was looking for someone to have a full relationship with. I was in the way. I was in the way whichever way I turned."

Still, it was Matthew who had finally put an end to the experimentation. He told Judy he had gotten it all out of his system ("like it was a poison, a drink," Judy said). He broke off with her friend. And several months later he confessed to Judy that he had been having a secret affair with a woman she didn't know, a woman he had come to love, and that this time he truly meant to separate.

"He took an apartment in the city," Judy said. "I was sure he'd want me back. After all, we'd done everything, everything together. I waited. We spoke to each other every day. He'd tell me it was driving him crazy being without me. I waited. He told me he couldn't think straight. I waited. I expected any day he'd say, 'Come back,' just like that night he'd asked me back to bed when we were kids. But he never did."

Judy was very often close to crying as she talked. What finally did make her tears come down was when she tried to explain that during the period she had pursued group sex with her husband, she had assumed that if they could arrive at intensely joyous sex, their relationship would be saved. "Sex was a salvation, a holy grail," she said. "I began to believe that if we could find it, find good sex, whether together or separately, it would keep us whole and together." It was almost the demise of a religious belief she was talking about, as well as the death of a marriage.

## Alexandra Newman / Handmaiden

I got a better grasp of why experimental marriage kept suggesting religion to me when I interviewed Alexandra Newman, a thirty-seven-year-old writer who was also now out of a marriage that had incorporated open adultery—group sex and partner sharing. Alexandra's marriage had been with a painter, avant-garde in his sexual style if not in his canvases. It had ended several years ago and she had just this year remarried. The past was far behind her, but she could remember her feelings and experiences well. In relating them, she made me understand how it was possible for some people to view sex not only as a personal but a societal salvation.

"I just got married but I was married before for ten years and it was in my previous marriage that I had extramarital experiences. My husband and I had a very strange marriage and in many ways the only thing that really defined it as a marriage was our getting a divorce. I was married to a painter and we lived in London and were very much involved with the artists and writers of the late fifties who were living abroad. By the early sixties most of them had already gone back to wherever they came from but we stayed on.

"We had lived together for three years before we actually

got married. We married mainly because my parents were absolutely out of their minds with grief that I was just living with him. That happened a lot to girls in those days. I wanted to get married to make my parents less alarmed. But Harold wanted to get married too. He was in analysis of some kind and in a way it meant he could 'graduate' if he got married. It would be proof that he had made it socially, that he was able to relate to another person. So we got married. But the marriage itself was horrible, the most unhappy period of my life, because by the time it took place, there were all kinds of negative things happening between us.

"In the three years previous to our marriage we had lived as a married couple. We were very monogamous, very intertwined and interrelated. But my husband had a friend who was a very strange person and had a great influence on him. This friend, a picture frame maker, was against marriage and was really very misogynous. He was against any man's having a monogamous relationship with a woman. I cannot say to what degree it was his friend's influence or to what degree this influence just reflected Harold's own feelings, but by the time we married, Harold had decided to try to alter our life. He was thinking of meeting other couples.

"I was very uptight about the group sex business. Remember, it was the early sixties. This stuff is so prosaic today, but then it was very daring. I was especially worried about it because our marriage was not sexually very good. It probably wasn't good on most levels, but sexually it really wasn't good. So I brooded a lot, thinking that if it were good, perhaps he wouldn't have been so interested in making it with other couples.

"Harold had problems, for instance with getting an erection, and he was never fully hard. Now, in a good relationship this might not matter because it doesn't have to be that important. In fact, I read an article recently that maintained that among Europeans impotence isn't considered quite the bugaboo it is here. What I read said that women are much more cooperative. They work around the problem. But at any rate, in those days, it seemed—at least to Harold—a very serious problem.

"I was fairly untutored. I had slept with a few other men, but just a few times, so I didn't really know much about anything. I didn't know what to expect, and I really just figured that things were going to kind of iron themselves out. But I didn't have sexual benefits, if you want to call them that—orgasms. And I didn't have a nice comfortable marriage. I was a real loser. So I went along with Harold on the group sex idea. He thought it was going to help his sex problem. He said it would help mine. But mostly I went along because I was from the generation where women were brought up to be handmaidens. Living in England just made it worse. It was impossible for me, at that point in my life, to think of saying no to something Harold wanted.

"Mostly I hated the group sex. As far as anything arousing goes, for me it was not very stimulating. I was even afraid to peek over and watch the other people. I guess I really felt it was kind of impolite.

"I have to admit that one time I did feel some gratification. It was a time when Harold had managed to get together for sex some quite well-known Londoners. Harold knew everybody who was anybody in those days. There was something about him, an intensity and intellect, that attracted people to him so that they let him just take them over. I wasn't the only person who let him do that. Anyway, on this particular occasion, there were some very important people present. We were smoking pot (who smoked pot in those days? just us; we were so special) and then we had not so much group sex as simultaneous sex. You have to realize that in the early sixties all of this seemed very radical and there was a kind of evangelism about it. I felt this small group of people wanted to change the manners of the world and that maybe if the world's manners were changed, all sorts of other things could change and be improved too. We generalized. If you could change sexual manners and habits, who knows? Maybe there'd be no more wars, no more brutality to children.

"I think the gratification I felt had to do with this kind of thinking and the fact that one of the men present was an internationally known celebrity important enough to make changes in the world's thinking, if not its actions. I felt very powerful. I felt like some sort of a goddess. If I took my clothes off, and then the rest of them did, we'd all of us be on our way to some sort of apocalyptic change.

"So I began. We were in a house owned by one of Hal's friends, a big old house with enormous quiet rooms. The living room had nothing in it but a fireplace, a huge bed, and oriental masks on the walls. There was music coming over the hi-fi, but otherwise everything was still. No one was even talking. There were four couples, and I undressed and started playing with one of the men, and he undressed and we got down on the floor and started making love orally, and then the others paired off in other parts of the room, and we never switched partners but we all stopped from time to time to look at what the others were doing. And while this was going on I did, that one time, look around me and have an intense feeling of gratification. It was as if I was a medium and I was feeling in my body what everybody else was feeling in theirs.

"But later that night I experienced a terrible revulsion toward Harold. It began as soon as the others had gone home and Harold wanted to make love to me. We always did that afterwards. But this time, I couldn't. I felt repelled by him. And I never quite got over it. I didn't want him to touch me anymore. We lived together a while longer, but I started staying away from home a lot, and a few months after that night I moved out and took my own place.

"That wasn't the end of my relationship with Harold. We were very intertwined, and at first I wasn't sure if I wanted to break away from him altogether. But I knew I didn't want sex with him or any of his friends. I'd meet Harold for drinks, but I was trying to start a life of my own. Finally, I got into a relationship with a man I'd met on my own, and he moved in with me, and I wanted to have him all to myself. I wanted someone who was just mine. But I never had known quite how to keep my distance from Harold, and I let him meet my lover, and then, before I knew it, he was trying to take over my lover. He wanted us all three to go on a trip together and share our nights together. And my lover got turned on by the idea and was willing. And I felt frightened at the thought and I finally realized that the only way I'd be able to have someone all of my own was to get as far away as possible from Harold, to leave England, to leave any part of the world he was in.

"I left and came back to the States and I went into analysis. My analyst suggested Hal had been homosexual, although just latently. He said it sounded as if his relationships were full of masochism and God knows what, and that he wanted to have me just so he could share me with male friends and please them by offering them his woman. I'm not sure about this explanation, but when the analyst said I had been masochistic, there I couldn't fault him. I really am very conventional. But I was going along with a lot of stuff that really brought me pain because I was scared of losing Harold. Today, when I hear about these communes and group sex, I think, in a way, they're lucky, these kids today. But in a way, maybe they're not. They're another generation but who knows what's going on inside them?

"Last year I remarried and I'm very happily married this time. My husband knows about some of the things I did with Harold but not about all of them. I wouldn't want him to know all of them. He's a very conventionally monogamous person and I love that about him. I love how possessive of me he is. I'm the same way about him, and I want us to stay this way. I can't say that it's wrong to sleep with somebody else when you're married or that it's right. It's just that the way I was doing it was not good for me."

## *Lydia Marks /*
## *Who Can Be Trusted When It Comes to Sex?*

With Lydia Marks, a modern dance teacher and performer, I found myself debating the unanswerable: what is best for women? Lydia had been married for fourteen years to her second husband, with whom she had had three children, and had separated from him a year ago, when she was thirty-seven. Few women I met were as appealing or exciting in their physical style as Lydia, a slim dark woman with long, straight brown hair, long graceful arms and legs, and what I came to think of as a long smile as well. Whenever she smiled, her face became so animated that even when she returned to deep serious thought, her eyes remained animated, sparkling, still smiling for long mysterious moments afterwards. Men must have found her as intriguing as I did, for she had, from what I could gather, no dearth of lovers in her current separated state. But despite popularity and self-confidence, Lydia fiercely regretted the end of her rebellious experimental marriage and her abortive attempts at pragmatism about sex.

"I had three affairs during my fourteen-year marriage," she said, "and each one of them was ridiculous. I always started out casually, thinking 'What's the harm in this?' but then somehow I'd screw myself up. I can't be trusted when it comes to sex. I'm apparently not yet ready to separate it from love. And I wonder who is. I wonder whether any woman is.

"Each time I had an affair I'd start to believe I was in love with the man, even though I always said it was sex, not love, I was after, or adventure, not love, I needed. You have to understand that marriage makes people grow together like fungus on a tree. Something happens because of this that kills the physical excitement. In the beginning I couldn't wait to touch my husband. There were all the corny things. We were magnetized like in the movies. I remember we once ran toward each other from opposite ends of an airport. But after a while, we lost that. It seemed to me that it was only when a man was really separate and outside myself that I could look at him and feel excited. My husband and I had grown so close that sex was like being physically attracted to oneself. We agreed, as a result, that occasional affairs would be permissible for either of us, provided we kept them slight."

Lydia wanted me to know that this had not been a unilateral decision. Both she and her husband were to have the same privileges. They had had the kind of marriage in which everything was discussed and shared—the children's inoculations, Lydia's work, her husband's job, their political attitudes—the trivial and the broad. "So I had the first affair," Lydia went on. "I was already interested in women's liberation, and I had very strong attitudes about affairs. For one thing, I always felt it was very divisive for single women to have affairs with married men. They shouldn't be taking men away from their sisters. So I also determined it would be wrong for me as a married woman to have an affair with a married man, and I chose only among the single or separated. And of course I thought I was choosing men I wouldn't love. I had three children and I wanted above all to protect their lives.

"My first affair was with an old boyfriend. We had kept in touch over the years, having lunch from time to time. Finally we went to bed. And that's when I began noticing how tricky this business of love and sex is. Here I was sleeping with a man I had previously rejected as a marriage partner, yet suddenly I found myself contemplating divorce and pursuing this old relationship again. I felt I was in love.

"It took enormous control for me to break it off but I did. I was able to do it only because I had now met someone else, someone I was absolutely convinced could give me what I wanted sexually but with whom I couldn't possibly fall in love. He was a hippy guy, a real kook. Forty years old and still bearded and barefoot. He couldn't afford to take me to dinner. Anyone could have seen he wasn't for me. And of course even I saw it, until I was into the thing. Then it started all over again—the worrying and wondering and wanting to be with him all the time. I even considered getting him together with my kids. I was lucky that time because he broke it off.

"I decided no more affairs. Too risky. But about two years later I got into another one. This last guy was even less appropriate than the one before. He was a chilly establishment type, the kind of guy who owns no shirts but his white ones and who wouldn't dream of having a conversation through the door while one of you was in the bathroom. But even so, overnight I was dreaming of shaking up my life and hooking up with him. I was wondering how the kids would take it while I knew inside myself he was no one I even wanted to take to a party. No one I even wanted to introduce to my friends. But sure enough, it all began all over again, and this time I even went so far as actually to separate from my husband. It was very painful. I was weeping all the time. My kids were weeping all the time. 'When are we going to see Daddy? Daddy doesn't love us anymore or else we'd all be together,' that kind of thing. I wanted to go right back home.

"But it was too late. My husband felt betrayed by me. His affairs had indeed been casual but mine had become inflated. He felt my love for him had become wobbly or else this wouldn't have happened. We're separated now, and in marital therapy, and I want to get back together but he's growing very distant. He wants a divorce. And of course, I blame myself. I see now that all affairs—even affairs with the unmarried—are dangerous because they can so quickly get out of perspective. The first thing you know, someone—it doesn't matter whether it's a man or a woman—is ready to run off from their marriage."

I felt when I left Lydia Marks that there was no question but that experimental marriages with open adultery carried within their soil the selfsame seeds of marital impermanence as did traditional marriages, either those that were monogamous or those with secret adultery. No marriage today is immune. Whether their marriage vows deny or permit extramarital sex, married people continue to fall in love with new partners or out of love with the old; usually, today, when either of these crises occurs, they then separate.

The fear of separation—not the loss of a mate's exclusive sexuality—is, I believe, what underlies most people's anxieties concerning extramarital sex. It is as insurance against our anxieties that we consent to ethical proscriptions limiting ourselves from extramarital sex. We do not fear sexual sharing itself, but fear it only because it can lead to the possible loss of a partner's emotional bond.

In experimental marriages the practitioners assume that they can avoid such loss of bonds by defusing sex, long a primary way of forming and experiencing attachment. But they fail. Sex keeps its volatility, at least when attachment is at issue—and often the participants in a sexual affair cannot themselves recognize what is at issue until after the fact of attachment. Therefore, I cannot see experimental marriage as the wave of the future, as some sexual utopians have predicted. It might even be argued that it aids new bonding by making the process easier, or at least more convenient. If extramarital sex were always about sex, perhaps open adultery might become popular. All too often, however, extramarital sex is not about extra sex but about extra marriage, extra emotional intimacy, or the need for a new or different primary bond of attachment.

# *Epilogue*

Throughout history men have courted women who were not their wives and I believe that even among women there was always considerably more adultery than was acknowledged. The fictional heroines, the wives on trial, the irate peeresses arguing to protect their rights to lovers, all give the lie to the dream that in some long-ago happy time all women stayed forever loyal to their husbands. Adultery has persisted —unacceptable—but as human as passion itself.

Still, it seems more in the air today, and certainly more women are talking about it or about having experienced it. This is not a mere matter of happenstance; it is part and parcel of a great change among all of us, men as well as women.

Longer lifespans, greater leisure, freedom from many of the medical and economic ills that once plagued us, have encouraged many people to raise the levels of their emotional aspirations. More of us pursue more education; we go to psychotherapists not just for mental illnesses but for crises of identity or chronology; we divorce in droves; remarry readily; and, curiously, even in marriage report high levels of sexual satisfaction unknown among people in the past. Extramarital sexual experience is simply another one of the innumerable activities engaged in by people preoccupied with personal happiness. This happiness is our society's prime ethic.

I know it is fashionable now to decry the current worship of self-fulfillment with its attending handmaidens of love and sexuality. It is tempting to look back and pronounce the past more glorious or at least more secure. But there is no returning to the past. And moreover, those who speak and write longingly about it and particularly those who express disdain for our current mode of marriage and periodic divorce seem to me to be indulging in mere wishful thinking. The past wasn't really so glorious or even so secure.

Certainly it was not for women. Indeed, Simone de Beauvoir has suggested that women's adultery is in itself a response to the inequities of the female condition, an angry time-tested response. Woman, she wrote in *The Second Sex,* is "fated for infidelity; it is the sole concrete form her liberty can assume. . . . only through deceit and adultery can she prove she is nobody's chattel and give the lie to the pretensions of the male."

Yet despite the fact that women are clearly as subject as men to the climate of the times, despite sympathetic voices like de Beauvoir's and those of a host of female fictionalists, women's adultery continues to be judged in our society in a more pejorative way than is that of men. In part this is a hold-over from the days when a male-dominated society made the rules concerning adultery. Wives were property and the privileges of a property owner were of course more generous than those accorded to chattel; additionally, men wanted to be sure of the genetic heritage of their heirs and, in the absence of birth control, women's sexual fidelity was essential if this was to be accomplished.

But these arrangements between the sexes have changed, and still we are more pejorative about women's adultery than about men's. It has to do with the fact that we consider men to be more sexual than women. Thus, when men are adulterous we tend to explain their experience in terms of their biologically-ordained needs for physical variety or their manly inability to control the passions of their bodies. By granting them such physiological urgencies, we also grant their adulteries to be personally imperative and not therefore directed against their spouses. But when women are adulterous, we do not ascribe to them the same physiological necessities or indeed, any clearcut personal urgencies. Instead we make do with a different—and subtly more demeaning— explanation. We tend to view women's adultery as rising out of reaction rather than self-propulsion. Thus a woman's adultery becomes retaliatory, directed *against* rather than prompted from within.

I don't mean to suggest that the prime cause of women's adultery is uncontrollable physical urgency. I don't even believe that this is the prime cause of male adultery. But I do believe that because we do not admit that there are impulsions and imperatives in women, we therefore view women as meaner than men when they are adulterous. We see them as passive-aggressive and thus we condemn their adultery more pejoratively.

During the course of my research on this book I have come to see that women have many non-retaliatory, urgent personal reasons for their extramarital affairs. I met some women who were indeed angry at their husbands, whether for their emotional remoteness, their sexual inadequacy, or their own non-monogamous inclinations. These women did seem to seek affairs in reaction to their husbands. But I met others whose marriages were sound and even successful, who bore no grudges toward their husbands, and who acted out of imperative personal longings for adventure and variety.

There were no universals, there was only a wide variety of patterns. I met women who engaged in extramarital activities because they were trying to wend their way out of unhappy marriages and women who engaged in them because they believed such activities would help them hold on, help them preserve their marriages. I met those who followed the romantic tradition and fell in love with their lovers, and others who had sexual relations quite casually, totally in opposition to the myth of the sexually cautious woman. It became clear to me that women are as disparate in their motivations and capacities for extramarital sex as they are in their appearances, and that affairs, like thumbprints, have whorls and markings and histories that are absolutely unique and individual.

Because of my own personal biases and upbringing, I did believe that most of the adulterous women I spoke with had turned to extramarital sex because there was something lacking in their marriages or in their own self-esteem. But here and there I met women who defied me to view them in this way, who claimed to have marriages and egos which were perfectly intact, and who felt that when I judged them as deficient I was merely clinging to something long-ago learned and not sufficiently re-examined, to a mindset that would not yield to fresh perception.

Listening to the personal testimony of these diverse women seemed to me to have many values. One was that it enabled me to evaluate some of the prognostications concerning the future of marriage which are so often linked to the statistical evidence of increasing extramarital sex among women. The linkers, usually sexual utopians, tell us that in view of the statistics, it is clear that women no longer want to live in sexually-paired relationships. They prophesize that the marriage of the future will undoubtedly consist of partner-sharing or group arrangements and urge us to prepare by ridding ourselves now of jealousy. But their conclusions are based on misinterpretation, on palm-reading of statistics. Extramarital sex, at least as I encountered it among an urban and suburban group of well-educated, middle-to-upper-class women, was only minimally the province of sexual radicals. For most of the women I met it had far more to do with holding onto or obtaining a partner—with living in pairs, albeit sequentially—than with living in threes and fours and at sixes and sevens.

But no matter how one prophesizes the future, it is the

present that is our biggest concern. And it is in helping us to sense the temper and tone of our own times in regard to extramarital sex that the personal testimony of women who have had the experience is most important. It enables us— men and women—to see that women are, after all, the same kind of animal as men, as prone as men to feel compelling sexual and emotional drives. We respond as intensely as men do to inadequate marriage, to feeling ignored, to starting to age.

There seems to me little point in bemoaning the fact that women's fidelity in marriage seems to be weakening, in tilting at social windmills. This is the way it is, where we are now. Rather, I think there can only be service and not disservice to marriage to admit what is happening and examine as closely as possible how, why and for whom fidelity cracks. Whether the prevalence of extramarital sex makes us nervous or cheerful is clearly a highly individual matter, but I can't see that sweeping it under the rug or hanging it up in the back closet or restricting its examination chiefly to the pages of fiction has ever done much for anyone, or any marriage, or, for that matter, for marriage itself.

# Bibliography

Bell, Robert R. and Peltz, Dorthyann. "Extramarital Sex Among Women." *Medical Aspects of Human Sexuality,* vol. VIII (March 1974).

Birstein, Ann. *Dickie's List.* New York: Coward, McCann & Geoghegan, Inc., 1973.

Birstein, Ann. *Love in the Dunes* in *Summer Situations.* New York: Coward, McCann & Geoghegan, Inc., 1972.

Bullough, Vern L., and Bullough, Bonnie. *The Subordinate Sex: A History of Attitudes Toward Women.* Urbana: University of Illinois Press, 1973.

Castamore (pseud.). *Conjugium Languens* or *The Natural, Civil and Religious Mischiefs Arising From Conjugal Infidelity and Impurity.* London: 1700.

Chopin, Kate. *The Awakening.* New York: Avon Books, 1972.

Chopin, Kate. "The Storm." In *The Complete Works of Kate Chopin.* Edited by Per Seyersted. 2 vols. Baton Rouge: Louisiana State University Press, 1969.

Crawford, John. *The Cases of Impotency and Virginity Fully Discuss'd* [*or The Genuine Proceedings Between the Hon. Mrs. Weld and her Husband, in a Cause, wherein she Libels him for Impotency*]. London: 1731.

Dante, Alighieri. *The Inferno.* Translated by John Ciardi. New York: New American Library, 1970.

De Beauvoir, Simone. *The Second Sex.* Translated by H. M. Parshley. New York: Alfred A. Knopf, 1953.

De France, Marie. "The Lay of Gugemar." In *Lays of Marie De France and Other French Legends.* Translated and Edited by

Eugene Mason. New York: Dutton, Everyman's Library, 1911.

De Lafayette, Marie-Madelaine. *The Princess of Cleves*. In *Seven French Short Novel Masterpieces*. Edited by Andrew Comfort. New York: Popular Library, 1965.

Dostoyevsky, Fyodor. *The Eternal Husband*. In *Three Short Novels of Dostoyevsky*. Translated by Constance Garnett. Edited by Avrahm Yarmolinsky. New York: Doubleday & Co., Inc., Anchor, 1960.

Euripedes. *Hyppolytus*. Adapted by Ian Fletcher and D. S. Carne-Ross. In *Joseph and Potiphar's Wife: An International Anthology of the Story of the Chaste Youth and the Lustful Stepmother*. Edited by John D. Yohannan. New York: New Directions, 1968.

Flaubert, Gustave. *Madame Bovary*. Translated by Francis Steegmuller. New York: Random House, The Modern Library, 1957.

Fox, Charles. *The House of Peeresses or Female Oratory*. London: 1779.

Haller, John S. and Haller Robin M. *The Physician and Sexuality in Victorian America*. Urbana: University of Illinois Press, 1974.

Harper, Robert A. "Extramarital Sex Relations." In *The Encyclopedia of Sexual Behavior*. Edited by Albert Ellis and Albert Abarbanel. New York: Hawthorn Books, Inc., 1967.

Hawthorne, Nathaniel. *The Scarlet Letter*. In *The Portable Hawthorne*. Edited by Malcolm Cowley. New York: The Viking Press, 1971.

Herold, J. Christopher. *Mistress To An Age: A Life of Madame De Staël*. New York: Time, Incorporated, 1964.

Hochman, Sandra. *Walking Papers*. New York: The Viking Press, 1971.

Hunt, Morton, *Sexual Behavior in the 1970's*. Chicago: Playboy Press, 1974.

Jong, Erica. *Fear of Flying*. New York: Holt, Rinehart and Winston, 1973.

Jong, Erica. *Half-Lives*. New York: Holt, Rinehart and Winston, 1973.

Joyce, James. *Ulysses*. New York: Random House, Vintage Books, 1966.

Kempe, Margery. "The Book of Margery Kempe." In *by a Woman writt*. Edited by Joan Goulianos. Indianapolis and New York: Bobbs-Merrill, 1973.

Kinsey, Alfred C., et al. *Sexual Behavior in the Human Female.* Philadelphia: W. B. Saunders Company, 1953.

Lessing, Doris. *The Summer Before the Dark.* New York: Alfred A. Knopf, 1973.

Kazin, Alfred. "Lady Chatterley in America." In *Contemporaries.* Boston: Little, Brown and Company, 1962.

McCarthy, Mary. *A Charmed Life.* New York: Harcourt Brace Jovanovich, Inc., 1955.

Maspero, Gaston. *Popular Stories of Ancient Egypt.* New York: G. P. Putnam's Sons, 1915.

Masters, William H., and Johnson, Virginia E. *Human Sexual Response.* Boston: Little, Brown and Company, 1966.

Maurois, André. *Lélia, The Life of George Sand.* Translated by Gerard Hopkins. New York: Harper & Bros., 1953.

Montagu, Lady Mary Wortley. "Letter to the Lady R. [Rich]." In *by a Woman writt*. Edited by Joan Goulianos. Indianapolis and New York: Bobbs-Merrill, 1973.

Power, Eileen. *Medieval People.* New York: Doubleday & Co., Inc., Anchor, 1954.

Pushkin, Alexander. "The Gypsies." In *Pushkin Threefold: Narrative, Lyric, Polemic and Ribald Verse.* Translated and Edited by Walter Arndt. New York: Dutton, 1972.

Raskin, Barbara. *Loose Ends.* New York: Bantam Books, 1973.

Rossi, Alice S. *The Feminist Papers.* New York: Columbia University Press, 1973.

Rossner, Judith. *Any Minute I Can Split.* New York: McGraw-Hill, 1972.

Salzman, Leon, M.D. "Psychiatric and Clinical Aspects of Infidelity." In *The Psychodynamics of Work and Marriage,* vol. XVI. Edited by Jules H. Masserman, M.D. New York: Grune & Stratton, Inc., 1970.

Seaman, Barbara. *Free and Female.* New York: Coward, McCann & Geoghegan, Inc., 1972.

Sherfey, Mary Jane, M.D. *The Nature and Evolution of Female Sexuality.* New York: Random House, 1972.

Simmons, Ernest J. *Leo Tolstoy.* New York: Random House, Vintage Books, 1960.

Steegmuller, Francis. *Flaubert and Madame Bovary: A Double Portrait.* rev. ed. New York: Farrar, Straus & Giroux, Inc., Noonday, 1968.

Strindberg, August. *Getting Married.* Edited and Translated by Mary Sandbach. New York: The Viking Press, 1972.

Tolstoy, Leo. *Anna Karenina.* Translated by Constance Garnett. Edited by L. J. Kent and N. Berberova. New York: Random House, The Modern Library, n.d.

*Trial Between Lieut. Trelawney, Plaintiff and Capt. Coleman, Defendant, for Criminal Conversation with the Plaintiff's Wife.* London: 1817.

*Trial of Mrs. Ann Wood, Wife of William Wood, Esq., for Adultery with Quintin Dick, Esq.* London: 1785.

*Trial of R. J. Fergusson, Esquire, for Adultery with the Countess of Elgin.* London: 1807.

*Tryals of Two Causes Between Theophilus Cibber, Gent., Plaintiff, and William Sloper, Esq., Defendant.* London: 1740.

Walters, Ronald G. *Primers for Prudery: Sexual Advice to Victorian America.* Englewood Cliffs: Prentice-Hall, 1974.

Weems, Mason Locke. *God's Revenge Against Adultery.* Philadelphia: 1828.

West, Anthony. *Mortal Wounds.* New York: McGraw-Hill, 1973.